The Big Empty

THE BIG

EMPTY

Contemporary Nebraska Nonfiction Writers

Edited by Ladette Randolph and
Nina Shevchuk-Murray

University of Nebraska Press | *Lincoln and London*

Nebraska ARTS COUNCIL

Publication of this book was
assisted by a grant from
the Nebraska Arts Council.

Acknowledgments for the use
of previously published material appear
on pages 293–95,
which constitute an extension
of the copyright page.

Library of Congress
Cataloging-in-Publication Data
The big empty : contemporary Nebraska
nonfiction writers / edited by Ladette
Randolph and Nina Shevchuk-Murray.
p.cm.
ISBN-13: 978-0-8032-9011-2 (pbk. : alk.
paper)
ISBN-10: 0-8032-9011-x (pbk. : alk.
paper)
1. Nebraska—Description and travel.
2. Nebraska—Social life and customs.
3. Nebraska—History, Local. 4. Natural
history—Nebraska. 5. Nebraska—
Biography. I. Randolph, Ladette. II.
Shevchuk-Murray, Nina. F666.5.B54 2007
978.2'034—dc22
2006025175

Set in Minion.
Designed by A. Shahan.

For the young writers of Nebraska

Contents

Preface

Nebraska, depending on your perspective, is either an empty place or a place teeming with life and history. Its geography is of no distinction or it is home to one of the most unique of ecosystems: the sandhills, an area covering much of the west central section of the state. Either Nebraska's inhabitants are as normal as they insist they are or their very insistence leads to the conclusion that Nebraskans are anything but normal.

Nebraska is rarely a destination unless you come for the sandhill crane migration in the fall and spring, or you have tickets to see the Cornhuskers play football, or you have a particular interest in American Indian culture and wish to visit the important sites of the Plains tribes. Nebraska is a state outsiders readily admit to driving through or flying over.

By chance, the two women who helped compile this volume, my coeditor, Nina Shevchuk-Murray, and a remarkable student intern, Elisabeth Chretien, consider themselves outsiders to Nebraska. Nina tells me,

> I did not even know where Nebraska was until May 22, 1999, when the phone rang in my parents'

apartment in Lviv, Ukraine, and we were told that I would be studying at the University of Nebraska in Lincoln, courtesy of the U.S. Department of State. We pulled out an atlas and an encyclopedia, which helpfully informed us that Lincoln, Nebraska, was a strategic railroad station and Omaha was home to an airbase we'd need to blast off the face of the earth in a hurry if ever an opportunity presented itself. It was, after all, an old Soviet encyclopedia we were using.

Both Nina and Elisabeth still feel like outsiders to Nebraska and the state's culture: Nina, for the reasons stated above, and Elisabeth because her family only arbitrarily settled in Omaha after many years following her father's military career. Neither of them has traveled west of Lincoln. I was intrigued by their sense that Nebraskans seem to have an inordinate desire to fill the flatness of the state with the contours of its history, or knowledge of its flora and fauna, or the details of its unique characteristics and famous past residents. I am hardly objective in my understanding of the place I have lived all of my life, but I wondered if they were right about this impulse.

Nina again:

This ontological tug [to understand the state] is best felt "out there"—in the infinite spaces of the sparsely populated eight-tenths of the state. There, it exerts its power in truly mytho-logical proportions, forcing one to undertake the archetypal task of naming the smallest things, much like the first humans must have had to do, to combat the vertigo of the man-dwarf-ing plains' horizons.

The writers we have brought together in this volume seem vital to this process of naming. To start, Ron Hansen writes an over-view of the state's attributes. John Janovy Jr. describes in minute detail the story of a wren and its increasingly endangered habitat in western Nebraska. Ted Kooser creates a memorable portrait of

the small town he calls home, while Kem Luther, Joe Starita, Lisa
Knopp, and Michael Anania provide the reader with new ways of
thinking about the rich history of westward migration through the
state and its early settlers. Bob Gibson and Michael Rips describe
an Omaha few of us know. Other writers make the overland trek
across the state the point of their focus. Instead of sleeping away
the drive through, they are awake and taking notes. Alan Boye re-
traces the steps of the northern Cheyenne in Nebraska in the tragic
last days of their attempt to return home after being forced to re-
locate in Indian Territory; Merrill Gilfillan, in the tradition of the
flâneur, takes the reader on a pleasurable trip full of the digressions
essential to the form; and Robert Vivian writes in exquisite prose of
his daily commute across the Platte. Mark Monroe and Delphine
Red Shirt portray contemporary American Indian lives. John Price
and Kenneth Lincoln grapple with modern masculinity, while Ruth
Thone looks back at an earlier era, and Bob Ross writes about fixing fence with humor and elegance. Bob Kerrey tells the story of his
evolution from ignorance to awareness before leaving for Vietnam,
and Jack Todd details the events leading up to his own decision to
desert during that same war. Paul Johnsgard and William Kloefkorn
write about the significance of rivers; Mary Pipher and Eamonn
Wall write about the immigrant experience. With characteristic deadpan Plains humor, Bryan Jones and Roger Welsch keep us
laughing at ourselves.

All of the writers included in this anthology have at least one
published book of nonfiction (the exception being Ron Block, who
has published books of poetry and fiction only, but whose excellent
keynote address at the Nebraska Literature Festival in 2004 was, we
felt, a perfect ending to this volume). There were many fine writers
we had to omit. I regret their absence and the page constraints that
led to such a difficult decision.

As always, there are people to thank. The staff at University of
Nebraska Press who edit, design, print, and sell beautiful books year
after year without expecting thanks or special notice, and whose

support and kindness I depend upon daily. Thank you all. Thanks to Nina Shevchuk-Murray for her tireless research, reading, sorting, note-taking, advice, and otherwise good help which made this volume possible in the first place. Elisabeth Chretien came to the Press as an undergraduate student intern for the summer and made herself invaluable. She provided just the boost I needed to make it to the finish, and she gave counsel wise beyond her years. Thanks, finally, to the writers themselves for creating works of art that are a tribute to our state and enrich us immeasurably.

The proceeds from this anthology, like its predecessor, *A Different Plain: Contemporary Nebraska Fiction Writers*, will benefit the Friends of the University of Nebraska Press.

The Big Empty

The Land That Time Forgot

RON HANSEN

I first think of the weather. Stunningly hot summer days, the July sun a furnace, grasshoppers chirring in the fields of alfalfa, and nothing moving, no one but me fool enough to be out, the shimmer of heat waves warping the farmhouse in the distance, and the asphalt road beneath my sneakers softening into tar. Or January and its zero cold stiffening my face on my predawn paper route, my gloves and galoshes not enough to protect fingers and toes that hurt as if hammered, and a fierce snow flying with the sting of pins as I slog forward through high drifts, twelve years old and near tears.

The hottest temperature ever recorded in Nebraska was 118 degrees, and the coldest, -47. And there's a wide range of climate even within the state, with flooding possible in the southeast while the parched west worries through weeks of drought. Our thunderstorms are the stuff of horror movies: lashing rain and a far-off flash of light in the heavens, then the scratchy sound of sailcloth tearing until the fifty-megaton bomb goes off and children scream all over the neighborhood.

Also, of course, there are tornadoes, more than two

thousand of them in the last fifty years. Once an Omaha friend driving home from his office noticed the May afternoon becoming strangely cool and gloomy and he glanced into his rearview mirror. His initial impression was of a sepia cloud and the churning turmoil of hundreds of crows. And then he realized he was seeing the swaying funnel of a tornado and what he saw flying around in the whirlwind were not crows but, as he gently put it to me, "things." I have read aftermath articles about horses in flight, about straw pounded through planks like ten-penny nails, about a dead woman found sitting stiffly upright in her front porch rocker but a mile away from home, about a house destroyed except for the dining room wall with its ornately framed print of Leonardo da Vinci's *Last Supper*.

Nebraska, meaning "Flat Water," was a Plains Indian name for the swift, shallow, brown Platte River that streams eastward the length of the state, sistering what is now Interstate 80. The first settlers used to lament that the Platte was "too thin to plow and too thick to drink." Locals still maintain it's "a mile wide and an inch deep," and Mark Twain claimed the Platte would only become a respectable river if it were laid on its side. The geography that the Platte slides through was part of what was once called "the Great American Desert" when the Nebraska Territory included all the states between the Missouri River and the Rocky Mountains and from the fortieth parallel of southern Kansas northward to the Canadian border. When Nebraska became the thirty-seventh state in 1867, it was scaled down in size, but its area of seventy-seven thousand square miles is still gigantic by eastern standards, large enough to contain all of New England plus New Jersey. Wayfarers on the Oregon Trail who got through the wide emptiness used to congratulate themselves by saying "I have seen the elephant."

A hundred years ago a Nebraska geologist maintained, "Rainfall follows the plow," and it's a fact that once European immigrants with nothing more to lose began cultivating the prairie of Nebraska, the Sudan of the first explorers gave way to some of America's richest farmland: waving acres of corn, wheat, sorghum, soybeans, and sugar beets, or sandhill grasslands where most of the state's six million cattle feed. Hidden underneath that land is the Ogallala Aquifer, a huge underground reservoir roughly the size of California that was formed by geologic action eons ago. Wells needed to reach into the earth no more than fifty feet before they tapped into a pure water source that seemed everlasting. Windmills and irrigation have made such use of that great lake that now, with an annual farm income of six billion dollars, Nebraska trails only California and Texas in agricultural prosperity.

And it's rural in the extreme: only Alaska has less land devoted to metropolitan areas. So there's still a great vacancy in the dunes northwest of Kearney, with less than seven people per square mile. (Omaha, for example, has one hundred and fifty). Which means in half the state you have six-man football teams, volunteer fire departments, houses that are unlocked, two or more grades conjoined in the schools, weeklies that list the wedding presents the happy couple received, five hundred–watt radio stations whose way of giving the news is to read aloud the front page. There the hired hands still ride horses. Some roads are scarcely more than Caterpillared cattle trails. Houses are starkly exposed on the topography, as in a painting by Edward Hopper. Rarely is there landscaping: with so much potential for loneliness, privacy is not a high priority. There you know the names and kin and histories of everyone you see. Once my brother-in-law surprised the sunrise occupants of a sandhills diner by wandering in and sitting alone at a booth. While he scanned the breakfast menu he could feel the men in feed caps and bib overalls staring at him until one finally strolled over and said, "We all want to know who you are and why you're here." No fear or warning was involved; it was sheer curiosity.

Ethnically, the heritage is primarily German, then Irish, then Scandinavian and English. In a population of one million, seven hundred thousand—Philadelphia has as many people—only a little over 5 percent are Hispanic, 4 percent are African-American, 1 percent Asian, and less than 1 percent American Indian. I was in high school when I first sampled Mexican food or had a Chinese dish that was not chop suey. I was ten years old when I first saw a Jew, a red-haired kid at a bowling alley, wearing jeans, a cowboy shirt, and a knitted yarmulke. A friend once insisted his town of sixteen thousand was not as insulated as some outsiders thought, declaring, "We even have a black family now."

Up-to-date as the state sometimes strives to be, there's still a land-that-time-forgot quality to much of it. I once drove through a small town on the Fourth of July and felt I had happened onto some Disneyland version of an America long gone: a white gazebo in the main square; girls in shorts writing their names in the twilight with sparklers; the old folks licking ice cream cones; a purple-costumed marching band just finished playing and the haggard members sitting on the street curbs, hugging their instruments, their high hats off, eating hot dogs and sipping Coca-Cola through straws; a grinning boy racing his Schwinn beside my car with an American flag flying from his red rear fender and balloons tied against his spokes in order to make a blatting, motorcycle noise. It could have been a movie set for Thornton Wilder's *Our Town*.

Middle American normalcy is still the main draw. Whenever I have asked people why they moved here from the East or West Coast, their initial reply is virtually always, "Well, it's a great place to raise kids." At last look Nebraska was number one in job growth, increasing 2.6 percent while the nation as a whole declined. Wages are low—the state ranks forty-fifth in teaching salaries—but so is the cost of living. A full breakfast at Cecil's is $3.70. And reading real estate ads can be hallucinatory to those who've just moseyed in from overpriced regions: 12 rm mansion, $300k. Small wonder Realtors claim Nebraska has the highest percentage of home ownership in the nation. It also has America's cheapest coal and, thanks to a mixture of corn-derived ethanol, startlingly inexpensive gasoline. But the telling statistics have to do with the concerns of families. Ranked sixth among the fifty states in "livability," Nebraska is twelfth in books per capita, seventh in public libraries, fourth in community hospitals, third in percentage of government expenditures going to education, and first in the public–high school graduation rate, at 91.9 percent. Nebraska's students score one hundred points higher than the national average on the Scholastic Aptitude Test. And if they stay put, they tend to achieve senescence in Nebraska, which is ranked fifth in the percentage of the population older than eighty-five. (The snide may recall singer and sausage-maker Jimmy Dean's comment on those who forsook worldly pleasures for a more healthy lifestyle: "You may not live to be a hundred but it'll feel like it.")

The old can-do spirit is alive and well here. With no available wood or stone for housing, the pioneers chopped blocks of sod and called it marble, heated and cooked with cow manure and called it Nebraska coal. In civic response to the area's treelessness, Nebraskans sowed fast-growing, fast-spreading cottonwoods, invented the spring rite of Arbor Day, created near Thedford America's largest hand-painted timberland, and achieved in Omaha the Lied Jungle, the world's largest indoor rainforest. Cyclical flooding losses have been curtailed by the most extensive system of flood mitigation projects in the country. The architectural wonder of its gorgeous state capital building was paid for as it was constructed, without the aid of bonds or sales and income taxes, levies that were still a generation off.

South of Omaha is Offutt Air Force Base, home of the United States Strategic Command, the national control center for the Navy's submarine launched Polaris missiles, the Air Force's bombers, and the intercontinental ballistic missiles hidden in silos, as well as "warfighter" space operations, warning systems, intelligence assessments, and global strategic planning. Arguably the most significant military installation in the world and the subject of great wrangling in Congress and among the military services, Offutt has managed to maintain a strikingly low profile in the community, hardly a word of it in the nightly news. This is no Fort Benning or Cape Canaveral; it's the picture of laconic restraint and muscular, just-doing-my-job-ma'am dutifulness that perfectly correlates to the personality of its home state.

Characteristic of Nebraskans are sincerity, independence, friendliness, stoicism, piety, and caution. Conservative values are predominant, good citizenship is honored, and the Armed Forces have no problem recruiting. The percentage of registered voters is twelve points higher than the U.S. norm. Independent Republican George W. Norris, who represented Nebraska in Congress for forty years, promoted the state's one-house, unicameral legislature, and because of that Nebraska ranks last in the nation in its number of state politicians. I have never met anyone who did not consider that a good thing. Although the statewide vote generally tilts Republican in presidential elections, there's a surprising disinclination to vote along party lines—the state legislature is at least nominally nonpartisan—and there's even a contradictory, nuisance tendency to split the vote, with a governor of one party and a lieutenant governor or attorney general of the opposition.

Owing to its position on the map—it's slightly north of the geographical center of the nation—Nebraska commands attention in a way that more outlying states do not. But the general notion seems to be that it's a dull, deadly, *Children of the Corn* kind of place, each steely-eyed and taciturn face concealing a friend with a rifle. Theodore Sorensen, the head speechwriter for President Kennedy, once dismissed his home state as "a place to get away from and a place to die." Even those who have not gotten away sometimes convey the same impression. Omaha is the mecca of the state, the flourishing, hilly, spottily cosmopolitan city where people honeymoon, have their larks, celebrate high school graduation, and find jobs or objects they can't get elsewhere; yet there's a bumper sticker that reads: "Omaha—Where the West begins and the East just sort of peters out." And when the *Omaha World-Herald* ran an article about the local ballet troupe, its headline was: "NYC DANCER FINDS OMAHA AS GOOD A PLACE AS ANY." The idea for many is to never single yourself out or get too big for your britches, but to accept your measliness and stolidly accomplish your chores.

The grand exception to that is the majesty of Big Red Football. Since 1970 the University of Nebraska varsity has won five national championships, and in the years 1993 to 1997 the football team won sixty times, including three unbeaten and untied seasons, for the finest five-year record in NCAA history. Memorial Stadium in Lincoln, which can accommodate over eighty thousand fans, making it Nebraska's third-largest city, has had 255 consecutive sell-outs, another NCAA record. And the list goes on. City streets can be without traffic when a game is played. Elderly women in retirement homes are rooted in front of television sets. Red jerseys, jackets, seat cushions, memorabilia, and the other stuff of fandom are everywhere, no matter the season. Nebraska football is not just the primary feature of sports pages, not just the common religion and language of the state, but the overriding id of the psyche. I have seen people who never even thought of higher education become sick with desolation when the University's football team loses, wild with exaltation when they win.

Still, when I think of Nebraska I first think of its climate and wide, blond cornfields, the green windbreaks that shield a farmhouse, windmill, and barn, skies that are blue as a jay. Sixty percent of its days are sunny. Well above average. And each season has its intimations of paradise. Cloudless October days when it's just cool enough to hint a sweater, giant harvesters rolling through the fields of sorghum while the operator tunes his Walkman to the Cornhusker football game. Or the first soft snow of December, the elm tree branches being mittened in white and the flakes hanging above you like God just shook the paperweight. Warming afternoons in March, shrubs burgeoning pinkly with their new buds, water quietly trickling beneath the final holdouts of ice, a baseball smacking a glove somewhere. August nights when the twirling sprinklers have made their crawl of the yard and the pale moon is rising, but it's just so pleasant out it's a shame to go inside, and the sultry air is sweet with the tang of mown bluegrass, a smell that seems to heal the lungs with each inhalation.

Myths of the American West: Two Views of the Oregon Trail

MICHAEL ANANIA

The man standing beside me is a retired stockyards drover from Sarpy County, Nebraska. The steel-guitar Western twang in his voice is real; so are the stiff curls in the toes of his cowboy boots. When he lifts his straw hat, it leaves a deep sweat-band furrow in his hair that no Sunday-morning douse of Wildroot or Brylcreem will erase. The wrinkles at the back of his neck are as sharply cut as cracks in dry soil. At the end of a small boat landing in front of us, his youngest son and my daughter are dangling night crawlers into the dust-colored waters of the Platte River. The exhaust fan of the bait shop–diner behind us is pumping the air full of the smells of patty melts and french fries. He points across the water to a stand of cottonwoods. That's his camper, an Apache, half-shaded from the midday sun. Massive corporate farms stretch off in every direction. We are standing on the Overland Trail. All the pioneers, the Mormons, and the forty-niners who set off from Council Bluffs passed by here early in their long journey west, and it is impossible not to transform his camper and the others circled in the trees into covered wagons. This is the same ground, after all, the same slow, murky river, the same flat western horizon, and my companion, who seems more American by half than I do, makes a plausible pioneer. The landscape fills quickly with images from State House panoramas and Hollywood movies, but what I want to hold in my mind with conviction eludes me, as it always has — the sense of distance and empty space that had to have settled on each voyager at about this point in the journey, the sheer awe and terror of it mixed with the hard labor of each day's progress and fashioned by the arduous dream of the infinite possibilities of what awaited him in California or Oregon.

The great overland migration to the Pacific Coast is a primary element in American mythology, and as such, it has been the subject of legend, folklore, political rhetoric, and pure fantasy since the day after the first wagons set off across the plains. It has served as an emblem of national purpose and proof of the American strength of character, and it has been the source for countless novels and hundreds of movies. The imagery of the covered-wagon pioneers has been so fully developed that most of the real, historical journey is lost or deeply buried. Some of the most common depictions of life on the trail are completely inaccurate or hopelessly exaggerated. The picture of the small, single-file wagon train, threading its way across an immense, empty space, is largely false. For most of the period the trail was crowded with wagons, and by 1850 travelers complained about the difficulty of finding empty campsites along the way. Popular accounts have often concentrated on the Platte River segment of the trip for their dramatization of hardship and valor, though the first half of the trail was the easiest. It was referred to as a highway, and some fortunate, well-stocked travelers compared it to a Sunday outing. The most popular image, the circle of wagons on the high plains surrounded by attacking Indians, is perhaps the most erroneous. Hostile encounters on the plains were extremely rare. Ninety percent of the deaths due to Indian encounters occurred in the Far West, beyond South Pass. Pitched battles were almost unheard of, even among documented hostilities, and in the end more Indians were killed than emigrants. Even the stalwart figure of movies and television series, the trail leader scout, is largely a dramatic invention. After a few years the trail was well enough known and crowded enough to make professional guides and scouts unnecessary.

Historical rendering, as well as popular imagery, varies. Early trail histories are dominated by a need to see the adventure as highly individualistic. Later accounts are often bent on finding a typical trail year and extrapolating a typical chronological narrative. John D. Unruh's *The Plains Across* is an attempt to view the migration as a whole, from 1840, when the first avowed emigrants disembarked, through 1860. It is a massively researched, readable, engaging book, well supplied with illustrations, and rich in anecdotes. The overland experience is the second most thoroughly documented, popular episode in nineteenth-century American history, exceeded only by the Civil War in the number of surviving journals, diaries, and letters. The overlanders knew they were being historic and left extensive accounts of their adventures. Unruh's mastery of this material is simply amazing. It is apparent in the meticulous development of his major arguments and in the ease with which he balances familiar trail lore with unexpected, even comic detail, to build a more textured sense of the experience than has been given before.

Unruh calls *The Plains Across* "revisionist," and two alterations in our view of the Overland Trail dominate. The first, and most significant, is that the overland venture was not essentially individualistic but was, instead, a cooperative venture, involving westbound travelers with one another, with returning, eastbound "turn-arounds" and traders, with the Indians and the Mormons. What he presents is not "humanity on the loose," as one contemporary called the migration, but an elaborate, evolving system of cooperation. His second major revision involves the attention he gives to the changes the trail and the journey underwent in twenty years. That the emigrants cooperated with one another along the way seems commonsensical, but the degree and complexity of interaction is remarkable. Goods and labor were traded fluidly on the trail. A system of messages established along the route so often made use of animal skulls that it was called "the bone express." Messages were left for stragglers; rendezvous were set; and one courtship was carried on through trail-side markers, despite the disapproval of both families. Our image of the hearty isolation of the pioneers is somewhat lessened by Unruh's accounts of the work of doctors, blacksmiths, and barbers along the trail, and by the early development of a fairly reliable mail system that used Indians and "turn-arounds" to carry letters from the wagon trains to friends and families in the East.

The most remarkably documented cooperative relationship on the trail is the one that evolved between the pioneers and the Indians. Early in the migration, the Indians are most often noted for the help they provided the emigrants. Sometimes they served as guides, often as traders. Some tribes improved the trail itself, then traded with the travelers for the right to use their improvements. In the more mountainous portions of the trail, Indians were prized for their ability to swim draft animals across swift rivers, and some diarists said that it was foolhardy to attempt most river crossings without Indian help. The danger from hostile Indians was always exaggerated, and some of the most notorious massacres of the period were pure fabrication. In what is probably the most impressive use of source materials in a generally impressive book, Unruh documents the decline of emigrant-Indian relations at several specific locations. By looking at a sequence of diaries dealing with an Indian bridge, for example, he is able to show how a hostile encounter was created when successive trains complained about tolls, then refused to pay, and, at last, shot at the Indians for having the effrontery to ask for payment at all. The unsuspecting fourth train in this series was attacked without warning and no doubt sent back warnings to those that followed that the Indians thereabouts were dangerous, thus perpetuating the problem. Most diarists, even in the

1850s, when white and Indian relations had suffered through many similar encounters, said that the greatest danger from Indians was theft, not violence. Moviegoers, who have seen thousands of whites and redskins bite the dust, will be amazed to know that at the end of twenty years along the trail, 362 emigrants and 426 Indians had been killed.

Unruh's sense of the trail as cooperative rather than individualistic is aimed at revising not only our sense of specific overland images and myths but our sense of the cultural importance of the whole adventure. Throughout American history the overland experience has been used to solidify our sense of isolated, individual effort and the isolation of the family unit. If we look back on the trail, crowded with people, wagons running often twelve abreast, with complex interactions taking place at all points, we have a completely different model. What we see is not the fabled abandonment of social and economic institutions but their persistence and flexibility under stress. Even the accounts of what was cast off along the trail change the common view of the pioneer. Chests of heirlooms, rockers, and the tear-stained spinets the movies treat so fondly were cast aside, but so were anvils, bellows, law books, grindstones, and bookcases. Even a diving bell was reported left by the trail near Salt Lake City. One of the most successful Oregon pioneers carried fruit trees the whole way. If we are to judge by what they carried along, the pioneers were expecting to build lives in the West not so different from the ones they left behind.

John Mack Faragher's *Women and Men on the Overland Trail* is a good supplement to Unruh. Faragher is interested in family life on the trail, particularly with the role of women on the frontier. Much of this study is devoted to understanding the population that made up the migration. Most of the emigrants came from farms in the Near West, and Faragher describes family life and farm labor in the Midwest in the 1840s in great detail. The labor of day-to-day farm life, especially for women charged with cooking, weaving, sewing, gardening, childbearing, and childrearing, is almost unimaginable.

The trail seems excruciating to us in part because we have had very little sense of the normal work of the people who set out for the West.

Faragher depicts the emigrant wife as someone totally identified with the work of the home. Because of her place in society and marriage, she was denied any real chance of participating in the decision to emigrate. Diaries written by married men on the trail rarely talk of loneliness or isolation. As we have seen, the trail had no shortage of company. Women's diaries complain of loneliness and isolation almost constantly. They were bound to the same duties that kept them busy from dawn to dusk on their abandoned farms, but on the trail these duties had to be compressed into "rest" periods. When the train stopped the women set to work, cooking, cleaning, and mending, and there was generally a lack of social contact, even in busy trail camps. The common picture of the bonneted pioneer wife seated in a covered wagon while her husband drove the team is also a false one. More often, the women walked behind the wagon, collecting kindling and buffalo chips for the next campfire.

Faragher develops his picture of farm and trail family life from personal accounts, but he also relies heavily on farm statistics and demographic data. The result is generally persuasive and occasionally interesting, but it makes for a slow text, and at times the statistics, however persuasive, stand in the way of his developing a clear sense of the actual lives he is describing. Still, the book is the first effort to deal with the family dynamics of the trail and to focus, specifically, on the women who made the journey. Faragher's conclusion is compatible with the sense of society on the trail in Unruh. Although the decision to go west meant immense changes for the family, the basic marital relationship was not expected to change at all. The male pioneers expected to transport their family units intact, with all the assignments of work, responsibility, and power unchanged. Some women argued against going: a few flatly refused. Not a single female diarist recounts having initiated the idea. The hope of change was a male prerogative.

Both of these books are valuable to our understanding of the great migration west. Unruh's *The Plains Across* is also vivid and engaging enough to have a chance at changing our images of the trail. It is not at all a bad thing to have in one of America's most cherished myths a potential model for social and economic cooperation, even though we will have to look elsewhere for our models of equivalent flexibilities in marriage and family roles.

Preface from *Local Wonders: Seasons in the Bohemian Alps*

TED KOOSER

Contrary to what out-of-state tourists might tell you, Nebraska isn't flat but slightly tilted, like a long church-basement table with the legs on one end not perfectly snapped in place—not quite enough of a slant for the tuna-and-potato-chip casseroles to slide off into the Missouri River. The high end is closest to the Rockies, and the entire state is made up of gravel, sand, and silt that ran off the front range over millions of years. Across this plain the Platte River meanders side to side, like a man who has lost a hubcap and is looking for it in the high grass on both sides of the road. Its sluggishness as it presses forward to join the Missouri is expressed in patches of quicksand, at the bottom of which lie dozens of cautionary tales about toddlers who wandered away from family picnics and were sucked out of sight.

About seventy miles in from the eastern edge of the state is a north-south range of low hills known with a wink as the Bohemian Alps. These "alps," which in the late 1870s began to be settled by Czech and German immigrants from that region of central Europe once known as Bohemia, run about forty miles north and south and five or six miles east and west. No more than a hundred feet from bottom to top, they're made up of silty clay and gravelly glacial till with small red boulders that look like uncooked pot roasts. My wife, Kathleen, and I own two of those hills and the wooded crease between, where we have two dogs, a house, a barn, a chicken house, a corncrib made into a studio for art projects, and a shack where I read and write and look out over our small pond shining in the sun.

Our closest neighbors are coyotes, raccoons, opossums, badgers, field mice, fish, frogs, and birds. For birds we have flickers, blue jays, mourning doves, robins, wrens, red-bellied and downy woodpeckers, nuthatches, several kinds of sparrows, catbirds, brown thrashers, goldfinches, siskins, dickcissels, orioles, great horned owls, great blue herons, red-tailed hawks, northern harriers, turkey vultures, and, early each spring, the same pair of Canada geese that have come to our pond for ten years. They stay a couple of weeks but have never nested. But, as the Bohemians say, "A guest in the house, God in the house." We're glad for their annual visits.

People who know about such things tell me these gullies and the rises between were eroded out of a plain by water melting from a finger of the last glacier. That's their term, *finger*, and when a professional geologist, who usually uses terms like *Ordovician* and *anticline*, uses a word like *finger*, I know she's really trying to make me understand. But what I see in my imagination's eye is not a great ridge of melting ice but a real finger, an index finger, huge and wrinkled and white, with a dirty nail the size of a county, under the edge of which are packed all the little rocks that lie scattered in the fields where I live. I see not only that finger but also the whole last glacier, an enormous naked man who has caught his toes under the northern edge of Canada and fallen forward, flattening the continent. One arm is outstretched, and at the end of that arm is a dead snow-colored hand with a pointing finger. The finger points south, the direction in which he was trying to go. It is the direction many of the people who live in these hills would like to travel in mid-January, when the last glacier's death rattle blows down our necks.

With mediocre cropland—at best, thin, rocky topsoil—these alps were settled by people who fled Europe during the conflicts for ascendancy between Bohemia and Germany during the last quarter of the nineteenth century. The church was seen by many of the Czechs as another of their oppressors, and a sizable number of these immigrants came to this country as freethinkers. Others have remained faithful Catholics.

The Slavic tribes had lived at the center of Europe for centuries, and it must have been hard to pack up and leave. One of their proverbs reads, "A horse has four feet, but yet it falters." By the end of the nineteenth century, however, the population of Bohemia was crowded, 315 people to the square mile, and in the distant hills of Seward County, Nebraska, there were only a few families to the square mile. The news got out. Their proverb says, "Tell it to the pig, and the pig will tell it to the boar, and the boar will tell it to the forest." They came in droves, with children, overcoats, and kettles.

In Bohemia, 65 percent were Czechs (including the Moravians) and 35 percent were Germans. They arrived in Nebraska in about the same proportions, and I'd guess the population of the Bohemian Alps is apportioned about the same today. They got here a little too late to claim the best land, but they accepted what they found and took good care of it. "As the thing is cut and sewn, so it must be worn," their saying goes.

In taverns and cafés in little towns like Loma, Dwight, Abie, and Bruno (formerly Brno, after the capitol of Moravia), you can hear older Czechs, now in their seventies and eighties, speaking their native language, but the old European card games of euchre and pinochle have been set aside in favor of pitch and hearts. The youngest descendants of the original settlers, sitting at other tables, may know a few Czech words but prefer to talk the hard yardage language of Nebraska football. They eat microwaved Tombstone pizza, burgers and fries. No *jaeternice*, spicy blood sausage, for them.

Old and young prefer the least expensive American beers—no pricey European pilsners bought in Lincoln—and I can attest from picking up litter that 98 percent of the cans thrown out along the road these days are Busch Light. The other 2 percent are Mountain Dew, a modest gesture toward sobriety and a salute to the salubrious effects of caffeine.

Every summer, the little town of Dwight, a dozen miles north of my home, has a Czech festival, and young and old put on bright peasant costumes decorated with colorful embroidery. For a few dollars, you can buy a plate heaped with roast duck, kraut, and dumplings. At another festival in the town of Prague (pronounced *prāg*) the Czechs bake the world's biggest kolache, a doughy roll with a sweet filling of apricots, prunes, blueberries, figs, poppy seeds, or cherries. The world's biggest kolache is twice as big as the Nebraska governor's Lincoln Town Car and is baked in an insulated shed heated with gas burners till its tin walls shudder and ping. When the day is over, as the Bohemians say, "it is easy for the satiated man to fast."

And there are a few people who still cook thrifty European peasant meals for their families. A friend was at the meat counter in a grocery store looking at a display of pig's feet and pig's ears, and out of pure curiosity he asked a nearby shopper, a woman in middle age, how a person might go about cooking a pig's ear. "Oh," she said, with a little Czech accent, "I don't know how others do. I fry them up real crisp and then crumble them over my husband's oatmeal."

The Czechs who live in the alps, with few exceptions, are Republican, and their neighbors, the Germans, are also Republican. In Nebraska, a "conservative" state despite the farmers' longstanding dependence upon massive federal programs, the Democrats are just another kind of Republican. The few Democrats who manage to get elected to office talk the standard fiscal-conservative, tax-cutting, state's rights, welfare-baiting Republican line and would probably be members of the other party if everybody could fit on that side of the ticket. "Where sheep are lacking," say the Bohemians, "the goats are honored."

Our postal address is Garland, Nebraska, a village of about two hundred people. Garland used to be called Germantown. In 1918, when anti-German sentiment was at its most intense, Germantown went the way of *frankfurter* and *dachshund*, which became *liberty sausage* and *liberty dog*. According to local lore, a soldier named Garland was the war's first casualty from our area. He died not under fire in France but in the States, having been run over by a truck and then dying of a gangrenous toe. The town celebrated its name change with a huge bonfire.

Garland has a co-op elevator, two taverns that open at noon and stay open late, a coffee shop that opens early and closes by noon, a body shop, an auction house, and a handsome little Greek Revival bank with four fluted columns. The Germantown State Bank has been the resting place of fallen plaster and castoff implement parts since the bank went on holiday in 1933 and never came back. The banker was a respected man who tried, but "he who goes seeking other people's sausages often loses his own ham."

If it's Friday night when you get to Garland, and you're hungry from the drive, you can get a slab of prime rib or an open-faced carp sandwich, baked potato or hash browns, and an iceberg lettuce salad garnished with a couple of saltines in cellophane envelopes. And you can pick up a six-pack of Busch Light for the road.

Go a mile and a half straight north from the bank, turn east, and follow that road along the ridge for a quarter mile. From there, you can get a great view of the alps rolling away toward Loma and Valparaiso — soft green pastures dotted with red cedars; shadowy groves of bur oak, cottonwood, red elm, and hackberry; fields of corn and soybeans with rows that wrap around the curving hills. Grant Wood's paintings of hillside fields in Iowa could be taken to depict this landscape.

Legend has it that during the Civil War, a man from Missouri drove his pigs north to keep them from being taken by the Confederate soldiers. In the dense oak grove you see just north of the ridge road, his pigs feasted on acorns and frolicked in the underbrush. When the war ended their owner was unable to drive them out, and though he went home to Missouri, they stayed in Nebraska. Though most of the early settlers had been discouraged by the rocky soil and severe weather of the Bohemian Alps, the pigs survived the hard winters and prospered. They were our first settlers, and for many years there were sightings of wild pigs north of Germantown.

Turn right at the first corner, go three-quarters of a mile, and you'll be at our gate. At the top of our lane, in that big tin mailbox with its flag flipped up to catch the attention of our route carrier, are the pages of this book, carefully wrapped in clean butcher paper and tied with grocery string, with proper postage in American flag stamps purchased from Iris Carr, the Garland postmistress, who counted the change back twice to be sure she hadn't cheated me. She's been known to send out a handwritten sticky note thumbed to the rest of the mail: "Ted and Kathy, your newspaper did not come today. Iris." That yellow note is just one of the thousand reasons we like it here.

The Bohemians say, "The cat makes sure whose chin it may lick," and I caution you that though this book is about the Bohemian Alps, you'll find me wandering off the track from time to time to talk about my family and the past. As my neighbors would say, "Sheltered by a wall, even an old man becomes courageous."

Nuts

JOHN PRICE

Several weeks ago I was having a driveway conversation with my neighbor, Todd, when we were interrupted by loud chittering noises. We turned and saw a red
fox squirrel chasing a black one up the side of a big bur
oak. I told Todd I suspected one of those squirrels was
running around inside the walls of my house.

"You know," he replied, "I read somewhere that red
squirrels will chew the nuts off black squirrels to keep
them from reproducing." Then he walked back to his
yard.

I took that as a threat.

This may seem paranoid unless you understand
that my neighbor and I are both trying to reproduce,
and failing. I know this because of other conversations
we've had in my driveway. It started just after Steph and
I moved into the neighborhood. I was out mending a
retaining wall when Todd walked over and said that it
sure seemed like hard work and that he wasn't looking
forward to terracing the hill in front of his house. He
said that if it were up to him, he'd leave the hill alone,
but "the wife wants our kids to have a pretty yard with

lots of wildflowers." I said I didn't know he had kids.

"We don't."

"Expecting?"

"Not yet."

He was smiling when he said this, but one year later, Todd has no baby and no terrace. I'd feel sorry for him except I've been too busy failing to impregnate my own wife. Todd knows this, unfortunately, because of another driveway conversation we had a few months ago. We were shingling the new roof when Todd wandered over to say how good it looked and that he was planning to build an entire second floor on his house to create more room "for the kids." I told him I understood, that that's why we had to get new shingles, it was leaking in "the baby's room." His face fell—"Expecting?"

"Not yet. How about you?"

He shook his head.

I immediately regretted sharing this with Todd; Steph and I already had enough pressure. Like many of our friends—like Todd and his wife—we'd put off having children until our thirties. We wanted to be settled inside secure jobs; we wanted a house, a yard, a life. The usual reasons. But now that we've decided to have children, we want to have had them yesterday. Last winter Steph and I sat down in the "family room" and came up with a game plan: she would get pregnant in April, the baby would be born in January, and with maternity leave and school vacations we would minimize day care. As each barren month passed we revised the strategy, emphasizing the positive: "Hey, look at it this way, if we conceive next month, the baby will be born in May—Grandpa Roy's birth month!" Now it's October and like the losing football coaches I'm watching on TV, we've thrown out the game plan. We're in the two-minute offense.

The reproductive process has left me vulnerable in surprising ways—ways I thought were private until Todd's comment about the squirrels. He of all people should have known better than to plant such a troubling image in my head where it would take root and, later that night, make intimacy more difficult between Steph and me than it should have been. While kissing, we listened to the squirrel scratch around in our walls and I wondered, for the first time, if it was a red squirrel or black squirrel, the aggressor or the victim, the chewer or the chewed. The thought grew, moving down my spinal cord, transforming into an overwhelming sensory experience. No matter where I ran in my mind, I could see it, feel it—the squirrels, the chewing, the horror.

The next morning it seemed clear: I had become a victim of sexual sabotage. Todd, my apparently benign neighbor, had drawn first blood in a campaign to prevent me from continuing my genetic line, from succeeding where he had failed. I started imagining counter strategies. I even did some research at the library, preparing for a future driveway conversation in which I'd be the one launching all the disruptive insights about the natural world. Like, hey, Todd, did you know bull fur seals will lurk offshore until their rivals start copulating and then attack them; or hey, how about the pungent stink fights between male ring-tailed lemurs; or hey, have you heard about how the bowerbird likes to demolish the home of his closest sexual competitor? *Why don't you try out those images in the cloacal bed tonight, Todd?*

I've since realized that Todd is not to blame for our failure to conceive, but at the time it felt better than blaming myself. Now I'm used to blaming myself. There's no rational reason to do so—I haven't tested sterile and six months isn't a terribly long time to try to conceive. Plus, I've been weathering reproductive pressures for years. For example, shortly after we were married, we were talking casually with friends about having children when their five-year-old daughter suddenly grabbed my hand and pulled me over to a pen near their barn. "See," she said, pointing at a pair of humping pygmy goats, "someday you'll plant a seed in Stephanie just like Sparky's doing and she'll grow a baby!" I laughed, of course, as I did when, years later, in the middle of Wal-Mart, an ex-girlfriend shoved pictures of her kids at me and asked, "Where's yours?" Or when, at my doctoral graduation, Grandma pulled me aside and told me that "smarts don't mean much unless you pass them on." Even when the day finally came, as it did for Sparky, to plant some seeds, the first few months were lighthearted, providing easy excuses to order pizza, rent French films, and experiment.

Something changed in September. Steph stepped into the bedroom doorway and I could tell by her face that we had failed, once again. The previous month, on the same occasion, we'd gone out to a restaurant, eaten fudge sundaes, criticized other people's bawling kids. Laughed. This time I spent most of the night holding her, listening to the sobs, understanding, perhaps for the first time, how strung out by hope we'd become. Steph fell asleep, but I didn't. I went downstairs and out onto the deck. The night was beautiful—no wind, the moon casting the woods into silver relief. Fireflies sparked in front of a young spruce where I knew a goldfinch nest was hidden. I'd been watching it for weeks, noticing the male at the feeder, peeking at the pale blue eggs, listening to the peeps. The goldfinch—a medieval symbol for the Holy Child, I recalled—had done his job. Now he was probably sound asleep in the spruce which, at that hour, seemed not so distinct as in the day. It seemed, instead, to have fallen back into the woods, back into the immense tangle of life from which, to my sudden grief, I had somehow become freed. When I crawled back into bed, I put my arm over Steph and whispered the only words that came: *I'm sorry.*

The next morning I wondered aloud what I had done wrong: *Was it the tight jeans in high school? The pimple medication? Was it too much lying around in front of the television while writing my dissertation? Too much microwave popcorn?* I went on and on until Steph slammed her hand down on the table and told me to knock it off, that it's not my fault. It's nobody's fault. If one of us is sterile or infertile, she said, it's just as likely to be her. Let's wait until we get tested before we panic. Steph was trying hard to be reasonable, I know, but what we felt the night before was beyond reason. It was also, strangely, beyond the circle of our love for each other. I think I realized this for the first time that morning, how the possibility of infertility had thrown us back into ourselves as individuals, John and Steph, male and female, to work through it in our own ways. And over the next few weeks, aside from the late-night sobbing, or maybe because of it, Steph seemed to be working through it better than me. She met with friends, took walks, weeded the garden. I, in contrast, avoided people, especially those with children. I also avoided the outdoors, moving quickly from front door to car door to office door. I found that if I lingered too long in the open air, I'd start feeling like the boy in the bubble, convinced that my body was a troubled, poisoned ecosystem sealed off from the fertile cycles of life around me. In such a state, every bug, every leaf, every wild cry mocks.

After a week or so of intense indoor activity—painting walls, reading, writing—I'd almost convinced myself that I could hide from the outdoors, from the daily reminders of my failure. But then the outdoors came indoors. The squirrel. It dug a hole under the new roof and started scratching around inside our bedroom walls. The first time I heard it, Steph and I were "trying" and it distracted me. Not that it took much. The squeaky bed frame, the faucet dripping, an Alanis Morissette song on the radio—any of these were enough to cause difficulties. But the squirrel was different. By visiting us in that moment, the creature seemed to be flaunting its reproductive prowess, its two litters a year, its ability to mate while hanging onto a tree branch, wrists rotating 180 degrees. I tried to change the mental channel to a different pest, but each time, obscure reproductive facts and the voices of various Orkin men surfaced to deflate me. What if the scratching wasn't a squirrel, but a mouse? *Mice can have twelve litters and over eighty young a year.* Roaches? *A roach can get his head cut off and continue mating for a week.* A bird? *In one species, the males have the human equivalent of fifty-pound testes.* It didn't matter—squirrel, mouse, roach, bird—they were all eating away at my home, eating away at the very foundations of my ability to reproduce.

So I gave up hiding indoors and returned to neglected yard work.

That's when I had the unfortunate squirrel conversation with Todd, and the weirdness intensified. Over the next few days, I became increasingly worried that Todd would impregnate his wife first, thereby exacerbating our pain and, through that stress, further reduce our chances. When I caught myself watching him and his wife in their front yard, studying them for signs of success—giddy laughter, hand-holding, flower-picking—I knew something had to give. I decided to turn to my closest male friends for advice. I planned to begin by asking them about fertility and then, if it went well, raise the psycho factor. It didn't go well. Most seemed reluctant to talk, hiding behind easy prescriptions like "boxers instead of briefs." In my altered state, I interpreted their reticence as further proof that all men, know it or not, are in genetic competition with each other and cannot be trusted for advice. There were, however, a few who tried to be helpful. One confessed that he and his wife had resorted to artificial insemination. For a guy we had nicknamed "The Mailman" during league basketball games, this confession took guts. His story got me thinking more about the promise of medical miracles. Fertility drugs, for instance—maybe we'd end up with septuplets like the McCaugheys and get a free house and minivan from the governor. At the time, however, I was still convinced I could do it on my own, using more natural measures like a better diet and exercise. But I was still open to suggestions. One friend recommended trimming the hair off the scrotum to keep it cool. This sounded like a risky procedure. And for all I knew, that was his intent.

I'm done talking to men now. I've been talking to God, instead, confessing, cutting deals. Late at night, I fill with remorse for the ways I've wasted my body's resources over the years, spilling them randomly and without purpose. I worry this wastefulness has been a kind of sin against God, for which I'm now being punished. So I've been praying for forgiveness. During these prayers I often recall the televangelist Steph and I stumbled upon a few years ago while channel surfing. The slicked-back preacher was hopping around the stage, spitting on and on about the evils of birth control, including withdrawal. His biblical reference was Genesis 38:1–10, the story of Onan. God had recently "slewn" Onan's older brother, Er, for crimes unnamed and it had become Onan's duty to sleep with his brother's widow, conceive a son, and preserve Er's patriarchal line. The preacher read, "And Onan knew that the seed should not be his; and it came to pass, when he went in unto his brother's wife, that he spilled it on the ground, lest that he should give seed to his brother." Whatever Onan's secret motives—lust, greed, genetic competition—they "displeased the LORD: wherefore he slew him also." The message then was laughable—*If I can't conceive a son, will Steph have to sleep with my cousin Steve? Should human males, like cats, have penile barbs to prevent early withdrawal?* But during these late nights the message has returned as a more serious question: Just how closely entwined are the ecologies of body and spirit? Have I, in squandering the fruits of one, squandered those of the other?

Sometimes, though, it helps to think of my reproductive self as a necessary sacrifice, as a rightly poisoned ecology, the demise of which will not be mourned by God or anyone else. On the contrary, it may be worthy of celebration. I recently retrieved two newspaper articles on overpopulation and stuck them to the refrigerator. One was covering the birth of "the world's six billionth child" in Bosnia. The boy and his mother had received a visit from UN Secretary General Kofi Annan which, I thought, probably wasn't as welcome as a new house and minivan would've been. Nevertheless, I was surprised to learn that despite the staggering numbers, world reproductive rates are actually slowing down. *Boston Globe* columnist Jeff Jacoby picked up this fact in the other article, declaring it further proof that humans are the superior animal, that people "don't breed like rabbits, multiplying without regard to their ability to support their offspring." *Right on*, I thought—and that goes for squirrels, too.

But then, in the second half of his column, Jacoby started worrying about an impending "baby bust," and that fewer people in the world would mean fewer minds at work to solve our problems.

"For babies are a blessing," he wrote. "And the more babies each generation produces, the more blessed is the generation that follows." My eyes filled with tears. I tried to fight it. I reminded myself that American children aren't like other children in the world, that they eat up more than their fair share of sugared cereals, crude oil, and trees. I reminded myself that it's easy to choose to have children when your ability to support them is subsidized by starvation half a world away. It's even easier when you believe that your child will grow up to solve the monstrous problems you've created or quietly amplified. Jacoby's breed of American selfishness makes me hesitant to start handing out blessings to our generation, or the next. Instead it reminds me of another Bible passage I wish I'd never heard: "Of those to whom much has been given, much will be required." When I think about that one for too long, I fill with fear that God may, in fact, be just.

Still, I wept over the article. Not because of what Jacoby understood, but because of what he did not seem to understand. This thing I'm feeling is *not* about the next generation or the last. It's about right now, me, my wife, our happiness, our desire to have a child, heaven and earth be damned. *Why do I feel this way?* The question had been frantically knocking around my brain, finding nothing close to an answer. Then, yesterday night, I had a dream. It occurred just after Steph and I—despite the squirrel—had successfully completed our seventh straight day of "trying." I was lying in bed, thinking that I finally understood how rutting elk die from exhaustion, when I drifted into sleep. I woke up in a tree. It was a large tree, with no top or bottom, filled with lots of people, billions of them. They were each holding a ladder that extended way down toward the bottom of the trunk, too far to see. The ladders were wobbly and fragile, but not more fragile than the arms holding them or the faces searching their lengths. I was holding my own ladder, afraid that whatever might latch on to it would be heavy enough to pull me off the branch, but even more afraid that nothing would latch on at all. So I held steady, even as my arms began to tremble and cramp, even as others around me fell or sobbed or shook their empty ladders. Even as they shouted and screamed because they thought they'd seen, just for a second, a small, dimpled hand reach out for them from below.

It had been a while since I'd shared with Steph any feelings or thoughts related to having children, but this morning I told her about the dream. At first she offered a safely scientific interpretation: the ladders are DNA strands, the rungs chromosomes. We're all up the same proverbial tree, trying to extend the genetic line. Then she abruptly got up from the table.

"How did we become so desperate?" she said, and walked into another room.

Desperate . . . I let the word reverberate through the bowl, the spoon, the bones. I became defensive—desperate was what I had been at the junior-high dances, skulking along the dark edge of the disco lights, watching girls dance with other boys, wondering if I might ever know the sweet privileges of flesh. That wasn't who I was now. Or was it? The dream, the feelings did indeed seem desperate, and despite what I'd thought, they had brought me closer to the natural world, closer than ever before. Especially to the squirrels—always in a hurry, high-strung, panicked like my adolescent self. Tree dwellers, as I was in childhood and even earlier, millions of years ago, when our species was cut off from the main genetic branch and cast out onto the savannah to fend for ourselves. How desperate might we have been then to feed, to reproduce, to move, leaving our footprints in the newly settled ash of volcanoes? I'd read about them somewhere, those ancient footprints. They were uncovered in central Africa, three figures moving in a straight line—the Laetoli apeman, his mate, and child. At one point, the prints reveal that the apeman paused and turned himself to the west. I wondered what he saw—Food? A rival male? A mirage of trees? *Was he desperate?* Or was he just amazed at a world once again changing, transformed by forces beyond his understanding, the thick volcanic air pulling across his future like the skin of a snake? Within that pause, he might have felt a twinge, an inward turn toward his mate, his child, the source so deep it was beyond his memory, beyond the place where memory matters. In that place, there is no he and I, no generations or species or nations, no blessings, no reasons to consider. In that place there is only the one reason: Life.

Then again, the ladder in my dream might represent the actual ladder in my garage, the one I should haul out and use to reach the gutters, desperate for cleaning. I can see from my window that they're clogged with leaves, which may also explain the tree image in my dream. I've been putting off cleaning them until, perhaps, I have a teenage son or daughter to do it for me. I look over and see that my neighbor has the same problem with his gutters. I haven't talked to Todd in a while. The last time I saw him he was standing in his still unterraced yard, dressed in a Chicago Bulls basketball jersey, swinging at dandelions with a nine iron. Winter is almost here and I wonder what he has been doing to prepare. Despite my lingering suspicions, I'm half-inclined to call him, to offer to help with his gutters. Maybe he'll offer to help me as well. Maybe in the coming years of this generation, as we and our houses grow older, he and I are going to need each other more than we think, learning to exchange one of the few blessings we may have in us to give: good will.

In the meantime the squirrels already cross the boundary between us, running from his yard to mine and back. I have no idea if what Todd said about them is true. At the moment I see both black squirrels and red, but neither seems interested in hurting the other. They just seem busy. Between the oaks in Todd's yard and the walnuts in mine, they have a lot of work to do. I can hear them now, the walnuts, thudding against the ground. One after another, as if there will always be plenty, as if none of it matters.

Far Brought
from *The Nature of Home: A Lexicon and Essays*

LISA KNOPP

On May 14, 2000, Ian and I strolled through the arboretum near Arbor Lodge, the Nebraska City mansion
where Carrie and J. Sterling Morton and their four sons
once lived. When I had visited this state historical park
over a decade earlier, I had sought nineteenth-century ,
Nebraska history. But this time I sought natural history: the lay of the land, evidence of what the land, flora,
and fauna had been, what it is now.

On this May morning the hilltop arboretum was
cool, damp, dark, and rather foreign looking. And for
good reason. Some of the more than 260 species of
trees and shrubs included in the arboretum are native to Nebraska. But most species are not. *Ginkgo bi-
loba*, Yulan magnolia, Norway spruce, sassafras, Chinese
chestnut, Scotch pine, swamp white oak, golden rain
tree, Japanese pagoda, tulip poplar, London plane, white
pine and bald cypress are native to other parts of the
continent or world and thus are exotics or aliens.

My son and I paused before a grove of American
chestnuts. In 1904 imported Asian chestnuts hosted
a fungus to which they were immune but the native

chestnuts were not. Within forty years of its introduction the blight had completely eradicated American chestnuts, once the dominant tree in northeastern deciduous forests. The Mortons' grove escaped the blight because of its location in a part of the continent where American chestnuts don't naturally grow and where people had not yet begun planting the blight-bearing imported chestnuts. But the Mortons' grove of white pines did not fare as well. Sterling had planted them in 1891 to prove that the eastern white pine, native to parts of eastern Canada, the northeastern United States, the Appalachian Mountains, and the Great Lakes region, could grow in Nebraska. This pine, accustomed to more moisture and less extreme temperatures, perished in the drought of 1937. Shortly thereafter the grove was replanted. The stories of the groves of these two imported species contrasts with that of the native Osage orange hedgerow that the Mortons planted almost a century and a half ago. Four of these spiny trees persist to this day.

Ian and I completed our stroll at the Prairie Plants Garden, which was added to the arboretum in 1979 by the Nebraska Game and Parks Commission. I suspect that Sterling, who preferred what he called "far brought" over native species, would have approved such an inclusion in his arboretum since it reminded visitors what the land was like before he had improved it.

From the moment they arrived in Nebraska Territory, the Mortons had designs upon the land. In 1854 Carrie and Sterling claimed and purchased a quarter section of land just west of Nebraska City, on the highest ground in the area, now the site of Arbor Lodge. When facing the Missouri River just a few miles east of their claim, they saw bluffs covered with the western edge of the oak-hickory forest and flood plains wooded with native ashes, willows, box elders, and cottonwoods. Because the then untamed Missouri flooded frequently and fiercely, scouring the lowlands of saplings and drowning older trees, the Mortons saw a riparian forest that was forever young. When they turned their backs on the river, they saw grassland, broken by woodlands clumped near rivers and streams and in the lowlands. Once this grassland extended, more or less, from the Rockies into central Illinois, from southern Saskatchewan into north-central Texas. Once prairie was our continent's largest and most characteristic biome. When the Mortons settled in Nebraska they saw prairie that was relatively healthy and intact. Periodic wild-fires, droughts, the integrity of plant communities, and grazing by bison, pronghorns, mule deer, and elk kept the prairie safe from the encroachment of trees and other woody plants.

Apparently the Mortons did not consider the grasslands com-forting or homelike. Sterling and Carrie spent their childhood and early adulthood in and around Detroit, Michigan, an area forested with aspens, beeches, birches, elms, maples, oaks, cedars, firs, hem-locks, white pines, and spruces. But their earliest memories were set in even more eastern forests: Sterling was born in Adams, New York, on April 22, 1832; Carolyn Joy French was born in Hallowell, Maine, on August 9, 1833. The bluffy, timbered Missouri River, that easternmost edge of Nebraska Territory, might have resembled the Mortons' geography of home. But the landscape that the Mortons saw when they faced west was entirely Other.

Because they broke the prairie on their claim in 1855, the Mortons knew something about prairie plants. In his 1871 address at the opening of the University of Nebraska, Sterling said, "One of the grandest of material labors is the reduction of untried lands to tillage." By "grand," I do not know if he was referring to what he perceived to be the lofty task of converting any landscape to pro-ductive cropland or orchard or if he meant that the job was "grand-ly" arduous. Certainly, the latter was true. Those who used wooden or iron plows had to stop frequently to clean the sticky prairie soil off the moldboard. In *Where the Sky Began: Land of the Tallgrass Prairie*, John Madson writes that the roots of the bluestems and prairie clovers were so tough and wiry that sometimes they dam-aged plows and injured draft animals. And breaking the tallgrass prairie was noisy work. The sodbusters called the leadplant "prairie shoestring" because when its strong roots were cut by a plow, they popped like breaking shoestrings. Nor was one plowing enough to subdue the prairie. The aerial and subterranean parts of the dominant tall grasses—Indian grass, big bluestem, and switchgrass—are roughly equal, with the seed heads waving six to ten feet above the ground and roots burrowing as far into the earth. While the aerial parts of little bluestem rise only a couple feet, the roots plunge twice that far. The roots of prairie forbs are even more remarkable. The roots of members of the sunflower-aster family can extend eight to twelve feet. The fleshy taproot of the purple coneflower extends ten or more feet. Roots of the leadplant extend sixteen or more feet. In healthy, undisturbed prairie, the sod is so crowded with roots that alien species—blue grass, leafy spurge, maple trees—can't gain a toehold. Because most of the prairie's biomass is beneath the earth's surface, the plants are safe from droughts, fires, harsh winters, hordes of insects, and big native grazers. Thus the Mortons and other sodbusters found that the tough, deep roots of prairie plants had to be broken again and again before the land was safe for corn and wheat, planted fence row to fence row.

Because the Mortons farmed and kept orchards, they knew something about the extraordinary fertility of prairie soil. But they probably didn't know what accounted for it. When the last ice sheets of the Pleistocene melted about twenty-five thousand years ago, vast stretches of dried mud remained. High winds carried the fine dust particles (*loess*, an Old German word meaning "light" or "loose") south into what is now Nebraska, Iowa, and western Missouri. Because glacial drift contains a larger variety and greater quantity of the soluble minerals that plants use for food, the soil formed from loess is superior to soil formed from native bedrock.

The fertility of "prairyerth" is also due, in part to an abundance of humus, the dark, organic residues formed when bacteria and fungi break down dead plants, animals, and insects: plant food. Madson says that in forest soils, the twenty to fifty tons of humus per acre are concentrated on or near the earth's surface. In unbroken prairie soils as much as 250 tons of humus per acre are distributed from the surface to the subsoil. Prairie plants are well nourished from seed head to root tip.

Yet no matter how much the rich, fertile soil yielded, Morton failed to see that treelessness and barrenness are not equivalent states. No matter how much money Morton made from the hogs, corn, and fruits he raised on prairie soil, he spoke of and acted with hostility toward the native landscape. In the March 12, 1870, issue of the *Nebraska City News*, of which he was the editor, he wrote of the need to "battle against the timberless prairies." In his 1872 "Fruit Address" to the Nebraska State Horticultural Society, Morton proclaimed that his goal was to make Nebraska our nation's "best timbered state." Sterling's biographer, James C. Olson, writes that on Christmas, 1876, Paul Morton gave his parents letterhead stationery that bore an engraving of their house, Arbor Lodge, in the upper-left-hand corner. Stuck in Sterling's farm journal is a sheet of this stationery on which he had scribbled: "From a photograph of house taken by Dr. Smith of Nebraska City in summer of 1876. Had the Dr. set his camera in the same place twenty-two years before it would have been a picture of barren prairie so far as the eye could see without a tree in sight."

Of course Morton wasn't the first to be distressed by the "timberlessness" of the plains. When the first white immigrants arrived in what is now Nebraska, 3 percent of the state was forested, or rather, 97 percent of the area was grassland—tallgrass prairie in the eastern third of the state; mixed grass in the Sandhills and south-central part of the state; short and mixed grasses in the Panhandle. This landscape didn't satisfy the overwhelming majority of the immigrants who were what Kansas historian James C. Malin called "Anglo-American forest men." Part of the baggage these newcomers brought with them from Europe or the eastern United States was, in Malin's words, the belief that "the presence of forests was natural and the absence of trees was an unmistakable sign of deficiency or abnormality of nature." So, when immigrants, who rarely if ever had seen the sun rise or set on an unobstructed horizon, arrived on the Great Plains, they felt overwhelmed, frightened, or diminished by the open land and sky. Many of them were so fixated on the lack of trees that they could not see the grasses, the rich soil, the integrity of the prairie communities. Shortly after his arrival in Nebraska, Judge Edward R. Harden of the territorial supreme court wrote to his wife in Georgia that he was catching the first boat home and would never return to Nebraska Territory: "It is poor country no Timber, sickly, and out of the world and settled up with Savages." One of those savages, Omaha chief Big Elk, told members of Major Stephen H. Long's 1819 expedition, "If I even thought your hearts bad enough to take this land, I would not fear it, as I know there is not wood enough on it for the use of the whites."

Nor was Morton the first immigrant to dream of remaking the prairie. In "Women and the 'Mental Geography' of the Plains," Sandra L. Myres writes that many newcomers to the plains "believed that the real physical world which they saw about them could be transformed by an increased population and the application of modern science and technology." The science and technology offered by Samuel Aughey, a land speculator, chairman of the Natural Sciences department at the University of Nebraska and first director of the University of Nebraska State Museum, was simple though arduous. Aughey believed that one had only to plow the grasslands to produce a more agreeable, more eastern landscape. In his 1880 *Sketches of Physical Geography and Geology of Nebraska* Aughey asserted that by breaking "primitive" prairie soil, one could increase absorption of rainfall, which in turn increased evaporation, which in turn increased rainfall. Aughey's views, popularized by Charles D. Wilbur, were repeated in the diaries and journals of diverse grassland settlers. For instance Elizabeth (Mrs. George) Custer wrote, "The cultivation of the ground, the planting of trees, and such causes, have materially modified some of the extraordinary exhibitions that we witnessed when Kansas was supposed to be the great American desert."

Morton did not come to Nebraska Territory because he loved the land; rather, he came, according to his biographer, "for the express purpose of achieving fame or wealth, preferably both." Immediately upon his arrival Morton went to work on his dual goals of becoming rich and famous and of creating a home place that resembled the home he had left. He succeeded on both counts. Among Morton's worldly accomplishments were the founding of Nebraska's first newspaper; election to the territorial legislature within a year of his arrival and several times thereafter; appointment as secretary of the territory by President Buchanan in 1858; appointment as secretary and acting governor of the territory for a term running from 1858 to 1861; selection as the Democratic nominee for governor in 1866, 1882, 1884 and 1892, as well as to the U.S. Senate and House of Representatives (he lost each race); an attorney for several Chicago corporations; coauthor with Albert Watkins of the three-volume, posthumously published *Illustrated History of Nebraska*; and appointment to the cabinet as U.S. secretary of agriculture during President Cleveland's second administration (1893–97). According to his biographer, Morton was "a conservative from a section of the country that seemed for a time to produce only radicals; a man, who, though virtually always in the minority, was ever a force to be considered." Morton supported free traders, the gold standard, the rights of labor, and the Confederacy. As a well-paid lobbyist-publicist for the Burlington and Missouri River Railroad, Morton opposed the Granger Movement, the farm organization that secured the passage of laws limiting railroad rates.

As Sterling's wealth and fame grew, so did Arbor Lodge, from a four-room cabin in 1855 to a thirty-room, neocolonial mansion at the time of his death on April 27, 1902. Sterling and Carrie's son, Joy, the founder of the Morton Salt Company, continued his parents' expansions and renovations. When Joy and his family donated the property, which had served as their summer getaway, to the state of Nebraska in 1923, Arbor Lodge included fifty-two rooms.

Sterling was also successful in his goal of recreating his estate in the image of his old home in the East. Immediately upon arriving on his quarter section, he began planting trees. Dr. George L. Miller, founder and editor of the Omaha *Herald* (now the *Omaha-World Herald*), wrote in the May 13, 1868, issue of the paper of his friend's landscaping activities: "The farm itself bears the most gratifying evidence of Mr. Morton's early appreciation of what was needed to make it yield the solid as well as the luxurious comforts of Home. His orchards, numbering hundreds of apple trees, remind one of those a century old in the East. . . . All around that splendid farm may be seen proof of the constancy with which Mr. Morton has given direction to fruit and tree culture. He is constantly sticking the 'cuttings' or roots or fruit of forest trees into the ground."

Morton was not content to transplant native cottonwoods from the riverbanks and bottoms. When County Commissioner Oliver Stevenson brought seed potatoes back from a trip to Pennsylvania, Morton wrote in the February 2, 1867, issue of the *Nebraska City News*: "If every Nebraskan who visits the East would look after matters of this kind, and emulate Mr. Stevenson by introducing new and improved kinds of grains, vegetables, and fruits the whole State would be much benefited." Morton hoped that tobacco and hemp would become "staple products of Nebraska." Likewise he introduced Suffolk pigs into Otoe County, adding imported fauna to the imported flora. When Carrie returned from a trip to Pike's Peak, she brought an Engelmann spruce seedling in a tomato can to add to the arbor. Sterling's only opposition to alien species was that "far brought" trees didn't grow as easily as native trees, which added ammunition to the arguments of those who believed that apples and pears could not be grown on Nebraska soil.

Nor was Morton content to forest just his own property. On January 4, 1872, he offered a resolution to the State Board of Agriculture, of which he was a member, to establish a tree-planting holiday. The board accepted the proposal and offered one hundred dollars to the Nebraska county agricultural society and twenty-five dollars' worth of books on farming to the individual Nebraskan who properly planted the largest number of trees on the holiday. Two board members wanted to call the holiday Sylvan Day, which Morton rejected since it referred only to forest trees. Arbor, on the other hand, referred to all trees. The name Arbor Day was unanimously accepted.

The next step for Morton in reconstituting the landscape was to compel individual Nebraskans to plant trees. In his famous "Fruit Address" before the State Horticultural Society, also on January 4, 1872, he linked the planting of trees with home, culture, and morality:

> There is comfort in a good orchard, in that it makes the new home more like the "old home in the East," and with its thrifty growth and large luscious fruits, sows contentment in the mind of a family as the clouds scatter the rain. Orchards are missionaries of culture and refinement. They make the people among whom they grow a better and more thoughtful people. If every farmer in Nebraska will plant out and cultivate an orchard and a flower garden, together with a few forest trees, this will become mentally and morally the best agricultural State, the grandest community of producers in the American Union. . . . If I had the power I would compel every man in the State who had a home of his own, to plant out and cultivate fruit trees. (Olson 163)

Such sentimentality and boosterism were readily accepted and repeated. On Nebraska's first Arbor Day, Lincoln's *Daily State Journal* charged every property-owning Lincolnite to "put out a tree or two, if not more, with his own hands, if necessary." Moreover, the editor wished that "business of all kinds could be suspended" so that every person "capable of making a hole in the ground" could plant something—tree, shrub, or even a rose bush—in recognition "that this is a treeless country, and that what nature has left unfinished, the enterprise of Nebraskans will complete. Nebraska only lacks trees to be the Elysium of the continent."

On April 10, 1872, the first Arbor Day was celebrated. Much to Morton's disappointment, the eight hundred trees that he planned to plant on his farm didn't arrive in time. James S. Bishop, a farmer who lived four miles southwest of Lincoln, planted ten thousand trees—cottonwoods, soft maples, Lombardy poplars, box elders, and yellow willows. He won the state fair premium for the finest grove of cultivated timber in the state. On the first Arbor Day, Nebraskans planted more than one million trees, though the editor of the *Nebraska Farmer* claimed that twelve million was a more accurate count. On that first Arbor Day, Morton was positively effusive. In a letter to the *Omaha Daily Herald*, he wrote: "Then what infinite beauty and loveliness we can add to the pleasant plains of Nebraska by planting forest and fruit trees upon every swell of their voluptuous undulations and, in another short decade, make her the Orchard of the Union, the Sylvan queen of the Republic" (Olson 165).

Arbor Day sponsors wanted a celebration every year and a forest for every farm. In 1874 the legislature set aside the second Wednesday of every April as Arbor Day, a legal holiday. In 1874 Morton's sometimes friend, sometimes foe, and fellow orchardist, Governor Robert W. Furnas, issued a proclamation encouraging Nebraskans to celebrate the new holiday. That Arbor Day Morton noted in his diary that he set out two hundred elms, ashes, and lindens on his farm.

In 1885 the Nebraska State Legislature moved the date of Arbor Day to April 22, Morton's birthday. (Ironically, Earth Day, first celebrated in 1970, coincides with the celebration of Arbor Day.) By 1892 forty-one of the forty-two United States (Delaware being the one exception) as well as several other countries celebrated the tree-planting holiday. In 1895 the state legislature passed a resolution that Nebraska be known as "the Tree Planter's State," a nickname that persisted until 1945 when Nebraska was redubbed "the Cornhusker State." By 1900 seven hundred million trees had been planted in the Midwest alone. In 1972 the centennial of the first Arbor Day, Nebraskans planted seven million trees. Now the holiday is celebrated in every state on a date or dates established by each state's legislature. Now the green road signs welcoming travelers to Nebraska identify our state as the "Home of Arbor Day," asking us to identify ourselves by a movement that sought to make Nebraska look like something other than Nebraska.

The movement to forest the grasslands has had almost a century and a half of political backing in the form of cash incentives from both the state and federal governments. In 1869 the state legislature exempted one hundred dollars' worth of property for every acre of trees planted and maintained. Since most farmers paid their entire tax bill by planting trees, the incentive became too costly for the government and the law was repealed in 1877. Under the federal Timber Culture Act of 1873, anyone who qualified for a homestead could acquire an additional quarter section by planting forty acres "of the same trees" and tending them for ten years. Later the law was revised so that one had only to maintain ten acres' worth of trees for eight years.

The Kincaid Homestead Act of 1904, sponsored by Congressman Moses P. Kincaid of O'Neill, Nebraska, provided 640 acres for homesteaders in northwestern Nebraska and free tree seedlings to any homesteaders or farmers living west of the hundredth meridian. In 1924 this legislation was replaced by the federal Clarke-McNary Act, by which two million trees per year were sold to Nebraskans at cost for farmstead and feedlot windbreaks. Through this program more than sixty million trees were planted in Nebraska. New Deal projects planted many thousands of miles of shelterbelts in the Midwest and the Great Plains to reduce erosion. In 1902 University of Nebraska botanist Charles Edwin Bessey persuaded President Theodore Roosevelt to provide 206,028 acres of land in the Sandhills, an area dominated by mixed-grass prairie, for what would become the largest human-made forest in the United States: the Nebraska National Forest.

Planting the prairie with pine forests, orchards, windbreaks, and arbors may seem benign compared to turning it under and either asphalting it or replanting it with nonnative grasses and crops. Yet each of these activities were and are inspired by the same mind-set: seeing the land and those who dwell upon it as a commodity or resource. According to this philosophy, land that lacks immediate and practical use is without value and can be remade according to the owner's desires—desires that are usually inspired by economic self-interest, such as Morton's. And so forests continue to be leveled, wetlands drained and filled, deserts forced to bloom like a rose, and the grasslands broken.

To the Anglo-American forest people, the planting of almost any tree was and is desirable, since it converts the ugly and barren into the beautiful and productive. Yet tree planting can have disastrous consequences when the species planted is inappropriate for a place. Alien plant species steal moisture, nutrients, and sunlight from native species. In the absence of natural predators, "far brought" species have no checks on their ability to reproduce and can quickly overtake a habitat. Since ecosystems are comprised of complex, intricate interdependencies, the insertion of an alien species into an exquisitely balanced ecosystem or the displacement of a native species from its exquisitely balanced belonging-place affects countless other organisms, in great or small ways.

The Russian olive, a native of southeastern Europe and western Asia, was introduced in the United States in the late 1800s and widely planted as a windbreak. Since then this aggressive species has invaded riparian areas that were historically open and has lowered the water table. Those riparian areas dominated by dense stands of Russian olives do not host the same rich diversity of bird species (piping plovers, least terns, and sandhill and whooping cranes, to name but a few) found on open sandbars, fields, and prairies dominated by native plant species. Likewise, the Siberian elm, native to northern China, eastern Siberia, Manchuria, and Korea, was introduced in the United States because of its fast growth and ability to withstand summer droughts and cold winters. Consequently, this species was the most widely planted shelterbelt tree in the 1930s and

the dominant species in Nebraska's urban forests. This elm produces many hundreds of samara (one-seeded, winged fruit) per
tree. The wind-disseminated seeds sprout quickly and easily, forming dense thickets of seedlings on disturbed prairie, making it even
more unlikely that the land will return to a vigorous, healthy state.
In short, tree planting is desirable only if one selects species that
preserve the integrity and stability of the native ecosystem. In some
cases the best way to contribute to the well-being of an ecosystem is
not by planting trees but by removing "weed" trees.

I do not hold Morton, Furnas, Kincaid, Bessey, and the other forest people accountable for what they could not have known. Since
the prairie was one of the last biomes to be studied, there was little information to challenge the cultural stereotype of prairie as a
deficient, monotonous wasteland. Nor could they have known the
value, nay, the necessity of genetic, species, and ecosystem diversity. Wallace Stegner writes that most people in new environments
were and are driven by "the compulsion to impose themselves and
their needs, their old habits and new crops on new earth. They don't
look to see what the new earth is doing naturally; they don't listen
to its voice."

But I do hold accountable Morton and anyone else who refuses to become acquainted with the place they call home and who
fights so hard against what is natural and right for a place. Nothing
in Morton's writings indicates to me that he grew to appreciate the
economy, productivity, diversity, and complexity of the tallgrass
prairie that he encountered on his political and business trips into
central Nebraska. Nor have I found evidence that he grew to see the
beauty of the grasslands. No accounts of bronze-purple stalks of big
bluestem or the golden plumes of Indian grass nodding in the wind.
No accounts of finding pleasure and solace in the seam where sky
and land meet. No mention of the leadplant with its silver-green
leaflets and its cones of purple blossoms and gold stamens or the
abundance of orchids (lady's tresses, prairie fringed, showy orchis,
bracted) or the scent of prairie roses or the brilliant red-orange of

the Illinois bundleflower. It appears to me that the high spot near the Missouri River where Morton lived, worked, and dreamed remained for him an estranging place. In his efforts to fill the emptiness that he projected onto the land with what did not belong there, he squandered his time, energy, intelligence, and prosperity. If Morton had not had such contrary designs on the land, he might have experienced the freedom and discipline that comes from living in and with nature.

In one respect, Morton and the other forest people were a magnificent failure. Despite their tree-planting zeal, despite Morton's legacy of 128 years of tree-planting incentives, at the turn of the millennium, only about 3 percent of Nebraska is forested—the same percentage as was forested a couple of hundred years ago. What has changed, however, is where one is likely to find trees. The native deciduous forest on the west bank of the Missouri has been cleared for agriculture and the expansion of such Missouri River cities as Omaha, Bellevue, Papillion, Plattsmouth, and Nebraska City. Native red cedars have moved out of the river valleys and onto range and woodlands. Dams and reservoirs have reduced floodplain forests; yet flood control has permitted trees to clog rivers and streams, robbing sandhill cranes and migrating waterfowl of their preferred habitat. At the same time, tree planting in cities—the only tree-planting efforts on the Great Plains that I support, since trees reduce the heat island effect, clean the air, and create the rather sheltered, rather private, outdoor enclosures that we want near our living spaces—is far below what it should be. According to Assistant Nebraska State Forester Dave Mooter, Nebraska's urban forest is less than 50 percent stocked.

But in another respect Morton and the other forest people were a magnificent success. According to a recent *National Wildlife* report, only .2 percent of the prairie remains, making it the rarest and most fragmented ecosystem in the United States, the one in gravest danger of disappearing altogether. John Madson observes that "[t]oday, it is easier to find virgin groves of redwoods than virgin stands of tallgrass prairie." Even when one does find a stand of never-broken prairie, it is usually but a fenced-off plot, a museum piece, too tiny and isolated to accommodate those species with large territorial needs, too tiny and isolated to even suggest its former range and glory. Now we can only imagine what once lay outside the Mortons' back door—dark bison moving through bright, seemingly endless acres of big bluestem, golden sunflowers, white asters, and purple gayfeather.

Excerpt from *In the Kingdom of Grass*

BOB ROSS

Fencing is agreeable enough, as are most ranch chores, but the obligation of it weighs like leaden shoes. Pasture contracts start the first of May, and most ranchers "turn out" between May fifteenth and June first; fences should be up and tight so that the cattle, who make it their first duty to investigate the fence, stay where they belong. I don't start fixing fence until April (after all, we *could* have a late storm, and nothing takes down wire worse than the heavy snow of spring), and I don't go early in the day; I don't fence at all if it isn't pretty weather. I throw a dozen posts and the post-hole diggers in the back of a pickup truck, get the bucket of staples and a hammer and fence pliers, reach the Goldenrod wire stretchers down from their nail. I find a pair of gloves that are already ripped and drive out to one of the pastures. If I work it right, I'll run out of posts and quit around four o'clock.

In principle, one fences to keep one's own cattle "in"; that is the law in the state of Nebraska. In practice—provided the neighbors aren't thieves—keeping others' livestock "out" is as often the problem. Two brothers to the south of me used to have a fine old Angus bull who dropped in for a visit every spring; they always came and got him when I called, fixing the wire he had disregarded, and it was comical to see them leading him home, one of them sitting on the tailgate of the pickup rattling a Folgers can of cattlecake. All the same, I wished he'd kept his nose out of my heifer pasture, because his timing was wrong.

Anyway, here we are. I've come through a couple of gates (no need to get out of the truck, the pasture gates lie open this time of year) and am driving at walking speed alongside the fence. For ranch work it's helpful to have a pickup with an extra gear on the low end; I drive along with the engine idling, reach out with the hammer handle, and give each post a good poke as I go by. It sounds lazy not to walk, but if I have to replace a post I've got them with me.

Our fences contain several kinds of posts; the oldest, and the most likely to need replacing, are white cedar, probably from Minnesota or Canada, and eastern red cedar, one of the tree species native to Brown County. (Red cedar heartwood is commonly used to make bridal chests and "moth-proof" closets. White cedar is familiar as decorative rail fencing; the wood is soft, coarse-fibered, and when sawed through it has a balsamy aroma.) The farm that Dad grew up on was finally lost to debt in 1942; before leaving, my father took off every cedar tree big enough to make a post, and when he and my mother moved to the ranch in March of 1943, his first job, once the ground thawed, was to begin building fence. That makes some of these little red cedar posts, often not two inches across, near fifty years old. Truth be told, there aren't many left, but they've done good service. White cedar rots away to a dull point; the only ones left now have broken off once and been reset, top end in the ground. With red cedar, the sapwood disintegrates, leaving the heartwood core to hold the post upright—if nothing leans on it—for an extra twenty years.

Two more old kinds of posts, cussed when encountered, are oak and osage orange. Scrub oak grows along the Niobrara and its tributaries, and makes fairly long-lived posts; sometimes the big ends are charred to help keep them from rotting. Oak posts are distinguished by their dark-gray, crumbly, wormshot appearance. Osage orange or "sage" posts are trucked from Oklahoma and Texas, where the tree is known as "bowdark," or *bois d'arc*. The big straight ones are virtually eternal and correspondingly expensive. Dad once bought a load of the smallest, two to four inches across and "so crooked you had to screw 'em into the ground." Most of them are still screwed in, but they're no one's favorite. Osage orange turns out to be nearly impossible to drive a staple into, and the tiny posts must be steadied against the palm of your hand, so your left hand stings as if you'd hit a baseball with the shank of the bat.

The next oak post I poke with the hammer handle swings back and forth like a "howdy hand" in the rear window of a psychedelic vw bus. Here's a case of the wire holding the post up, rather than vice versa. I turn off the pickup motor and listen for a moment to the jabbering of a Western kingbird—Dad calls them "bee martins"—a rod or two down the fenceline.

First I pull the staples and put them in the bucket. (I make it a rule never to spend more than fifteen minutes hunting for a dropped staple.) Fifty-year-old oak posts make wonderful firewood, so I toss this one into the pickup box. Next I get out the post-hole diggers. The kind we use has two handles (in Montana, where the soil is 85 percent rocks, a one-handled type with a sort of boulder-scooping lever is preferred). I begin digging by holding the handles as wide apart as they'll go (the blades therefore together) and stabbing the sod, taking out little wedge-shaped chips. Looks silly, but it's the correct technique for getting through the first inch or so. After that, I hold the handles together, stab, pull them apart, and raise the blades, lifting the soil out of the hole.

Once the sod is pierced, the digging takes two or three minutes. At first, it's pleasant exercise; the sand has a fine cool texture and a clean-earth smell, and I get a hint of the blue world's suburbs: root life, grub life. I go down two and a half feet, piling the sand near the hole—some of it always falls back in and has to be dug out twice—and get a new creosote post and the tamper, a slender axle from some ancient spidery automobile. I hold the post so it just touches each of the wires, and begin kicking and tamping the sand back in. (Here's an oddity: if there were loose, absolutely dry sand nearby—no cohesion, the Lawrence of Arabia stuff—I could put that down the hole instead of the moist sand I've just dug up. I'd simply wiggle the post and pour the dry sand in, and it would set up tighter than I could tamp it.)

A fellow who used to ranch along Plum Creek would cut a pick-up-load of cedar posts, haul them to town, and sell them. Then he'd use the money to buy just half as many creosote posts, which he'd take back home to set in his fence. Creosote posts are pine poles that have been peeled, cut into lengths, and pressure-treated in a vat of licorice-colored carcinogenic goo. Their durability depends on whether the poles are dried after they're cut, how well the creosote penetrates the wood, and the concentration of the mix. Similar to creosote posts are tan or yellowish "penta" treated posts. They were a lot nicer to handle than creosote, cost and lasted about the same, but the stuff they were dipped in was so deadly that the EPA won't let them be manufactured anymore. A new greenish copper-treated post is being sold to those who don't like the way creosote ruins their clothes, gloves, and skin, but there is some skepticism as to whether they'll last. Untreated pine lasts maybe five years; a green hackberry limb I once set rotted off in a year.

I've set the post so it barely touches each strand; this is curious-ly important and worth some trouble, because the straighter the fence the easier it is to stretch wire. Next I staple the wire to the post; nothing very technical here. There's a place below my knee that feels right for the bottom wire, a place on my hip that's about right for the top, and the middle wire goes between. (Four-wire fence—most of our perimeter fence now has four wires—requires different spacing, which I have to measure with the hammer han-dle.) The fence my father bought with the land mostly had just two wires; it takes a despondent and unimaginative cow to be kept in by a two-wire fence. In the first year and a half Dad built most of the corrals and nearly all of the cross fences, setting every post he'd brought with him and buying more. He, my mother, and my mother's father also built a pole barn and a five-room house, all this with a war on, materials hard to come by, and hardly any money. There was also the usual business of running livestock, trying to get the ranch going. Conceived near the middle of this wad of work, it's a wonder I wasn't born with a backache.

I throw the diggers and the tamper in the pickup, dust my hands, start the motor, and proceed along the fence, poking posts with the hammer as I go. It doesn't pay to be too particular; if there's a bit of sound wood left, that's good enough. Once when I was little I went out with a cousin to "help" my Uncle Oz fix fence. He sent us ahead of him to find the broken posts, unstaple the wire from them, and lay them down; he would come along and set new ones. He wondered why he was having to put in so many new posts, until he caught sight of the two of us, far ahead of him, one on each side of the fence, rocking back and forth. We were breaking off every post that seemed to make a cracking sound when we tested it. He ramped and roared, but we were too far away to hear. One thing about it, that section of fence didn't need much attention for years.

As I approach the crest of a knoll I notice slack in the wires, and when I get to the top I see that in the swale below me two of them are broken. I coast down the hill looking around first to be sure I can drive out again; my pickup doesn't have four-wheel drive. This time when I shut it off a meadowlark salutes me: *per-twee-oop-whee-wheedlydeedidde.* Something like that. A cloud the shape of Paul Harvey's head is traversing the sky from the northwest.

Little flakes of snow have broken this fence. What happens is that wind blows snow off the ridges and into the low places, where it drifts. Snow is denser in a drift than when it first falls, because as the flakes rub and rattle along, their corners get knocked off. If it stays cold and the wind changes, blowing this way and that, the fluffiest white stuff will pack down into drifts a cow can walk across. When the weather warms up this hard-drifted snow settles and sags, taking the wire downward as it goes. The wire stretches until it breaks, nearly always at the foot of a hill, where the drift is deepest.

All three wires have broken here before. The top wire, which is very old, has given way at the end of a previous splice; the splice on the second wire has held, but the wire itself has broken at the nearest staple. The bottom wire's not broken, but it needs stretching. I get the stretchers and fence pliers and a piece of loose wire from the pickup box and go to work. First thing is to loosen staples on the nearby posts; where the wire broke at a staple, I pull the staple and put it in my pocket.

Next thing is to stretch the fence. I start with the bottom wire and attach the stretchers across the old splice. The wire stretchers have a toothed jaw at each end that's supposed to catch the wire, and these get pounded tight with the fence pliers. Now I work the lever to tighten the wire. This is a delicate matter; you don't want the fence to break in another spot, and you don't want the ratchet mechanism to slip back and pinch you. Banjo-tight barbed wire is said to sometimes curl back on breaking and whip itself around you. Though I've never had this happen, I'm always a little nervous when I put tension on the stuff.

Once the fence is snug and I'm sure the jaws are holding, I undo the splice. To an electrician or a trout fisherman, this "splice" would be a crude joke; it's nothing but a foot-long piece of wire with loops at each end attaching it to equally unaesthetic loops at the ends of the broken wires. I stretch the wire tight, stopping to wiggle the barbs through the old loop, and then re-bungle the splice. Some men pride themselves on making small, tidy loops; I make big ones, the size of a tablespoon. That way I won't have to untwist both loops next time. This bottom wire is still pretty flexible, so there's no trick to splicing it.

The middle strand is inferior, lightweight wire, maybe bought during the Depression or World War II; it's hard to tell just how old it is. Instead of splicing right at the post, I snip off a foot or two with the fence pliers and put in a length of new and heavier wire where the staples will go. That way, next time it'll break somewhere else.

The top strand is . . . well, people collect this stuff. Once a white-haired man in an old green Chevy stopped and asked me for a piece of my fence. I said sure, hoping he'd roll up half a mile of rusty old wire and replace it with new, but he only wanted a couple of feet. Modern barbed wire has two-pronged barbs, but these barbs have four points each, and the wire itself is of a heavier gauge; now a rind of rust surrounds what's left of the steel, making it even fatter. This ancient, brittle wire is the reason for my habit of making splices with big loops. Sometimes it helps to bend it around a hammer handle; sometimes you have to try three or four loops, progressively farther back, before you get one that won't break on you. Today, though, I'm in luck. This particular wire feels "soft"—bends easily—and old wire that has a soft feel usually splices well. This is no exception, and soon I'm stapling the wires back to the post.

When the land was first fenced a hundred years ago, it must have been fine business for the steel companies. The earliest barbed wire came in a lot of styles and was mostly vicious-looking stuff, made for fencing "out" at a time when Texas steers could live four or five years and grow to weigh a thousand pounds without ever seeing a fence. They tried razor-ribbon wire and single-strand wire with sharpened spurs welded to it; nearly all of it was of a heavier gauge than what's used now. Early cowboys hated the wire passionately and with reason. Horses, unlike cattle, will panic and fight the wire if they become entangled, and a wire-cut colt is a sickening sight. Imagine the harm that old razor wire might have done.

One more thing needs mending here, I see. At the bottom of a valley you need something to tie the fence down, because as the wire is tightened it tends to pull the posts up out of the ground. To hold it at the bottom, something called a "dead man" is used. A tire or any handy piece of junk is buried a couple of feet in the ground, and a vertical wire fastens the fence to it. Here the tie-down wire has broken; I make a loop, attach a new piece, start the pickup, and drive off, poking posts.

I've mentioned bee martins' gabbiness, and a barn swallow on a wire in the evening can be quite loquacious, but my candidate for champion chatterbox is the cowbird. That's what I hear when I stop the engine next. A bit smaller than a robin, this character is the color of scuffed black leather, or, not so fashionably, week-old cow manure. He compensates for his south-of-the-tracks accoutrements by charming his lady love with talk; this one does go on, hovering in the air, clicking and whirring and twittering like a small-town telephone exchange. Though we deem her drab, the female cowbird expects a glib approach. The reason I sit and stare so gloomily on such a warm blue breezy cowbird-chattered day is that I've come to the section line, and find that the cross-fence's corner has pulled out.

Like the cornerstone of a building, the corner of a fence is that on which all else depends. Cantilevered in the ground, it resists the pull of three or four (or six or eight) taut wires. This force is sustained year after year, and over that long a period soil behaves more like Silly Putty than like bricks. Therefore, in order to hold, a corner post must be big; it must also be set deep, it should have an anchor (a board or two nailed crossways near the bottom), and it must be braced. What's happened here is that the big old cedar post has come vertically partway out of the ground. It's huge, full of knots and bumps so that you'd think nothing could uproot it, but there it is, the fat gray top looking embarrassed with its knobby pink underparts exposed. Though it seems heavy and strong, it's been in the ground longer than I've been on top of it, so here's one for the firewood pile once I get the wire unwrapped.

First I pull all the staples I can dig out, including the ones on the brace post. Once that's done, it's a matter of mind over barbed wire. The fence has been re-stretched to this corner countless times, and wire that was already old when this post was set has been untwisted and rewrapped each time, with the result that it has broken and been spliced, and now the splices are part of the wrap, loops and all. Prickly stuff. It springs loose suddenly, snatching at my shirt and gloves (piece of advice: wear a long-sleeved shirt to fix fence). As I get each wire loose, I walk it aside, several steps from where I'll be working.

Next step is to remove the brace wire. This is "number-nine" wire, hard, obstreperous steel, part of a sort of box-truss arrangement that ties the brace post to the corner. You have the corner post, the brace post about six feet away, and an "x" between them with a crossbar at the top. The crossbar and one of the "x" pieces are wood, either posts or two-by-fours; the number-nine wire forms the other leg of the "x." It is looped around the outsides of the two posts, then twisted tight at the two open places by inserting a stick across the loop and winding the wire against itself, tensioning it to the breaking point. From an engineer's point of view, the idea is to make the corner and brace into a solid unit, so that the corner responds to the force of the fence by wanting to rise vertically rather than lean. This idea gets translated into actual fence corners with varying degrees of accomplishment, and not all corners look like the one I've described.

(After the telephone company switched from high line to buried cable, there was a bonanza of corner posts and corral poles around here; they pulled up all the phone poles and left them lying in the hills, some only two or three years old and a foot thick at the butt, ready to be dragged in behind a tractor and chain-sawed. The one I'm about to set is the last of those, so I suppose I'll have to start buying corner posts again. They're expensive suckers, too.)

Next I dig out the old corner. I do more digging than you'd think necessary. This post weighs maybe forty pounds, not all that much, but if two knobs of cedar rub against opposite sides of the hole, I'll be trying to lift the ground under my feet as well. There's no elegant way to lift it; squat, wrap both arms around it, grunt. A chiropractor can do pretty well in ranch country. Folks who are serious about fencing usually own a tractor with a loader on the front and a power-takeoff-driven auger mounted in back. A swag of chain hangs from the loader bucket; a wrap around the post, a hiss of hydraulic fluid, and the post is out. Sensible. A few years back my father and I pulled up a mile of posts in a couple of hours; Dad drove the tractor, ran the Farmhand loader, and smoked cigarettes, and I walked ahead and whipped the log chain over each post as we came to it. It was easy walking, and it made us a good day because it seemed like we were getting a lot done. That was about the last time we did an afternoon's ranch work together.

I take another bird break, but all I hear this time is the distant rumble of an airliner five or six miles overhead. Sometimes National Guard fighters play tag fast and low over these hills; usually you won't see them coming or hear them until the jet noise hits you as they blast overhead. Here's another scary flying critter, a bumble-bee. Western kingbirds are called "bee martins" because they catch bumblebees and eat them, holding them down on a fence post and thoroughly hammering the life out of them. Once while mending fence I found a mallard hen's nest, high on a hill and a long way from water, in the tall grass of the fencerow. I guess if you're born a mallard duckling, you have to walk before you can swim. Won't need to walk far if a hawk sees you.

All I have to do now is reconstruct the corner. I've got a corner post in the truck; I'll need to find something to nail crossways at the butt for an anchor (the old knobby cedar post didn't have one). I dig the hole a little larger, set the post, tamp it, saw a brand-new fence post to replace the gray two-by-four across the top, and notch the corner a bit to hold the down brace. Now I loop some number-nine wire and twist it, and I'm almost done. I've got the fence wires to re-stretch, and then I can take the rest of the day off.

Funny, it's almost suppertime. The sun's butter yellow and the warm spring day is cooling a little. On my way across the pasture I chase up a flock of prairie chickens, and they wing and glide, wing and glide toward the hay meadow, leading me home. My old green truck purrs softly, until I slam across a cowpath and it rattles like a wedding car trailing a string of cans.

Hereafter in Fields

ROBERT VIVIAN

The way the sun shimmers in the long Nebraska grass just off the highway can make you feel hope again, like there's still time for lovelier, finer things. It hovers in every reed and dust mote, rippling out into the tiny eyes of grain that burn with winter's fire, an ember so small and subtle you know something is burning inside you, too. It's a destination that breaks the spell, that teeters into dread. Dusk can make the fields remote, haunted, the patchwork of all your silent prayers. I drive because I have to. I drive to get where I am going, making the fifty-mile commute between Omaha and Lincoln three days a week. But what about these fields, these grasses? Why do they suggest something about time, about eternity? I'm just another pilgrim in his crude bark boat, making his way across the waters; I'm just another commuter fiddling with the dial. But more and more I wonder what it is to arrive; more and more arrival becomes the thing bequeathed, but not desired.

If only we could keep going, out of harm's way, and take with us only the best part of ourselves; if only we knew why we dream at the wheel or think more clearly while moving down valleys and across rivers. Driving toward the horizon on Interstate 80 can make you feel this. Driving anywhere flat and endless can. It can wear you down to sheer seeing, to that mesh of changing light just over the horizon that blooms like sunflowers drenched in a cut glass vase. Sometimes the clouds above the Nebraska plains contain such towering beauty that you sense the sky is exploding around you in myriad waters, bearing down on you like grace before dying. The grooves of the highway moan, and just outside Lincoln the view north is endless in rolling fields, undulations firm as a roadkill's thigh, a rigor mortis of earth chipped from the moving plates of time.

⊕ ⊕ ⊕

I could never really know these fields anyway; they are meant to be regarded from a distance, because distance is what they are all about, the tan, variegated earth I have grown—begrudgingly—to love. Who lives on this gradual, curving earth anyway? So many people I know curse this Nebraska landscape, saying it is dull and uninspiring, stripped of beauty; one acquaintance I know even called it "the bland aftermath of oblivion." For most of my life I have been in this camp, too, disparaging the state where I grew up because it could not compete with oceans and mountain ranges, soaring skyscrapers and the frenetic pace of urban life. It just sat there outside town like an existential flat tire, devoid of inspiration. Horizon was all there was, a threadbare rim that took you to the edge of nowhere and plunged you deep into sky, leaving your imagination with nothing to cling to. But now I have come to think that even here the landscape can work its way into you by the dreamy process of driving across it, a constant revelation of blue heaven that will never know boundaries, the land beneath it filled to the brim with distance for all comers. Even Nebraska can be a holy place if you are willing to take on the cosmos and yourself, mile by passing mile. I have learned this the slow way, as I learn most things. But see how the earth drops off just beyond the rest stop off Exit 432 on

I-80, how the fields to the north define the rough edge of distance like a skinned drum, sounding the hollow notes of forever.

You could taste this north in the wind it brings down, carrying rumors of the pole. You could lose yourself in distance, the metaphysical equivalent of emptying your mind of all worry. Then flatness becomes a virtue, the keen edge of your heart in extended space. I drive between swales cupped like a lover's arm, those secret places we love to kiss and lose ourselves in: valleys that bottom out, humming with fine cirrus of light; the sense of wonder and time that these confer, again and again, driving among them because I am here. You are alive, too, as you read this, and may regard these plains as a boredom to be endured, or as a chance to daydream with your eyes open. But I think the pressure of the plains could change you, the invisible pressure of the land beneath your tires.

Where are the unbroken spaces where the soul can go to be itself? We put so much burden on these fields, we mow them down and cut them up. I want the wide-open spaces where the earth drops off; I want to see the winter fire in the eyes of the hunkered grouse, where the sky moves in a whorl like the drying, spilled ink of the sun. This could sustain you for a lifetime, maybe longer. We can enter the hereafter in fields, moving over the earth, sifting through the fine grains of fire, lighting the sparks that take our bodies home.

I am not the same person after this fifty-mile drive to and from. It doesn't matter who I am in either city, but who I am in between.

I see the brake lights of other cars and the necklace of city lights as I approach Omaha. They hover in a timeless space above the horizon, these jewels, the forethoughts of city planners. They would go on a long time, or as far as the last prefab home, bleak strobes of progress that won't let us down. But progress does let us down, every time. They glow with a threadbare yellow leached of solar nutrients, tired, worn out, a jaded string of lights that loops around midwestern dreams. Your only defenses against them are the radio and spinning tires. Drive into any city on the plains and you will see them from far away, blinking and hovering like a lasso made of burning embers. But beyond the city limits lie the fields unfolding in countless variations of repose, from the pure potential terror of snow fences banked against the sky to those fields of stubbled corn whose nappy heads ripple as if they were asking the universe a thousand questions at once.

I return to Omaha each time a little tired and fatigued, a cleaned-out feeling the fields work through me mile after mile. The drive gives you nothing you don't already carry inside, waiting only for the appropriate time and space to come forth. It gives you back your thoughts, spread out as if upon a smooth white table. The exact dimensions are not important. They come out only in hints and intimations, nudgings so small they're like a puff of warm air on the back of your neck. The drive can speak to you in barely heard murmurs, or in the wind-hollowed silence of the landscape. What is it they have been trying to tell me all this time? For years it has been like this, a moving whodunit, where I reevaluate my own small life and think of those who make it into my dreams. Then the fields ring me out in their long-grass sieves, soundless harps that play with tiny fingers.

I would go into them if I could, wandering knee-high to the bend of a meandering stream. I would look into their tentlike gaze for some brief, fleeting notion of grace. But no doubt this is a fanciful delusion, half-crazed, because what they do best they do at a distance, as a moving panorama, the texture of the earth's body entire and not a particular vale or region where I stand rooted to one spot. I am a temporary voyeur of the moving earth, rolling over it a few times a week, wondering each time at the subtle mysteries of where the land meets the sky, how they meet in changing juxtaposition, and how these work their wonder in fields. Then, sometimes, if I am lucky, I can get the whole feel of it, and I am sucker-punched by grandeur, by my mote-like presence in a world that is meant to knock me to my knees. It has become the difference between hearing and listening, singing and saying, watching and seeing. It's the hereafter in fields, waiting at the edge of every city and small town, beckoning you to lose yourself in contemplation of the land and sky and your brief sojourn between them, joined by the speed of memory.

Boring, wide-open Nebraska, unbroken by drastic change, unfurled paper of an endless map, you have been nudging me more and more insistently toward the beauty of the sky and your own dipped hollows that move like shadows into the thistle of your reeds. I drive across you to get where I'm going. I drive across you to come from where I've been, and you lay it all out before me, a long and ideographed scarf that contains walking pictures and voices.

If your fields wake, we are dead; if you lie still, or move so slowly that even graves cannot hear you, how better for us that we do not know it, that we cannot sense your awful turning, that we cling to the skin of your cheek like mites on a granite face, making our way into the thin creases of your forehead.

I drive because I have to. I drive because I must. But now the drive between Omaha and Lincoln has become the deepest part of my day, the deepest part of my week, the deepest part of my life. The realization has come upon me slowly, like shadows moving out over the fields pulling their slow curtains, giving the threadbare world a dark clarity. I do not know why this is, why certain curvatures of earth should visit this mystery upon me in the declining hours. I suspect it has something to do with memory and how the earth exacts devotion. I am relieved when I cross the Platte River either way, and a little sad. I do not know why this is. Maybe it is the way the winter trees hang near the water's edge like some keening tribe of women whose sorrow would rock me to the core, or the gray way they gather sunlight into the nethermost part of themselves, giving back nothing but deepening shadows and partly reflected light.

I have seen these fields before dawn covered with mist until they become insubstantial in the clouds, haunted by the gravity of their own churning. I could drive eighty, ninety, two hundred years and not know why it is they haunt me so, why it is I keep coming back to them, chastened, wanting to know their secret and the secret of my-self. But neither shall be disclosed, not now, not ever. They lie back always just beyond the meaning of time, waiting to come forth in small offerings of silt and clay. Duly I note my passage across them and come up with little to say, no dirt beneath my nails. This must be why some farmers seem touched with a far away spirit, their blue or brown eyes ineffable for the kinds of sun they see there, and the fields that call to them in dreams like the susurration of in-land tides. I drive over the earth but do not penetrate the cusp of it. Only in the glancing, improbable hereafter in fields do I sense a reason behind this sloping distance, or how this distance works itself in me, or how they work together to create a yearning for a dif-ferent kind of life.

Organic Vertegration
from *The Farming Game*

BRYAN JONES

Organic farming has gained adherents in the past twenty years. Most of the technology used is rather elderly, dating back to ancient China; however, some practices, such as organic pest management, are comparatively new. Basic organic practices, such as crop rotation, green-manure plowdown, and composting, are proven superior farming techniques and should not be controversial. The total abstinence from the use of chemicals, herbicides, pesticides, and fertilizers, as practiced by some organic zealots, is the issue that has generated most of the heat and very little of the light between pro- and antichemical farmers. Farmers who have mastered the use of Treflan and 2,4-D generally view organic farmers as left-wing weirdos who want to turn back the clock and cut yields for everyone. Organic farmers tend to perceive chemical farmers as backward sinners who, if they would only see the light, could grow bountiful crops without poisoning their farms or using a lot of high-cost petrochemicals. University researchers, who might be expected to resolve the fuss with some timely research, have only poured gasoline on the fire. Organic farmers believe that chemical companies have an undue influence on university research results and do not believe tests that reflect badly on organic practices. Prochemical farmers tend to believe university test results that reflect favorably on chemical methodology and to ignore evidence of organic superiority. Some folks in the organic camp believe that the high cost of commercial fertilizers and chemicals has made a switch in farming practices inevitable and that the rising cost of imported oil will force American farmers to go organic in the very near future. While there is no evidence that any big change is imminent, many farm communities now have an organic practitioner for the neighbors to study. Any successes will be noted, and if repeated often enough, imitation will follow.

The most successful organic farmers resemble successful chemical farmers in that they tend to be well established and in a position to take a few financial knocks without going under. Most farmers who have given up chemicals have suffered up to three years of lower yields, increased insect activity, and weed problems. Most say such difficulties abated in the fourth year of changeover, and then the milk and honey of healthy soil, balanced insect populations, and weed control through crop rotation began to take effect. Farmers laboring under a heavy debt load have a difficult time surviving one year of reduced income, let alone three. This is one reason for the popularity of organic farming among relatively well-heeled farmers and those just entering on a part-time basis. The latter often have another source of income and can afford to experiment.

My favorite organic farmer fits into neither of these categories. Tony needs to maximize farm income every year. If he doesn't, his creditors will force him into a different occupation. Tony's career as an organic farmer has been marked by one fiasco after another. First, the banker wasn't impressed with the new way of farming. "If it's such hot stuff, why isn't everyone doing it?" Then there were the inevitable bug and weed difficulties that reduced yields and confirmed the banker's suspicions. Living one mistake away from bankruptcy is not a particularly desirable position, and the pressure did not contribute to Tony's domestic tranquility. His wife, Thelma, reluctantly took an off-farm job to meet living expenses. There were dubious neighbors, like Shaky Ed, who bequeathed Tony forever the nickname "Organic Tony." At first Tony patiently explained his views on nonchemical agriculture but gave up in the face of merciless banter. Working under a crushing debt load, Tony was locked into producing maximum cash returns. This led to a concentration on organic pinto beans, edible soybeans, and wheat. Some organic processors would orally contract for a truckload of organic pinto beans, only to drop the price or renege completely at harvest. Tony found himself marketing his production door-to-door at city health-food stores to obtain the prices he had counted on. His marketing costs were terrific and his net income fell below everybody's expectations.

"I felt I had reached the bottom. I had a thousand bushels of organic, edible soybeans and I couldn't find a store that would take over fifty pounds at a time. The banker wanted me to sell them at the elevator to pay off a note I had coming due. I knew I could get eighteen bucks for them somewhere, but I was running out of time. That's when Thelma thought up Organic Tony's Cosmic Cereal. I guess I oughta give Ed some of the credit, but Thelma really pushed it. We scraped up some money and took out an ad in a couple of national health magazines. Two months later I'd sold the whole works for twenty bucks a bushel, and the customers had paid the freight. Since then we've sold everything through the mail that we've raised. The banker smiles when he sees me, and we've been able to add some processing equipment without adding to our debt. I guess you could call it vertical integration, or vertegration, as Thelma says, although we're so small it doesn't seem appropriate. We grow the grain, process it, and market it, so there are absolutely no middlemen involved. We've got customers from as far away as Alaska that buy Organic Tony's Cosmic Cereal just like clockwork."

Some of us have tried a variety of Tony's organic products, with mixed results, but they all have flavor going for them, if nothing else. Thus far Ed claims he hasn't eaten any of Tony's stuff. Says it leads to immorality and international communism. Some folks think Ed's just irritated because Tony turned his teasing into a nationwide brand name. Of course, it doesn't help when some of us greet Ed as "Mister Organic Marketing Genius." Ed has always lacked a certain ability to laugh at himself.

Excerpt from *This Death by Drowning*

WILLIAM KLOEFKORN

For it is the source
Of Afton that I seek and dread,
Compelled to marvel at movement and
To worship visible fountainheads.

"THE SPRING HOUSE"

To know a river, float it in a twelve-foot johnboat every
summer for thirty summers. Try the Platte, and enjoy
it—the braided currents, the expansive shores, the in-
numerable sandbars and islands. As you half recline in
the boat, resting the oars, think of all those westward-
ho pioneers whose souls reached this river to follow
it—wherever. Of those who made it and of those who
didn't. Of locust. Typhoid. Bottlejaw. Kangaroo rat.
Grasshopper. Cholera. Smallpox. Tick. Blizzard. Colic.
Distemper. Think of this river as a haven for the crane,
the eagle, the goose, the tern, the plover. Think of what
one of the pioneers, James Evans, said of the Platte in
his *Journal of a Trip to California:*

My first impression on beholding the Platte River was, that as it looked so wide and so muddy, and rolled along within three feet of the top of the bank with such majesty that it was unusually swollen and perfectly impassable. Judge my surprise when I learned that it was only three or four feet deep. . . . The water is exceedingly muddy, or I should say sandy; and what adds greatly to the singular appearance of this river, the water is so completely filled with glittering particles of micah [*sic*] or isinglass that its shining waves look to be rich with floating gold.

Think of the Platte. Then, summer in and summer out, float the Loup.

Because of this: the Loup is a homegrown Nebraska river, its central and northern branches beginning in the sandhills of Cherry County, its southern branch with its fountain head not far from Stapleton in Logan County. And just as the Loup knows where to begin, it knows where to end: just below Columbus.

Spring, meaning a flow, a fountainhead, is a mystery I do not care to have explained. Heacock's Reservoir began with a fountainhead enshrined within a stone house, the clear cold water rising and rising into a trough that carried it from the house to drop it into a shallow gulley that carried it over red earth and through a grove of catalpas to the reservoir, so that by the time it reached the pool it was sufficiently roiled and muddied to suit the tastes of the carp and the catfish and the turtles. I loved to fish in that reservoir, to sneak away from home with a cane pole and a dozen obese night crawlers in a Prince Albert can, to hop a slow freight train if one happened along; but at times I chose to take an alternate route, to walk west beside the blacktop so that I might drink from Heacock's spring before moving on down to the reservoir.

On a stifling day—mid-July, maybe, maybe early August—you could hardly wait to reach the spring house. By the time you entered its side door you would have been drenched, sweat coursing the stomach and the spine in a sweltering aggravation of rivulets. You would place cane pole and can on the floor, then moving to the corner of the house where a large rectangle of concrete enclosed the spring, forming a basin, you would lie on your stomach to drink the cold clear rising water—to drink, and to press an open eye all the way to the gravel-scoured bottom of clarity.

On certain extra-hot occasions I drank that cold and immaculate water until I swear I became the heavy-bellied catfish I had come for. I remember how difficult it was on those occasions to disengage my fins and force myself to my bulky clumsy landlocked feet. I would stand immobile for several seconds, blinking, then walk half-drunkenly in a circle, trying to find my legs. When my vision had cleared, and the legs were steady, I would pick up the cane pole and the can of worms and hike appreciatively, as if with eyes reborn, down to the reservoir.

The sources of the North and the Middle Loups must be the big brothers to the source of Heacock's Reservoir. Covering an area of more than 19,000 square miles, the Nebraska Sandhills make up one of the largest sand dune areas in the Western Hemisphere. They measure, east to west, about 265 miles; south to north, at the widest point, 130 miles. Some say its shape resembles an egg; others say a diamond. I opt for both: eggs for its fragility—eggshell and topsoil vegetation not much thicker than a shim—diamond for its priceless and hard-headed inclination to stick around.

To appreciate both sides of this apparent contradiction, drive with me to the northwest quarter of the State. After a cheeseburger and a beer at the corner hotel in Hyannis, we will take Highway 2 west to Ellsworth, where we say we are stopping for gas, but where in fact we use the fill-up as an excuse to buy something made of leather put together by a craftsman who supports his talents through the sale of gas and oil. From Ellsworth we head due north on Highway 27. Twenty miles later we will turn east to follow a couple of back roads that will take us to the grave of Mari Sandoz.

The lone grave is on the side of a sandhill overlooking Old

Jules's transplanted orchard—apple and peach and plum trees in long thick lines of open defiance, Old Jules himself having defied almost everything, weather and terrain and hearsay and his several wives included, to get the trees planted and watered. The grave is protected from the Hereford and the Angus by several tiers of barbed wire; you enter the protected arena through a small-slatted gate rigged with a pulley and a sash-weight. Inside, you walk uphill to the large granite tombstone and, standing behind it, you behold the Sandhills.

Or you *would* behold them, if you had eyes equipped to see forever. Beyond the myriad dunes and hog backs immediately before you, dunes kept pretty much intact with needlegrass and switchgrass, dropseed and bluestem, soapweed and grama, spiderwort, thistle, primrose, sand cherry, ivy, and redroot, flow the Snake and the Niobrara Rivers, along and between them a scattering of red cedar, pine, box elder, hackberry, cottonwood, wild plum, chokecherry, and elm.

Say that the month is March. Say that at the moment you do not need a sweater, though you brought one with you.

If your eyes are impossibly keen they might be seeing far away to the east the largest county in the Sandhills, the largest in all of Nebraska—Cherry. On one of the ranches—a modest though somewhat comfortable one, say forty-five hundred acres—a rancher with his hired hand is caking the cattle, after which they will ear-tag several of the youngsters, during which time they will undergo half a dozen interruptions to help a cow or a heifer with her calving. Now look closely. See that Angus heifer? She's in trouble; they'll have to use the calf puller. They affix the puller's clamp to the protruding hooves to winch the wet black blob to birth. Notice how the mother in agony dropped at the last moment to her knees, then fell on her right side. Notice how quickly, though, following the birth, she is back on her feet, how soon thereafter she is circling her calf—curious, bewildered—afterbirth trailing her like a slick bloody rope. And what is the hired hand doing? He is sprinkling the supine calf with what you'd hear him call "Calf Coaxer" if he weren't a hundred leagues away. Does it work? Yes—its blood aroma attracts the heifer, and she begins to lick.

That large space nearest the barn, the one teeming with cows and heifers whose bags appear tight to the point of bursting—that's the heavy lot; it is filled with those animals the rancher and his hired hand believe are closest to coming light. That one just there, for example—can you see her? She had dropped not only her calf but also her calf bed, a goodly portion of her innards. Now watch the rancher and his sidekick. They will place the dangling pear-shaped innards into a five-gallon can; the hired man will hold this can while the rancher works the innards back into the walleyed cow. Eventually, if all goes well, all of the entrails inch by gut-slick inch will be returned, and the rancher will sew the ruptured skin together, wash his hands at the pump, and be ready for another.

But note that most of the calves arrive without incident, several hundred on his ranch alone before the end of March. Watch them watch their mothers licking them clean. Watch them struggle to find their legs, how with the help of the mother each noses its way to where already the milk from her bursting udder is dripping. You ever have the feeling that whatever isn't round wants to be?

Sure, says the hired man (after supper, after roast beef and mashed potatoes and iced tea and macaroni and two types of cheeses with hot rolls and cherry Jell-O and a wedge of chocolate cake under an impressive dollop of vanilla ice cream with hot black coffee to wash it down—and when there is a lull out in the heavy lot), I'll answer a question or two, if I can.

Yep, most female bovines do have their little eccentricities, especially when they are about to give birth. For one thing, they prefer at least a handful of privacy. The cow by and large prefers hers at the top of a hill, but the heifer will take her privacy wherever it happens, ridgetop or otherwise. The heifer's offspring will ordinarily weigh around forty-five to fifty pounds, the cow's around fifty to sixty-five pounds. But exceptions—how do you say it?—*abound*, and one reason is that sometimes a heifer will be bred to a type of bull whose get produces large calves. The Galvey bull is one of those, and the Saler bull—that's a French breed with balls so prolific they rhyme with *beaucoup*.

Absolutely: The windmill had been a big part of the Sandhills since long before Hector was a pup, and I don't see it drying up in the near future. That one north of the house pumps water not only for the cattle, but also sends water down the slope to the pasture. We have five windmills on this spread, and all of them pump water.

Your ranch horse, if it's worth its feed, should be ambidextrous, part cutting horse, part roping horse—and it should be a horse willing to take its rider to either of two places: nowhere or anywhere. My own horse, Rowdy, used to be but isn't now; I tamed him with an ax handle.

Barbed wire? Some say barb wire, some bobwore. I spent a couple of lifetimes one summer in Texas, so you prob'ly know which one I prefer. Mostly around here you'll see red-strand bobwore. That's because the barbs are painted red—or were, when the wore was new. The barbs are double and are spaced about one dick length apart, give or take. This morning I saw a new calf attack two strands of that wore, and the wore won.

No, the Sandhills coyote is not extinct, and prob'ly never will be. Saw one a couple of days ago, but couldn't get off a shot. A good pelt during a good season will bring seventy-five or eighty dollars. Last year, though, the average was about fifty dollars. Nope, I don't skin them; I hang them up and keep them as cold as the weather permits until a fur trader takes them off my hands. Yes, there are indeed quite a few traders come through here. You'd be surprised. And even with the high cost of ammunition—six bucks for twenty shells—you can make money, if you can hit what you're aiming at.

Well, the blowout happens when the vegetation here, such as it is, gets overgrazed or trampled down, leaving the sand at the mercy of the wind. Ranchers don't care to see this happen; on occasion I have heard my own dear boss mutter improprieties when he comes across a fresh blowout. He doesn't even approve of the cattle socializing in clusters at the windmills, after they've had their fill of water. The more the cattle go to clustering in the same spot, the more likely that spot will become a blowout. It takes a long time, years most generally, for a blowout to recover its lost vegetation. Sand: it's what a lot of folks fly to to lie on to have something to call *vacation*. Here, sand is what you don't want to see unless most of it is being held in place with grasses. I need another cup of coffee. How about you?

You remain at the grave of Mari Sandoz, just off Highway 27 northwest of Hyannis and straight down from Gordon, to watch the dunes slowly darken into an eerie and mysterious void as the sun sets behind you. Sure enough, the Sandhills coyote is not extinct. If it is, how can you hear one howling? And the deer and the bobcat, the porcupine and the occasional red fox—out there in the void somewhere they sniff and lay their plans. They move and persist.

Move and persist. Under your feet as you leave the gravesite you can feel movement, the weight of your brief biped existence making itself known against nineteen thousand square miles of ancient and distinctive and bullheaded sponge. Sand, yes; hills, yes. Simple addition: sand + hills equals sandhills.

No. The Sandhills are more than the sum of their parts. Because above the sand grow grasses sufficient to sustain some of the largest cattle ranches in the country, if not the world. Because, wounded by blowouts, the prairie penstemon and other tenacious members of the figwort family come eventually to their rescue. Because in its own diverse and resourceful ways the loose earth collects and stores its rainwater, permits it to flow horizontally to the swales and flats to become, say, one of the seventeen lakes in Cherry County, lakes with nothing short of magic in their names: Shell, Pelican, Rat, Mother, Swan, Red Deer, Willow, Dads, Cottonwood, Beaver. Because these lakes, and countless others like them, are tangible liquid evidence of what lies below—the High Plains Aquifer, the

Ogallala Aquifer, 174,000 square miles of phenomenon that stretch from Texas to South Dakota, enough water to fill if not overflow Lake Huron.

And because it is the spring from which the North and Middle Loups begin.

To know a river, decide which river you want most to know. Then push your boat into the nearest current.

I did this for the first time thirty years ago. I did not own a boat thirty years ago—and I have otherwise well-intentioned colleagues who might venture that I do not own one yet—my vessel being a twelve-foot aluminum johnboat, Appleby by trade name. My argument is this: if it floats and gets you there, it is a boat. Their argument is—never mind. Their argument is nothing more than a canoe with holes in it, all of them on the lower deck.

My maiden voyage, as it turned out, skirted disaster. I had put my trust in an acquaintance who did in fact own a boat, a thick-gauged wide-hulled iron-masted aberration he had christened, appropriately, *Diamond-in-the-Rough*, and appropriately had sacrificed a long-neck bottle of Lone Star for the christening. My acquaintance said that he knew how to read a river, most especially the Loup, because he had gone to the State Historical Society and it had plied him with relief maps detailing the Loup River all the way from—hell to breakfast. I believed him. So did my brother, whose leg to this day carries the scar of the spurting artery. So did my brother's friend who, like me and Maclean and Eiseley and probably untold others, has a fear of water he loves not to resist.

We covered the dining-room table with maps until they spilled onto the floor; then we covered the floor. We penciled and planned far into the night; neither tactical nor strategic fine points were left uncovered. On our knees, beer in one hand and a highlighter in the other, we described a river route calculated to quench that thirst for adventure that the Falstaff could not touch. Finally, this question: Should we load the boat tonight?

By all means—or by any. Atop my Chevrolet Bel Air, the one that one day would take me to St. Patrick's Church to discuss the efficacy of baptism with Father Lightbody, we loaded my acquaintance's *Diamond-in-the-Rough*, one of us remembering, at the last moment, the oars.

That night a rain so gentle it scarcely interrupted my sleep—I was adrift on a mattress, reading the channel with impeccable foresight—fell, but by morning the clouds had floated far to the west and a brilliant August sunrise portended nothing but the dry warm smell of success. Having noted the sunrise through the living-room window, I stepped outside to admire the Bel Air with its boat, both poised streetward in the driveway as if for flight. I saw right away that we had not loaded the boat properly; we had placed her upright, intending to use her glandular space for the loading of gear. Into that space, or into much of it, the rain had fallen, enough rain to cause the ivory portion of my tan-under-ivory vehicle to collapse. The scene registered itself heavily upon the mammalian section of my brain. Christ, I remember thinking, what have we done?

I passed the word to my comrades; soon we were taking turns on the ladder, using a two-pound Folgers coffee can as a bailer. Last night, in our planning, we had not thought to include a bailer as part of the gear; now, bailing, I suggest that we take one—this very one, in fact, since it seemed to be doing its work efficiently enough, albeit slowly.

The boat at last free of water we untied and lowered her onto the lawn; then moving as if a well-trained unit we deployed ourselves deliberately and precisely inside the Bel Air—my brother and I in the back seat, my acquaintance and my brother's friend in the front seat—and on the count of three we pressed our collective palms upward until the top of my lovely Chevrolet exploded like an M-80 back to its predeflated configuration.

This time we loaded the *Diamond* upside-down, securing her with perhaps more rope and bungee cords than necessary. Into the trunk we forced our gear.

We did not take much gear because we had planned only a two-night float, and because August in Nebraska rarely calls for coats. And because I had promised plenty of catfish for the evening meals, we did not have to pack much food—an egg or two for breakfast, with some bacon and a couple of hotcakes, sardines and baloney and cheese sandwiches for lunch. And a bottle of something less than Royal Salute with a couple of beers to settle things down.

The drive from Lincoln to the Fullerton Bridge, where we would put the *Diamond* onto the river, was one hundred miles of sunlight and anticipation, of dawdling and of speeding up and of stopping—at Central City, for example, where we found a hardware store almost without parallel: yes, they did have tent stakes in stock, and, yes, they did sell them separately from the tents. We bought a dozen because my brother's friend, who was furnishing the tent, had forgotten the stakes, but luckily for all of us, he said, he remembered that he had forgotten them, and he did the remembering in time for all of us to chip in and buy four more stakes than we needed, just in case.

The shank of the day was pretty much history when after a snack in Fullerton, just to tide us over, we pushed the *Diamond* into the clean clear sand-scoured water of the Loup River. Four pioneer spirits in a single boat adrift on a current two-thirds of which, at least, had begun as seepings in the sandhills of Cherry County, the north branch with its birth not far from Piester Lake, the middle branch beginning its inexorable flow about twenty miles north of Hyannis—the other one-third, the south branch, oozing into the act ten miles west of Stapleton, near the line that divides McPherson and Logan Counties. O sweet Jesus! I know we are moving because the Fullerton Bridge, with its museum of artwork and graffiti, is slowly receding. This river, I tell myself, is the ultimate and the wisest compromise: it is not Shannon's Creek, from which my friend Oscar emerged grinning and gasping and sanctified, nor is it the Mississippi, Twain's lovely but sometimes ominous chameleon. It is instead a mid-sized river, its currents swift and plentiful enough to change from year to year the contours of some of the shoreline, yet not large enough to attract anything more exotic than an occasional airboat or a brace of youngsters with something more than wading on their minds.

Time is the stream we go a-floating in; almost before we know it the sun has taken on a tint of orange, and the owner of the boat, who has been doing the rowing and who has given all of us permission to call him either Captain or Skipper, allows that we should keep our eyes peeled for a good place to camp. This we do—because our Captain, after all, is our Captain, a man who knows the river because he had gone to the State Historical Society and it had given him a ton of relief maps detailing the Loup River all the way from hell to breakfast. These maps our Captain brought with him; he had bound them with brown twine into a bundle the size and heft of a Sears catalog, and he had stuffed them into a space at the back of the boat between the port side and the beer chest.

Our Captain is a rotund fellow who is perpetually good humored—until something goes wrong. At such a time his mood varies from slightly petulant to surly to downright unpleasant. At the moment, his chubby hands at the oars, he is happy; he has a round boyish face, its roseate cheeks, like the rest of him, a tad overweight, his brown hair going off in several directions. He sits with his back to the bow. He looks at me, grins, tells me to read the channel, then to pass my reading along to him: Heavy on the right oar, Skipper, for example, or hard on the left, Captain, or easy on both oars—I think we're smack in the middle of the channel and can let her float without much rowing.

When I misread the channel I hear for the first time a sound that is difficult to forget, a soft scraping of sand against the underside of the *Diamond*, a scraping that intensifies until our craft comes to a complete stop, the shallow water of the Loup moving on as if our hang-up doesn't matter. And it doesn't, not really; its irritation is so slight, in fact, that the Captain finds it more amusing than aggravating. He invites us to step out of the boat and push it back into the

channel. We do—for he is our Captain, after all, a man who knows
the river because . . .

After several further misreadings I and my fellow noncommis-
sioned swab-jockeys find it difficult to smile while pushing the
Diamond back into the channel. For one thing, the *Diamond-in-the-
Rough* is a heavy and cumbersome boat, even when empty; loaded
with gear—the chest of beer aft, our duffel bags and the tent with
its new sack of tent stakes fore, not to mention our Captain sitting
portly and ruddy amidships, shouting orders—the *Diamond* is a le-
viathan that might well have swallowed an anvil or two instead of
Jonah. And another thing: there really isn't much of a channel to
read, a bald fact that our Captain seems unable to assimilate. He sits
there on a bench of thick-gauged aluminum, his hands on the oars,
the business ends of the oars poised above the water as if at any moment the boat either on its own or at the behest of three barefooted
yeomen might discover the channel, whereupon the oars will come
to life to guide and encourage the *Diamond* downstream.

But the sad truth is that there isn't much of a channel to be
discovered—not by the boat on its own, not by the three yeomen
who pull and push until they have only enough strength left to
threaten mutiny.

Our Captain removes his red tennis shoes and rolls up his pan-
tlegs; he is wearing blue overalls and no shirt, meaning that his
sunburn at the end of the voyage should be more decorative than
any of ours, because we are wearing jeans and washpants and T-
shirts—and one of us has a ball cap to protect the skull, another a wide-brimmed straw hat, while my brother protects his cra-
nium with a sailor's cap loaned him by my Aquarian wife, who
came by the cap by way of her older brother, who after the Japanese
surrendered aboard the *Missouri* served long and honorably in the
Seabees.

Our Captain takes the lead rope, worries a peculiar slipknot into
the loose end and manages somehow to force the noose down over
his shoulders and chest so that, leaning his body, his midriff, against

the noose he can bring an impressive amount of weight to bear in an effort to offset the *Diamond*'s considerable drag. By this time we yeomen have caught our breath and are fully prepared to do our share of the hauling and heaving.

When we find the trickle of a channel near the shore our vote is unanimous: this would indeed be an ideal spot to camp for the night. And, in fact, the spot if not ideal doesn't miss it by much. The bank is steep and a bit too high to be easily negotiated, but the area is fertile with dry wood for a campfire, and several cottonwoods, high as skyscrapers, should give us plenty of protection from the sunrays the following morning.

So is it my fault that I do not catch enough catfish for supper that evening? Is it my fault that I do not catch *any* catfish? The water on this side of the river is much too shallow for any fish larger than a minnow, and my legs are much too spent to go splashing across to explore the other side. The Loup is not as wide as the Platte (the latter having been translated by the Indians as *flat*, from the French), except occasionally, but after all its branches have come together it cannot by any means be characterized as narrow. Thus do I suggest cheese and baloney sandwiches—with at least one can of sardines, a few crackers, and a beer. We can worry about the last day's lunch when the last day comes.

My brother's friend (mine also, alias Leon) supervises the setting up of his tent, shows us where and how to hammer home each of the new tent stakes. The tent is old—heavy brown canvas that, erected, forms an elongated A, though not quite elongated enough to accommodate comfortably four pioneer spirits, one of whom, our Captain, requires the better part of an acre, and two others, my brother and I, who aren't all that far behind. The fourth, alias Leon, though a virtual string bean, nonetheless deserves something more than a strip no wider than a Band-Aid to lay his string bean on.

But, as our Captain says (he has eaten, without outside intervention, two sandwiches and a can of sardines and a half box of crackers and has drunk a six-pack of Lone Star beer), who the hell cares?

Is this a river voyage, he asks, or a panty raid? Are we mice or men? Bill, he says, would you toss me another beer?

Night descends. It is a warm night, and humid, but there is a breeze just strong enough to discourage mosquitoes. My brother had started a fire shortly after the securing of the final tent stake; perhaps he believed that I would find a way to catch a mess of cat-fish, or maybe he simply wanted to amuse himself with flames and coals. And soon enough the embers burn orange to blue to orange, and during a lapse in our campfire conversation I look up from star-ing at these embers to see a long low fork of lightning upstream. I tell our Captain. But already he is in the tent, in his sleeping bag, his snoring as if a mating call to summon thunder. And how it works! Suddenly the breeze becomes a cool raging wind, flapping the tent, bending the cottonwoods. Just as suddenly the lightning is upon us, with its attendant thunder. And when the rain falls it falls both thick and horizontal.

Inside the tent, half soaked, we settle into our sleeping bags to lie out the storm. Fortunately, says the owner of the tent, I remembered that I forgot the tent stakes. Because now, he says (something philo-sophical in the way he says it), we have four extras.

Soon we are making use of them, driving them deep into soil that thanks to a layer of green sod affords a minimal purchase. We are not long at doing this, at driving the stakes and affixing four ropes from the stakes to grommets at the sides of the tent, but when we return to our sleeping bags we have been thoroughly immersed: in the name of the Father, and of the Son . . .

Our Captain meanwhile snores on. He has twisted himself and his sleeping bag so that now he is lying at an odd angle, usurping some of his crewmen's space. I sit on the dampening floor of the tent and with both feet push at the lower half of our Skipper's body, hoping to reduce the angle. Surprisingly, I succeed; the mass inside the sleeping bag both slides and snorts, and when it has been re-turned to a right angle I desist.

With my fellow Aquarians I do what I can to dry myself. In addition to four pioneer spirits, the tent shelters four duffel bags; we dip into three of them to bring forth a towel here, a dry pair of trousers there, a shirt that is only damp over yonder. The search for something waterless is not easy. No one had remembered to bring a flashlight. Fortunately, as Leon says, sotto voce, we have the incessant lightning to guide us. Another problem is that the wind is whipping the ancient tent so forcefully, and in gusts so menacingly violent, that it drives the rain through the brown canvas, refining it in the process so that it thickens the inside of the tent with a mist like a heavy fog.

Even so, we persist. Perhaps in our ears yet rings the rhetorical encouragement of our Captain: Is this a river voyage or a panty raid? Are we mice or men?

We lie without speaking, half dry, half damp, the other ten percent merely drenched. The wind and the rain slap at the tent, whipping and abusing and contorting it, until I begin to wonder whether we might not finally lose the tent to the storm, and all of us with it. I could imagine the water rising and rising until in a rush of indescribable power it would burst over the bank and carry away in a mad frothy swirling downward rush everything in its path. I had heard of rivers doing this, and had seen pictures. And now I see a picture with all four of us in it, four faces with four sets of open eyes staring quizzically into the eye of the camera they will never see.

As if to punctuate my half-dream, lightning strikes; the sound is that of an M-80 firecracker, say, exploded half an inch away from the eardrum. I can hear then the futile resistance of the cottonwood—a creek gives way to a groan that rises steadily in pitch and increases steadily in volume until—how many eons later?—a thousand twigs and limbs crash brokenly against and into the waterlogged ground.

I hear myself saying, Missed us.

I hear my brother saying, This must be the end of the world.

I hear Leon saying, Lucky I remembered I forgot those tent stakes.

I hear our undaunted Captain, snoring on.

Uncle Vic's Mule

ROGER WELSCH

Whenever Uncle Vic pushed back his chair from the card table in the Town Tavern, everyone used to run for the door. This explosive reaction always surprised tourists. It would happen just like that: Vic would push back his chair and say something like "Whelp," and suddenly everyone was throwing on coats and hats and gloves as if the fire siren had gone off. Vic never seemed to notice or to change his own pace but all around him there was this flurry of activity and then all these people trying to get out the tavern door all at once.

Out in the street five or six car engines would spring into full power and cars would be shuffling from one side of the main street to the other in a ballet, looking like a bunch of Shriners driving those little cars in the Fourth of July parade.

See, Vic had this great big old Buick, and what he would do when he was leaving for home, just a couple of blocks from the main street, was to start the car, get the engine moving at a pretty good speed, pop the clutch, and back up until he hit something. Then he would go forward all the way home. He didn't very often hit anything going forward, which always surprised me, since he had to look out through the steering wheel over that great expanse of sheet metal in front of him, but he *always* hit something when he was going backward because he never stopped going backward until he did hit something.

Well, everyone hoped it wouldn't be his car that signaled the end of Vic's backward movement. Even if you only drove a junker, you were concerned because that monstrous Buick could reduce it to scrap metal. Vic once drove right over the top of six bicycles and never so much as slowed down even though two of the bikes were jammed up underneath that Buick and the next day Herb had to use a cutting torch to get them free of the automobile.

All of that made good conversation, but Vic's driving finally got so bad it was dangerous. He scolded Hat for almost three weeks after they ran into each other with their cars at the highway intersection. "You damned fool," Vic shouted in Hat's face, "why did you run into me like that?"

"Well, you old idiot, you didn't even slow down for that stop sign," Hat responded, smiling. He smiled, I think, because it was one of the two or three accidents he had ever participated in that wasn't a result of his being drunk. Hat once got two drunk-driving tickets in one day, setting a state record that has never been broken. "I thought you'd at least slow down."

"Hat, how long have you known me?"

"Well, probably forty years, Vic."

"And haven't I left the tavern and gone through that intersection at precisely nine-thirty P and goddamn M every day of my life?"

"Well, I suppose so, but . . ."

"And have you ever seen me stop at that stop sign, Hat?"

"Well, no, Vic, but . . ."

"Then, you damned fool, what made you think I was going to stop *this* time?"

Hat didn't have an answer for that, and neither did the rest of us, but eventually the sheriff did. He finally asked the State Patrol to pull Old Vic's driver's license, and they did. The argument went that Uncle Vic was too old to drive, that he had become a danger to the community, and, most convincing of all, a real threat to his own safety and life. He was just too old, too blind, too deaf, too weak, and too stubborn to drive anymore, everyone pretty much agreed.

Except of course for Uncle Vic. He and Em lived about three blocks away from the tavern, and he could have walked over there for his daily card game with no trouble at all. In fact, the exercise probably would have done him some good, everyone agreed, but precisely because everyone agreed, Vic insisted on driving.

For a while after he lost his license to drive the Buick, he drove his 1937 Allis-Chalmers tractor, but then one day the crank kicked back and broke his wrist so Em sold the tractor to Slick for "parts." Vic warned Slick that if he so much as loosened a lug nut on that tractor he would tell everyone in town, especially Connie, about the time he got so drunk at a volunteer Fire Department meeting that one of the CPR instructors, a nurse from Rising City, had to take him out and help him take a leak. Slick said he wasn't sure Vic would ever tell that story to a woman anyway, or if he did whether Connie would believe it, or even if she did believe it that it would make any difference, since she seemed to think he was sleeping with every woman in town anyway, but I did notice that he never so much as loosened a lug nut on that Allis.

Anyway, next Vic took to driving his riding lawn mower to the tavern, but then one night when it was cloudy and there wasn't much of a moon he drove over Em's deaf cat while he was still in the garage. The only thing that bothered Vic about the accident, he insisted, was cleaning out the canvas bag that catches the grass clippings—or in this case cat clippings, but Em took it all a good deal more seriously, just as she always seemed to take everything a good deal more seriously than Uncle Vic.

Well, it got to be a bit of a game over at the tavern to see how Vic was going to travel those three blocks from his house to the tavern next. When the Buick had been sold, the Allis-Chalmers given away, and the lawn mower locked up in the garden shed, there didn't seem to be much left for Vic except walking.

Now, no one would think it at all unreasonable for Uncle Vic to ask Woodrow and Lunchbox for a ride over to the Thursday evening community action in Rising City, and so no one did. But if anyone had considered for a moment the time that Woodrow and Lunchbox took me over there, fed me beers, and then prodded me and encouraged me into buying sixty-seven baby ducks, they might have also wondered about the wisdom of letting Uncle Vic go to that sale with Woodrow and Lunchbox and no responsible supervision.

Any normal-thinking person might have raised some objection when Uncle Vic started bidding on the grizzled white mule toward the end of the evening, but that is not the style of Woodrow and Lunchbox. Far from exercising any sort of responsibility on their own part, they did whatever they could to relieve Uncle Vic of whatever self-control he might have had had he been enjoying more favorable company.

"You got the bid now, Vic," they goaded. "Don't let that Rising City square-head take that mule away from you now, Vic. Keep bidding, Vic. Show 'em how, Vic. Don't let 'em push you around," and when the auctioneer hammered a "Sold!" Vic had bought that mule for a price that even brought a smile to the mule's face.

Normal people might have wondered how they were going to get that mule led to the truck, yet home, but not Woodrow and Lunchbox. They "helped" Uncle Vic buy a saddle, reins, and a kiddie carriage, all for only $422. "We'll hitch him to the carriage, throw the saddle and tack into the carriage, and then Vic can sit on top of all the stuff and drive him home. It's only a few miles," reasoned Woodrow, while Lunchbox smiled and nodded in agreement.

To show you just how wrong a fellow can be, I thought that an eight-mile ride at night on gravel roads in a kiddie cart behind that mule would kill Uncle Vic, but I was wrong. The carriage had been brought up to the mule, but not a single piece of harness had touched his quivering hide before he unleashed four kicks with both of his spring-loaded rear hoofs that reduced that carriage to a pile of dusty wood and antique hardware.

And you would think that any reasoning human being would then just walk away from the kind of potential disaster that obviously headstrong mule represented. I've done that. You just pretend that whatever you've bought and paid for isn't yours, leave it lying right where it is, and the auctioneer will just sell it again, if he can find someone about as dumb as you.

Not Vic. He actually smiled at the pile of wire, scrap metal, and kindling that had been his kiddie carriage. Believe it or not, even before the dust settled, Vic liked this mule even more because of what he had just done. Vic liked the way all of us bystanders stepped back about ten yards from that mule because Vic had seen us do the same thing with him. Vic and that mule had, as the phrase goes these days, begun "to bond." Not a half-hour after they met, they were as close as kin.

Woodrow called Lloyd, who was looking for a reason to get out of the house and away from LaVerne for a while anyway, and he came over to Rising City with his stock trailer. The mule was no dummy and could see that the trailer was not something that would be as easily reduced to its elements as the kiddie carriage was, so he just stepped up into that wagon as if there was nothing in this world he would rather have done than cooperate with his new friends and owner.

Woodrow, Lloyd, and Lunchbox got the trailer to Centralia in fine condition, helped Vic get the mule into the old shed behind Vic and Em's place, taking great care not to wake Em up. They had the mule in the shed when the yard light came on and suddenly Woodrow, Lloyd, and Lunchbox remembered that they had lots of things to do at home, and they jumped in their trucks and took off, leaving it up to Vic to explain to Em just what the hell was going on with this mule and saddle and tack and the three cardboard boxes of carriage hardware.

It was several days before any of us saw Uncle Vic again. But when we did, it was a moment of glory. "Sweet Jesus," Slick exploded from behind the bar, "will you look at that?!" and we did, and there was Uncle Vic riding into town on that mule. We all went out onto the street to watch this marvel, and it was worth the effort. The mule was walking along just as if he was proud of being a mule. Vic had soaped up that saddle until it looked new. The mule was brushed and carried up nice. All in all there was not a soul who would have argued that Uncle Vic's arrival was anything but a triumph.

We helped Vic tie the mule to the Allis out in back of the tavern, and Vic played cards that night with a renewed enthusiasm. What had seemed to be an impossible situation now seemed to have been resolved more easily than any of us could have guessed.

At nine thirty P and goddamn M, as Vic put it, he folded his cards, smiled, finished his orange juice, and said, "Well, I guess Silver and I will be heading home."

Silver. He had named the mule "Silver." We all went to the back door of the tavern to wave Vic and Silver good-bye. Vic untied the reins, put his left foot in the stirrup, and prepared to swing his right leg up into the saddle. But the mule took a couple steps while Vic hopped along beside him, his left foot in the stirrup and his right foot still on the ground. "Hold still, you miserable oat-burner," Vic said. "Whoa, Silver, whoa!" He waved to us sort of, still hanging on to the saddle horn and reins, still hopping alongside Silver, as they went out of sight around the corner of the tavern.

"Hold still, you obnoxious beast," we heard Vic yell, and then, "See you guys in the morning," and we all laughed our farewells and went inside to congratulate ourselves on how well things seemed to work in our little town of Centralia.

We buried Vic Monday. Herb said he was just closing up the service station when Uncle Vic came by, waving and laughing and hopping alongside that mule, still trying to get his right leg over the saddle. "See you tomorrow," Herb said Vic yelled to him.

Herb said that Vic then hollered something like, "Silver, you no-good, lop-eared fool, whoa, will you? *Whoa.*"

Hat said that Vic went by his place north of town about nine-forty, still hopping, still trying to get up into the saddle.

"Need some help, Vic?" Hat said he hollered.

"What the hell kind of help would you be with a mule if you can't even drive a car?" Vic yelled, and then something like, "Silver, whoa, you miserable, spavined devil."

The sheriff followed the trail down the gravel the next day—a set of mule tracks and about ten thousand right shoe prints alongside, all the way to the Rising City community auction barn. It was there they found the mule helping himself to a pickup load of corn some-one had brought for the sale, and Uncle Vic, lying not far away, dead but looking as if he could sit up and cuss any time.

Silver was sold again at the auction house the next Thursday to a city fellow looking for a gentle mount for his wife, who had refused him a divorce only the week before. He said he'd read about Uncle Vic's unusual death and his faithful mule, Silver, in the Omaha newspaper.

Solomon Butcher
from *Cottonwood Roots*

KEM LUTHER

From the cemetery I drive three miles west to the place where the Ruckle and Luther homesteads were situated. To find the two homestead properties I use a high-resolution county map on which I have marked the two quarter-section homesteads. The locations were derived from the section, township, and range numbers in the homestead records. This is often the only way to find these ancient farms. At least they can be found. Genealogists who work with the metes and bounds system in the eastern and southern United States face a major piece of detective work to find the vanished boundary markings. The exact location of the homestead lands associated with Arthur's father and John Ruckle has not been well preserved in the communal memory of their descendants. My father was probably the last living person who could have driven to the right spot without recourse to the grid lines of a plat map.

I'm not really expecting to find anything on the Luther homestead, so I am not disappointed as I top the last hill and begin to parallel the homestead land. It's just a piece of middling land, part pasture, part plowed and ready for planting. There is no house, or even a vestige of a house. A hundred years ago there would have been several dwellings in view from here, at least one family every quarter section. Today the average farm size is well over a square mile.

Arthur's family held this land for a mere five years. Perhaps a dozen other farmers have owned and sold it since. This real estate is only important to my pilgrimage for two reasons. One reason is a picture. The other reason is that, among the crowd of subsequent owners, the Luthers were the first.

"First owners" only has meaning within the larger fiction that the land was created fresh and unclaimed minutes before some American or European settler signed a document in a land claim office. County histories raise themselves to an almost religious mania when speaking of these first claimants. The first ones are The Pioneers, whether they stayed for five years or fifty. The county histories written around the turn of the century will list page after page of these claims. They are the Book of Numbers in the narrative of beginnings. I have been through many county courthouses looking at the early land records. In none of these have I ever seen an entry of ownership predating the land patents of the settlers. (Even some of the land patents themselves were included retroactively, since the patent record was originally at a land office rather than a courthouse. The property would not usually appear in the official county records until the patentee sold or mortgaged it.) In almost every case, however, the Indian claims to these same lands were extinguished by a process of *purchase*. If the Indians could sell it, they must have owned it. If they owned it, why is their transaction with the federal government not recorded for this piece of land?

What is to be noticed here is the peculiar usage of the word "ownership" in land records which allows it to be applied to the pioneers but not to the Indians. Ownership, however, is a turtle word, as in the story of the missionary who had engaged the local wise man in a debate about the origin of the world. On being told that the world was supported on the back of a great turtle, the missionary asked, smugly, "And what does the turtle stand on?" The sage replied, "A larger turtle." The missionary, sensing a reductio around the corner, continued "And what does that turtle stand on?" The wise man, thinking for only a brief moment, replied, "It will do you no good, ma'am. It's turtles all the way down." The concept of ownership, like turtles, has no limit within itself. If it applies at all, it applies all the way down to the bottom. Someone owned the land as soon as there was someone there to own it who could fulfill the minimal conditions of ownership. Property, and the ownership of it, is one of those big, bounding, defining concepts which sets the horizons for discourse. We do not know how to change what such words mean without reworking sizable chunks of other parts of our language. When we use the word in a way that changes its meaning, we stand on the precipitous edge of ambiguity. So the Indians were, by all that language can discover, owners of this property.

But they are owners who are not in the official ownership records. It seems, then, that there are owners, and there are owners. Indians are one kind of owner, the homesteaders are another. Custom has the task of dividing what language unifies. To keep language from expressing itself requires a strong custom, firmly embedded in human nature and need. It calls for a turtle which can not only support all the turtles above it, but can stop foundational questions from being applied to itself. Even a custom as deeply entrenched as slavery was not able to hold language apart. The language of individual rights used in the revolutionary era contributed to the eventual emancipation of the slaves. Although the rights embodied in the U.S. Constitution were not originally extended to blacks under slavery, it did not explicitly exclude them. It could not have excluded them, or the high language of human rights would have been trivialized. And so the seeds of contradiction, cast into the soil of language, must either come up as hypocritical weeds or be rooted out. The Civil War was a mighty weeding of a badly overgrown semantic garden.

The same kind of semantic process gave rise to homesteading.

As it was practiced between 1840 and 1880, homesteading was an attempt to resolve ambiguities in the concept of property which were planted when the Europeans began to force the Indians westward. It was a way to keep turtle ownership from going all the way down. The government could not continue to hold and sell the purchased lands itself without crediting the previous Indian ownership as one of the prerequisites of a valid sale. The federals redistributed Indian lands in two ways at first. One was to give them away as bounty lands to soldiers who had fought in U.S. wars. The other was to sell the lands in large chunks to quasi-corporate entities (railroads, land companies) who would resell them to settlers. As means to get a mass of settlers onto the properties and the lands under development, both devices turned out to be partial failures. Land companies continued to hold large parcels of land out of development. Soldiers sold their bounty certificates for immediate cash to large developers, who in turn held these or resold them at inflated prices. Both of these outcomes tended to undercut the basic thesis underlying the alienation of Indian lands: that the land was required to accommodate the pressing masses who needed new lands for homes and farms. Instead of a potent social movement which was able to divide the notion of ownership, all the government got was political legerdemain. A modern political analysis might have accused the government of *laundering* the lands. What was needed was some social use of the land which would allow ownership to have two domains of application, one before the settlers came, and one after. For a brief time the corporations and soldiers were convenient recipients: the corporations, because by their bankruptcies and rechartering the thread of ownership could not be traced through time; and the military, because soldiers could be construed to have justly received the land without a sale, in compensation for wars in which the Indians, with a perverse instinct, had almost unfailingly chosen the wrong side.

Such laundering, however, can only hide ambiguity, it cannot resolve it. For these reasons the government was moved, first in the

Pre-emption Act of 1841, and later in the Homestead Act of 1862, to change the moral basis of land acquisition. Under the Homestead Act, persons who were heads of household were "entitled" to a 160-acre tract of western land, if only they would settle on it and improve it. Waves of pressing immigrations, coupled with the ideology of Manifest Destiny, provided the moral climate for the recreation of the western lands. The lands were indeed purchased from the Indians, but they were then given away to meet the strong social pressures of living space. And so the chain of ownership was broken. One set of owners, the Indians, had held the land by natural possession and had given it up by sale, and the other set of owners now held the land by the entitlement of social urgency. Thus did the notions of homesteading and property come to live quietly under the same roof.

Or so the story goes. Perceptions of moral trends are always easier in long retrospect. I frankly doubt that Arthur's father ever gave these issues a second thought when he moved his family onto this freshly laundered land. Twelve children and no money in the bank does not provide the best context for sensitive historical analysis. But I have dropped down these hundred years so easily in the last hour that the Indian ghosts under this pioneer land do not seem so far away. I can sense them just below my feet. They are not ghosts that I would like to awaken.

The other reason I wanted to see this homestead was to match it against a picture. The picture is one of the thousands taken by the frontier photographer Solomon Butcher in Nebraska's pioneer era. Butcher ranged this county from one end to the other doing his version of Matthew Brady. The battlefields he photographed were the nearly invisible demarcations between the hopes of the settlers and the intractable climate of central Nebraska. Butcher probably didn't know that he was photographing a war. At first he was just trying to support his homesteading habit. He opened a photographic studio about thirty miles north of Algernon, near Sargent. In 1886 he conceived the idea of a photographic history of Custer County.

Over the next seven years he managed to average nearly one Custer County photograph a day. Many of these have survived in the original large glass negatives.

The pictures are farm and family portraits. The first homes of hundreds of The Pioneers are on these plates. They are astonishingly clear in the fine detail. Though I had known the pictures for many years through Butcher's own books and through the prints and copies on file in historical societies, it was not until I saw the precise reproductions in John Carter's *Solomon Butcher: Photographing the American Dream* that I understood how attractive the first copies must have looked to those for whom he took the originals.

What makes Butcher's pictures unique is not their technical quality, though. It is the way he tells a minute piece of a larger story with each picture. The spirit of Butcher's interpretations is so far from what is considered to be the modern standard that it is difficult to apply the vocabulary of aesthetic criticism. In each exposure there is a compromise between what the families wanted and the part that the picture was playing in Butcher's vaster conception of frontier life. He was not above adding the silliest retouchings to the plates, or posing his customers in ridiculous theatrical stances. The naïveté of these pictures, however, calls attention to the fact that the picture itself was, for Butcher, the eye through which the spirit passed. The spirit was that of the Nebraska pioneer, and the almost daily struggle to turn a strange and uncomfortable land into a landscape of farm homesteads. The conflict between the dynamic of the events and the flatness of the image is an abiding tension in most of Butcher's photographs. These photographs are chapters in the story of the rise and fall of the pioneers' hope. Here is a family standing around the prairie grave of a dead child. Next to another family is the team of horses which were daily partners in the effort to wrest the means of life from a grudging land. A field of withered and widely spaced corn crawls up to the front door of a soddy. Hogs slop in foot-deep mud a few paces in front of another opening in a sod wall. Family pictures are hauled out to be included in the portraits, sad testimony to the loneliness and isolation of the dry lands. The night before another of Butcher's photographs was taken a rain soaked the roof, and in the morning it collapsed, just minutes after a widower and his three children had gone outside.

In the Custer County photographs of the 1880s the sod house predominates. Butcher was fascinated by the role of the soddy in the life of the Great Plains settlers, and later in his life wrote a tract on the construction of these houses. The sod house resembles from a distance a house built of largish brick. On closer inspection the resemblance disappears, for the bricks are hairy three-inch-thick rectangles of sod, the only building material within the settlers' meager budgets. Like a log cabin in a forest, a sod house could be constructed on the prairie in only a day by a small crew of men and women. A glance at the background of Butcher's photographs shows a land almost totally devoid of trees. The absolutely necessary wood components—window sashes, doors, and ridgepole—were often carted in from long distances.

For being composed of only earth, the sod house was remarkably durable. Some partially sod houses were still in use when I was growing up in the 1950s. But the goal of the pioneer was to get out of the sod house as soon as possible. Its drawbacks are all too apparent. When it was dry, a fine dust sifted down continually. When it rained it was no better: sod roofs were known to drip on the inside for three days after a rain finished on the outside. There were, of course, advantages. But it was never a matter of economic calculation. People with aspirations simply did not continue to live in dirt homes. Its most obvious advantage—that anyone could build one for minimal cost—was its most evident disadvantage. Despite the fact that marvelously large and complex versions of the sod house were built, their days were numbered by the same factors that doomed the rough-hewn log house as a building technology for permanent homes. Sod houses are shelters in the same way that gruel is food.

In the spring of 1888 Solomon Butcher and his photography

wagon passed through Algernon. Here he found the Luthers and the fourteen-year-old Arthur encamped on this quarter-section. Out of this encounter came a portrait of the family and their sod house. The picture has its complement of typical Butcher features: the central family ranged in front of the farmstead, less central persons (a visiting neighbor) in a further plane, the sod house, the teams of horses, the farm implements, and the heirlooms carried out to join the family circle. As though it were not enough to have the care of the nine children included in the picture, Arthur's father Henry holds a picture of another family group, perhaps the older children already married and out of the house.

Removing the picture from its folder, I hold it at arm's length. I had hoped, given the line of low hills on the margins of the photograph, to identify the place where the sod house stood, but there is a sameness to these rolling horizons that defeats my attempt to find Butcher's ancient perspective. Nor is it any use to examine the land. Sod houses had no foundations. A few years of plowing were enough to erase the evidence of a family's sojourn. An archaeologist turned loose here might be able to locate the house using a midden or the lining of the well. I remember as a child the small dumps with rusting stoves, parts of cars, and twisted barbed wire that marked the futile homesteads on each quarter-section of our ranch. But the ranch land had not been regularly (and should never have been) plowed. In this valley is enough rain, when the rains do not fail, to attract the plow. A hundred years of intermittent cropping have left me without a shrine. I slip my icon back in its case and leave the land to its spirits.

Two Wrens

JOHN JANOVY JR.

One is seen and one is heard. The one that is seen is also heard, but the one that is heard is very rarely seen. Both are living bits of their places: the marsh wren is a bit of cattail head, broken, still clinging to a stick in the wind; the rock wren is a small bit of Brule with some very small lichens. They are both full of steam, as must every wren in the world be, and they couldn't have chosen two more different kinds of places to live.

It is difficult, once a person gets beyond the snails, to express Keystone Marsh in any terms other than those of the wrens. It is impossible not to study wrens, the long-billed marsh wrens, in Keystone. There are times when a person "goes after" a species, with equipment and intent, in order to understand the manner in which that species makes its way in the world. There are times when a person goes after a species with the idea that maybe, just maybe, there will be something in the life of that creature that will add perspective to the life of the person. These times are laced with other times, however, when the unexpected species comes forth, stands out and up, gets the attention, makes the point.

A pair of fishermen drift down the canal. A canal has been dredged along the south side of Keystone Marsh, a canal to keep the water flowing, and there is a large sand dike, the dredgings, on the marsh side of this canal. Small strands of cattails have made it over the dike, and every stand has its pair of wrens. A wren comes to the top as the boat approaches. The insect buzz (the world *scold* has never been applied more appropriately) is directed at the fishermen, who appear not to notice, and the task is picked up by other wrens down the canal as the boat nears that place just past the bridge where the canal empties into the lake. The wrens have done their stunt for the day; they've gotten the fishermen down the canal! I am not able to understand how a fisherman can drift down that canal once and not become an ornithologist, a studier of wrens. I cannot understand what is going on in that boat, what kind of conversation, what kind of equipment preparations, that could override the marsh wren. A fisherman by all rights should simply throw the tackle overboard, beach the boat, and wade in after the wrens. That's about the effect *Telmatodytes palustris* has on me and all my friends, regardless of the reasons for entering the cattails. One can collect snails without thinking, but one cannot collect snails without listening to the wrens. Before long the listening pace quickens and the collecting pace slackens. Before much longer, the snail picking stops altogether while the back is straightened, and the knuckle sucked. The buzzing comes closer very rapidly. The wren is there, a few feet from your head, then all is quiet. Back to the snails, but the wren is there also, this time silent, slipping along beneath the cattails. Eye to eye with a marsh wren beneath the cattails, then the bird is gone and the person is back to the snails until, not long after, the ritual begins again. The marsh is alive and well.

There was a person that summer, a cheerleader, a Girl Scout, who always liked to do that kind of stuff.

"Sure, I'll do it, I like to do that kind of stuff!" she used to say. Such statements are statements of responsibility; they put the volunteer into any kind of position, usually one of responsibility. It is easy to foist responsibility off on a volunteer, and subsequently it is just as easy to forget that the volunteer is shouldering the responsibility. I have this impression, this feeling, this almost-dream, that there was a time, a prehistoric time when mastodons roamed the plains of Keith County, when a member of the Nebraska Game and Parks Commission drove a state car out to this place and asked for volunteers.

"We need a volunteer," he said, surveying the animals, "we need someone to take the responsibility of letting us know the cattail marsh is alive and well." He was a very serious person. People with state cars have a job to do.

"Sure, I'll do it," said the marsh wren, "I like to do that kind of stuff!" I also have this feeling that Game and Parks has forgotten the wren, has after these thousands of years come to take the thing for granted. The bird is still there, boys down at G and P, still doing its job, volunteer work. Maybe with a little support it could even become a tourist attraction. On the other hand, the Game and Parks commissioner went to the doctor today, and the nurse put her hand on his wrist. Feeling the pulse, she declared the commissioner alive and well. No pulse ever became a tourist attraction, no matter how long it has carried the responsibility of being a monitoring device.

People enter a marsh for various reasons. The act of entering a marsh is highly recommended, and as a teacher I find it comes close to being the very act that breaks the shell of inhibition, that cracks the unwillingness to participate, in a student. If the act of breaking and entering a cattail marsh does not do the trick, or if seining alone does not, then the combination is surefire. Any student who fails to participate after breaking and entering a cattail marsh, especially if the act comes on the heels of a good seining experience, has serious problems. Seining is an activity that really is not, in its finest form, readily available to the public.

Anyone can enter a cattail marsh, however, usually without permission, since there are plenty of discarded ones on public land. Just wade in. Just walk up and wade in. It's that easy. Just enter the marsh. Oh, most assuredly there is mud, often vile, beneath the water, and the cattails are difficult to walk through. You flounder, sometimes even fall right down in the stuff. It's the first step that's the big one. Ready now? Your shoes and pants are dry? Stand on the sand and go. Lift the foot and simply place it, shoe and all, in the water, then push the shoe down into the water and the mud below; keep pushing, knee-deep? Okay. Now try the other one; see how easily it goes in right beside the first? That smell? Oh, that's the marsh. Yes, your tennis shoes and jeans *are* going to smell just like that for the rest of their useful lives. That buzzing sound? That's the marsh wren. Now you've placed your muddy feet on the marsh, the wren-pulse is telling you the marsh is alive and well. Yes, every time you touch the marsh you will feel the wren-pulse. At least as long as the marsh is alive and well.

The wren is everywhere. Across the lake now in a canoe, hunting muskrats on the north shore. The muskrat stunt is tried, slipping very quietly along the cattails, not extensive but certainly all along the shore for almost a mile, looking at those places where muskrat might be sitting, nibbling, twitching its nose, waiting for a bullet. Then there is the buzz. A substantial attempt is made to ignore it. After all, this is a sneaky expedition. Not a chance. The buzz picks up as the canoe drifts; in the lee of the north shore, a canoe drifts and glides with but a touch of the paddle, for the north shore of Keystone Lake is also a dike. It is very hot, late in the afternoon, although Keystone Lake has no mosquitoes, none to speak of, only the wrens. The hunters are distracted now, the rattling buzz becomes more intense, but the muskrat is seen too late. There was a chance for a shot, had they been alert, but now there is only the most fleeting of backs and tails. The hunters will look well ahead this time, will find those runaways well before the canoe drifts by. It doesn't work. There is still this distraction, and not only that: a duck, flightless or injured, flops out of the cattails and is gone. Ripples wash down the shore for a hundred yards or so and there are a couple of responses from the wren-pulse.

Later the hunters will try the same thing with yellow-headed blackbirds. They will try the same thing with black terns. They will try the same things with mice, with small traps set at the edge of the marsh. Sometimes these things will work, sometimes not. The activities will be carefully watched, however, carefully recorded and upon occasion, I feel, passed on to the next generation of wrens, the keepers of the keys to Keystone Marsh. In the eons since the mastodons roamed, Game and Parks may have forgotten the wrens, taking for granted the work was being done. In those same eons of volunteer work the wren has extended its own responsibility to include a watch over the marsh. First the pulse, then the eyes and ears of the Keystone cattails; the roles are very different. A creature, given an onerous task, completes it willingly and easily, and in the course of time comes to view the task as not a task but a role, a place in the network of the world's living society, not simply some commissioner's idea of a way to keep busy, a way to ensure every tiny bit of the state's business is done. Sure, I'll do that kind of stuff, says the wren, I like to do that kind of stuff.

People enter the marsh now, people who have broken and entered before, young people, people who for the first time in their lives have a marsh at their doorstep. They walk across the heavy wooden bridge and turn west along the dredging dike for the spot. They linger along the way, picking at rocks, picking at empty snail shells, picking at killdeers, looking for killdeer nests, sucking their knuckles to tease the blackbirds, skipping rocks in an occasional spontaneous contest, sending someone back to get the gallon jars forgotten in the morning's preparations. They are not anxious, they are perfectly relaxed today; not like the first day, that first day when some felt a need to prove themselves, when some were very apprehensive about their own abilities to deal with any situation as complicated as the cattails.

On the other side of the dike, in a small pocket of cattails, the wren starts. They learned the wren the first day, they learned to suck up a wren on their knuckles, and it was almost the first thing they learned about the marsh. They learned it from the old man who learned it from another old man, the latter the best in the knuckle-sucking business. A sucked knuckle, if done properly, sounds like a baby bird in real trouble. When done by the best in the business, it sounds like a bird in so much trouble that there is no way in all living hell that poor creature is going to be saved, a fledgling blackbird being eaten in slow motion by a raccoon but screaming the screams of a whole marsh full of baby blackbirds in fast time. Back in those Oklahoma woods such a knuckle suck sent shivers down the spine of even the humans in the group. Come on now, adults, get here quickly, come on up, make this man stop this infernal sound. Out in the marsh even the most simple knuckle suck brings up the keeper of the keys, instantly. They all learned that the first day; now they all do it. They do it to the wren on the other side of the dike. They stop down at the entering place. A few gather their gear for a stomp through the cattails, but a few others always call up the wrens.

I stand in the morning sun. Today we are going after land snails in the cattails. The species is *Oxyloma retusa*, and although they live in the marsh they are land snails. They never get wet, to my knowledge, on purpose. We have never found an *Oxyloma retusa* with muddy feet, just as we have never found a *Physa* with clean feet. I wonder today, standing in the heating sand waiting for the group, what would happen if no marsh wren answered the suckers. I have this feeling that it would be first day all over again. The group has come to depend on the keeper of the keys. All it takes is once. One time, that is all. Step to the marsh, call the keeper, the keeper answers, and it is all right to go into the cattails. The feeling is gone now, and a sureness is there. I am totally confident that without this ritual, that if no wren answered, the young people would not go into the marsh. The animal that liked to do that kind of stuff volunteered back in the time of the mastodons, the animal served well and became the keeper of the keys, the eyes and ears, and now he gives permission. The humans require the permission; they have come to depend on the keeper to do his job. This morning there are wrens and they answer. Permission is given, and into the cattails we go after more snails. This is still a tale of wrens, however, for the life of *Oxyloma retusa* is intimately tied to the life of the wren; or so we say, since we refuse to kill enough wrens to find out for sure. Some questions are best left unanswered.

Below the cattails it is silent, the water is calm regardless of a gale that clatters the tops. The half-submerged stalks of last year's growth form an uncertain mat for human feet, and there are places where it seems a deer may have lain; or run. The water is warm; in small and almost dry pockets there may be some mosquito larvae, carrying protozoa on their backs. There is an unbelievable number of insects. There is an almost equal variety of spiders. There is seemingly a spider and a spider type for every insect and insect type, for there are many many spiders indeed below the cattails. There are caterpillars in the cattails. There are real caterpillars and fake caterpillars. The wren consumes all these things. The wren is the dominant form in this marsh, and one could study, as did Kale in Georgia, the flow of energy through the marsh into the wren. Energy flows from sun through plants through a layer or two of insects and spiders and into the wren. The wrens have much energy! Wait a moment, the fake caterpillar is also a part of this food chain, the fake caterpillar has plugged into the series of events. The fake caterpillar lives in the tentacle of *Oxyloma retusa*. The fake caterpillar is really the larva of an intestinal parasitic worm.

The worm is a member of the trematode genus *Leucochloridium* and lives as a larval form in land snails, but as an adult in the digestive tract, or associated organs, of a bird. The snails are difficult to see, normally. Often an effective way to collect *Oxyloma* is simply to stomp down the cattails, submerged, then let the affronted snails crawl up your leg. An infected snail is pretty easy to see, however, for the tentacle is a brightly colored fake caterpillar. The larval worm has worked its way up into the inside of the snail's tentacle, it has synthesized or stolen some pigment that it has laid down in green and brown bands, and it pulsates, throbs, in and out of the tentacle. The human stands there looking at the infected snail beneath the cattails. It is the tentacle that caught the eye, and most assuredly the tentacle that catches a human eye will be sure to catch a wren eye. The slender but vocal bill that snaps up *this* caterpillar will send to the digestive tract maybe a hundred, maybe a thousand, parasitic worms. Let's see, first a volunteer to act as the pulse of Keystone Marsh, simply to let us know the marsh is alive and well. Next as the years go by the eyes and ears, the dominant form in this discarded portion of the ecosystem. Now the giver of permission, the keeper of the keys. An onerous task well done, well done for the benefit of society, and now because of it a position of responsibility, stability, a role. Now comes the bitter with the sweet; the rip-off. I reach for the infected snail but the wren beats me to it.

"Don't." I say; but it is too late. The fluff has shaken the fake caterpillar and consumed it in one gulp. This cannot be the first time it has happened, nor can this event really have much effect on the dominance of this marsh by the wren population.

It is a football morning, silent, cold, crystal, and the lingering call of a magpie filters down from the next canyon, or maybe the next one, or maybe even the one after that; no one knows how far the magpie call will filter on a morning like this. The station is deserted, and I stand on the back patio, with coffee, looking over Keystone Lake. Way down the hill, fumbling around in the brush, is a cream-colored station wagon with a red picture of the state of Nebraska on the front doors. Surveyors. I walk toward the boat house and there are targets on the sand, aerial survey targets, large wooden sticks with radiating red plastic strips tacked to the sand. The surveyors are here to take the marsh. There is a hydroelectric plant scheduled for the spillway of Kingsley Dam, and the diversion dam at the eastern end of Keystone Lake will be raised three feet. The water level of Keystone itself will be raised three feet. It was not my feeling during the endless summer that this was actually going to happen, regardless of the local talk. Now the men are here for the marsh.

"What's this trash?" I say. There are three of them and they are burly. The station wagon is filled with survey equipment, poles, transits, what else, and the tires are worn. The Nebraska emblem is also worn. This is a field team. Engineers. The men look at one another, then back toward me. One goes back to work, the other two have very blank expressions.

"What's this trash?" I repeat.

"Ain't trash, mister; aerial survey targets."

"Have you asked the wrens?"

"Huh?"

"Have you asked the wrens, you dumb shits, have you asked the wrens' permission to take the marsh?"

"Who you callin' a 'dumb shit'?"

The conversation really does not take place anywhere but in my mind standing on the patio, watching the engineers fumble through the brush far down the hill below. Of course they have not asked the wrens' permission to take the marsh. If questioned, Game and Parks would formally state that the marsh wren is responsible only for telling whether the marsh is alive and well, not for permission to take the marsh. I turn back inside, wondering if there is in fact anyone anywhere whose permission must be asked before the marsh can be taken. No wonder the bird snatched that infected snail tentacle out of my grasp. A gut full of worms, now that I think about it, stoking the fire, is not much of a rip-off after all.

Salpinctes obsoletus is a very plain name for a bundle of fire known as the rock wren. It is heard, up on the bluffs, up in the rocks, but it is seen only by those who climb the bluffs regularly, and then it is seen only irregularly. Except today. For some stupid reason it had done the thing that wrens all over the world must do—fly into a small spot and get stuck, trapped, when the small spot turns out to be a cavern. Tom Sawyer and Huck Finn. Today it flew into the men's washhouse and was caught, caught and placed in a small hardware cloth cage. The cage was a bit of totally ingenious prior preparation by a field man's field man, for on one end it had a door.

The door was simply two strips of rubber inner tube, nailed so that a hand with a wren could easily be slipped between them, but a wren without a hand could never find the entrance from within. There was a worm man guarding the cage. To a worm man a rock wren is a dish full of intestinal contents. To a wren man a rock wren is a model to be painted. I bargained for its life, or at least for its temporary survival.

"I will put the damn thing back in the cage," I said, "I will put the damn thing right back in the cage and put the cage right back in this very spot."

He looked very suspicious and stroked his beard.

"I do admit this very publicly. This is your bird, your bird that you trapped while cleaning the washhouse, I admit this freely, and when I'm through with the painting I'll return your damn bird right here to this very spot!"

He was not satisfied, but the bird was taken away, back to my cabin, away from the din of business and curiosity. I had vowed not to release it. Not to release it, to relinquish it to its "rightful owner," meant sure death for the bird. None of this bothered me at the time, for I had spent a few hours in bird intestines myself. It did bother me to be accused of plotting to release the bird.

As you will read later, I am a painter of birds, although through no fault of my own. There are things you do because other people you know do them, and painting birds is one of these things. I am not a very good bird painter, and you will not learn much about painting birds from the chapter of that title. All of the value in painting birds falls to the painter rather than the painting. The pencil sketch took about thirty minutes. The pattern on the back of a rock wren is exceedingly complex and I simply had no idea of how to begin converting watercolors into that pattern. So I started with the eye.

I normally start with the eye, and the eye is normally the easiest. But I don't start with the eye because it's the easiest, but because if the eye is not the right shape, the pupil placed correctly, then the bird simply does not look alive. Incidentally, the foot is the hardest, anatomically the least understood, anatomically the most difficult to manipulate and represent on paper. The best way to ruin a good eye is to put a bad foot underneath it. Models are normally very cooperative with the eye, and this one was no exception. I held the bit of fire by the feet, between the fingers, so that it faced toward my left. Often a bird will calm down in this position, calm down somewhat. Not the wren—not calm, but then not jittery or uncontrollable either. Just a ball of fire. A twit. It glared; it was baleful, insulting, affronted, darting and full of the emotional stuff, with its tarsometatarsi wedged firmly between my fingers. I apologized. I almost asked its permission to drop some watercolors on my own paper. What is it about a wren that gives one the feeling that permission should at least be asked?

Something had come down out of the hills with the bird, something wild, something heard off in the toughest part of the canyon but never seen. It communicated; it told me of the hard times up on the outcrops, and I believed the story, but I believed the story knowing full well it was a lie. I was being put on; life on the outcrops was a bowl of cherries. There was plenty to eat up there, and any creature with the flitty equipment of a wren is made for life on the outcrops. This animal came from my backyard, but from a spot in that backyard where I really could not go. Something told me this one knew nothing of the marsh wren. If the rock wren had known anything of the marsh wren, I think the former would have had nothing but pure disdain for the latter. It's all in the test, I was told that day; live in a place where you are not tested, and you are living in a place of inferior quality. Come to the outcrops. Come to the outcrops and you will be tested. Come to the men's washroom, big shot, and you will also be tested, I replied; then I came to the feet.

Models may be very cooperative with the eye, but they are very uncooperative with feet, and if allowed to place the feet naturally will normally fly away. This one's feet were very gnarled, almost as if hopping around on the Brule outcrops was hard manual labor. I worked hard on the foot, realizing that any creature that comes with gnarled feet is a creature that does have, somewhere in its life, some contact with what is physically tough and hard. The picture was finished now, as best I could manage. The pattern on the back was hopeless. One might have to paint that rock wren fifteen or twenty times to get the feel of how to make the pattern, much less be able to make it. I was glad to finish the picture and rid myself of the hill thing that demeaned my every movement. I see now, after writing this, that I know and feel absolutely nothing about the rock wren aside from what was learned that day painting. I also have this feeling the rock wren prefers it that way. I returned the thing to its cage, not really caring whether it was converted into tapeworms. I returned the cage to the laboratory and covered it with a cloth. I went to dinner and played volleyball afterwards. The wren was forgotten; it belonged to the worm man.

"What'd you do with the wren?" he said in the morning.

"I put it back in the cage."

"No, you didn't."

"Yes, I did put the wren back in the cage and put the cage back in the lab."

"It's not there now."

"I don't know where your bird is; I put it back in the cage."

"You're sure?"

"I'm sure; I told you I would put the bird back in the cage. You're sure it's not hiding in the cage?"

"How in the hell could a bird hide in a cage like that!" (I agreed.)

We checked the lab. Wrens that are loose in the room have a very distinct way of flying about. The animal was gone.

"Could Cindy have let it out?"

"I have no idea." Cindy is my daughter; she will explode when she reads someone thinks she might have done something on the sly like that.

"Sorry, Rich, the wren is gone. I did not let it go."

He grumped for a while.

Later that morning, relaxed now, I climbed the hill in back of our cabin and picked a rock to go under the painted wren. The rock co-operated beautifully, and even seemed to enjoy having its picture made. I still have the rock. It is a wild rock, from the hills on the south of Keystone Lake, but it does all the things a pet rock from Bloomingdale's ever did or ever will do, and it has adapted well to human company.

The wren must be back on the canyon wall now, and I sense an overwhelming lack of knowledge, a lack of familiarity, a lack of in-troduction, to this creature that entered my life so suddenly and under such quick circumstances. It was here and gone. I go then to the library to find out about the rock wren and am shocked. After reading even the most elementary writings of the rock wren I am shocked at society's ignorance of this bird. Why has the rock wren not been discussed, over and over, in every textbook that has ever been written? Is it because no one has taken the time to read what is known about the thing? Dawson tells me the rock wren makes its nest in the rocks, in the nooks and crannies; but I knew that. Dawson also tells me the rock wren makes its nest *of* rocks, and that startles me. *Of* rocks? They are evidently flat little peb-bles, these rocks, selected with the utmost care by the frail bill, and placed carefully in a bed. A bed of rocks? The wren actually makes a bed of carefully selected rocks? Is there a creature like the marsh wren that becomes so at one with its environment that it becomes a busted cattail? The marsh is full of cattails; they are there by the hundreds, the thousands. The marsh wren makes many nests. Is the animal that has become a busted cattail trying to emulate the marsh and become many busted cattails? I accept the fact that it might be. Dawson tells me the rock wren does the same, makes many nests. Is the animal that has become a rock trying to emulate the Brule outcrops, the very bluffs where it lives? I also accept the fact that it might.

Dawson tells me the rock pile of the wren's nest makes a "pleas-ant tinkling sound" when the wren leaves. I know now what must be done the next endless summer: I must hear the sound of the wren leaving its nest. Oh boy; oh boy, oh boy! This defiant creature with the gnarled feet makes a bed of rocks that tinkles like a wind chime so many times a day for so many times a summer? I know the thoughts that will come when I hear the wren rocks: tens of thousands of years ago people lived in nooks and crannies in the bluffs, even in the bluffs of Keith County, and as they lived there they modified the crannies, making them art museums. I feel now they must have made them also concert halls, those caves in France where they drew the pictures of their bison and rhinos. They must have made some music, must have noted the sound of the wind in the bluffs and arranged something to make a sound, not an imitation, but a sound with the equivalent subtlety. I see Neanderthal now, entering his cave, stepping on the bed of small stones, noting the pleasant sound of crunch and tinkle, assuring himself that after all he was home. Yes, I will climb the bluffs and listen to the wren nest.

The Missouri and I

PAUL JOHNSGARD

In late May 2003 I stood at the officially recognized headwaters of the Missouri River, near Three Forks, Montana, where three rivers discovered and named by Lewis and Clark coalesce—the Jefferson, the Madison, and the Gallatin. The spring thaw was just starting, and the waters from newly melted mountain snows rushed past in wild abandon, carrying good-sized branches and even small trees along with them. It was a fairly pristine scene, probably not too different from the one that Lewis and Clark must have seen two centuries ago, with the Rockies rising to the south, east, and west, and the very edges of the Great Plains still visible toward the north. About a half-mile south, along the Madison River, an adult bald eagle stood regally with its wings partly spread, soaking up the warming sun. Wild chokecherries were just coming into full bloom along the river, just as they had done nearly a month earlier in southern Nebraska.

I had followed the Missouri northward through the Dakotas and Montana for the better part of two thousand miles, from the eastern edge of the Great Plains just north of Kansas City, to its western edge, at Three Forks, Montana. I was in a personal search for the American past, as well as trying to evoke some nearly lost memories of my own North Dakota childhood. Most of the past along this ancient river route had long since been swallowed up by the present, but there were places and times, as with the sun setting on a placid and remote stretch of the Missouri River in central North Dakota, where time seemingly flew backward, and a simpler and much quieter America reappeared in its place.

At Cross Ranch State Park in North Dakota, I spent a night in a log cabin a hundred yards or less from the Missouri River, and only a dozen miles or so from the explorers' 1804–1805 wintering site at Fort Mandan. There, under massive and ancient cottonwood trees, one might fall asleep while listening to the ageless voice of the river, supplemented by those of Canada geese and great horned owls, all sounds that were certainly familiar to Lewis and Clark. With luck one might also detect the distant yipping of coyotes, or perhaps even imagine hearing the sounds of bellowing bison on the adjacent Cross Ranch Nature Preserve.

I stayed at the John Colter cabin, where there was a bookshelf of Lewis and Clark references. These included Gary Moulton's transcriptions of expedition journals, as well as a book on John Colter, an expedition member who later became famous for discovering the Yellowstone region. I got up one predawn morning to watch the full moon set as the sun rose, and to listen to the dawn serenade of Baltimore orioles, house wrens and least flycatchers.

When Lewis and Clark came upstream into what is now Nebraska and Iowa in early July 1804, they encountered steep hills built of wind-carried silt, or loess, on both sides of the river. On the Iowa side of the river, Waubonsie State Park near Nebraska City offers a splendid view out over the middle Missouri Valley from these "baldpated hills" that were thus described by Lewis and Clark as they passed this region. The "bald" aspects of the hills were a result of the native prairies that replaced the hardwood forests on hilltops and dry south-facing slopes. Over the past two centuries these prairies have nearly disappeared. They were supplanted initially by red cedars, and later by mature oak—hickory forests, largely as a result of increased protection from periodic fires.

Another Nebraska highlight was my search for Blackbird Hill, near Decatur, which Lewis and Clark visited August 11, 1804, to pay homage to the grave of the recently deceased Chief Blackbird of the Omaha tribe. He had died of smallpox brought in by fur traders. The gravesite is located atop the highest of the loess hills overlooking the river within the present-day Omaha Indian Reservation, and its exact location still remains unmarked, probably owing to the wishes of the Omaha tribe. I finally found it after wandering over hilly back-country dirt roads in October 2002, after the goldenrods had deposited a rich yellow blanket over the lowlands, the sumacs had roasted the hillsides into a burnt crimson, and the bluestem and Indian grass in scattered prairie remnants provided a bronze and Indian-red tapestry. It seemed a perfect site for a chief's final resting place.

In my searches for signs of Lewis and Clark, I drove roads I have never before driven, and learned the names and locations of tiny villages that I had never heard of. One such village was Lynch, near the mouth of the Niobrara, where Lewis and Clark made their first major mammalian discovery on September 7, 1804. They found a colony of black-tailed prairie dogs at the base of an eroded sandstone and clay promontory that they called The Cupola, but which is now known as Old Baldy. After a day of hauling endless buckets of water from the nearby Missouri River and pouring it into burrow openings, they finally evicted and caught one thoroughly waterlogged prairie dog. Later, they obtained several more live specimens of this heretofore unknown species, and even managed to send a living animal back to President Jefferson. He evidently appreciated it more than do present-day ranchers, who have since managed to eliminate it from more than 99 percent of its historic Great Plains range.

During the past two centuries the Missouri has shrunk greatly in width but has also speeded up in velocity, as a result of unending efforts by the Corps of Engineers to make the river straight enough and deep enough as to make it ever more suitable for barge traffic. In straightening and deepening the channel, the Corps evidently didn't realize that they were also greatly increasing the risks of annual downstream flooding, and perhaps didn't care that they were eliminating the sandbars and shallow riverine habitats of several now-threatened or endangered animals in the process. Wide and slow-moving river bends, such as DeSoto Bend in Iowa, were cut off to shorten the river route and form isolated "oxbow" lakes. Only a few of these, such as DeSoto National Wildlife Refuge, still survive as protected natural habitats.

There are other sites along the middle Missouri to be savored in my memory, such as visiting "Councile Bluff," now Fort Atkinson State Historical Park, where in midsummer I lingered for a time in the shade of an enormous and ancient bur oak. It must have already been present when Lewis and Clark stopped there in early August 1804 to have a council meeting with the Otos and Missourias, in the first of the explorers' attempts to make formal contact with the many Native American tribes of the Great Plains. They could not have known that they were also witnessing the final phase of a major civilization, which would soon be decimated by alien diseases and the loss of its lands and natural resources to the succeeding waves of frontiersmen, cavalry, hide-hunters, gold-seekers, and, finally, settlers.

These next two years of the Lewis and Clark Bicentennial celebrations will be a time for each of us individually to remember our country's history, including both its high points and its low ones, and especially to remember the brave men (and one equally brave woman), who risked their lives on a daily basis for more than two years to learn what was on the other side of the Rocky Mountains, and to describe the wonders of western North America to others. They proved to all Americans that it is indeed a marvelous land. It is now up to us to try to preserve for future generations as much of it as is humanly possible.

The Factory

MICHAEL RIPS

The failings of my eyes had made me curious enough about the process of seeing that when my father suggested that I come to work at his factory during the summer, I agreed.

Each morning at seven thirty I was delivered into the hands of Siegfried Christianson, the manager of the surfacing room. If my grandfather and father had searched to find the most intimidating man to manage their optical factory, they could not have done better than Siegfried Christianson, who was both taller and broader than any other man on the floor. With his light hair, large jaw, and powerful arms and fists, Siegfried ("Fred") inspired obedience. Even if one were inclined to protest, it would have done no good: Fred had the confidence and authority of my family and for that reason there was no appeal from his orders.

In the middle of the twentieth century, the optical industry was little different than it had been for a hundred years: lenses were ground and glasses assembled by local laboratories, with each laboratory comprising a small number of highly skilled men.

My father had no interest in this system. As soon as he took over the optical factory, he began experimenting with machines that could mass-produce lenses, and when he was satisfied that those machines could do the job, he advertised across the country, offering prices that were the lowest in the nation, and as a result he received orders from doctors in nearly every city in America.

For the system to work he needed to produce an enormous number of glasses quickly. Fred, with his authoritarian manner and his mastery of making glasses, was able to help my father achieve this.

During that summer Fred moved me from one job to the next, always making certain that my incompetence would in no way interfere with the pace of production. I, on the other hand, spent my days avoiding Fred, my assumption being that a man like Fred had a temper and, if provoked, would unleash it.

When an order first came into the plant, the prescription was written down on a sheet of paper, placed in a box, and then sent up to the room where the lenses were kept. Lenses were selected from inventory based on the size of the "correction" (the term used for the prescription), the dimensions of the frame, and the color of the glass. The lenses were placed in the box with the order and the box was sent off to a room where plugs of metal were affixed to the back of the lens. The box was then delivered to Fred Christianson and the surfacing room.

The first stop in the surfacing room was the generators. Each generator had a long arm with a clamp on the end. The clamp held the lens. The lens was then dragged across a diamond-coated wheel spinning at high speed, which produced the desired curvature.

The heat created by the wheel was so great that if the lens was not cooled it would explode. For this reason, a continuous stream of liquid was applied to the lens. The liquid rained on the operator, and the noise of the machines was something close to the noise that I imagine a cat makes when it is fixed.

Because the arm of the generator was four or five feet off the ground and heavy, it was assumed that the machine could only be operated by a tall man of some strength. But standing next to me that summer was a woman who was shorter than any man in the plant.

When she first came to the factory she was assigned to a clerical position. Intrigued by the generators, she approached my father. No woman had ever worked on the generators. My father looked at her and then the generator. She was shorter than the arm.

Without a word he walked over to a box that was sitting on the floor and dragged it in front of the generator. She got up on that box and stayed on top of it for another thirty years. Among lens grinders, there were few better.

Once the lenses were correctly cut and polished, they were sent on to be fitted into a frame. This was usually accomplished by aid of a pattern that was the precise shape of the frame. A machine cut the piece of glass to match the pattern. In some cases, where the frames were unusually shaped or the lenses too cumbersome to fit into the machine, the lens would be cut by hand. There were two men who did this, and they were located in the back corner of the surfacing room.

One of these men was named Charlie, and it was Charlie to whom I was assigned.

When Charlie was not cutting lenses he would wander around the factory and talk to people. He told me that he was raised on a ranch. He had the polite manner that I identify with people who are from the countryside of Nebraska. Despite living and working in Omaha, he continued to wear his cowboy boots, cowboy shirt, and a belt with a silver buckle.

Charlie and I would have lunch together and every once in a while we would have a drink after work. There was a bar across from the plant, and it filled up with workers when the plant closed.

There was a jukebox in the bar and not infrequently people danced. Workers, who flirted with each other in the factory, would meet and dance at the bar.

So that I would be able to join in with the others, Charlie offered to teach me the two-step. There was no doubt that Charlie was a good dancer. No woman turned him down, and he seemed to be as good as, if not better than, the other dancers. There was even a point in every dance when Charlie, holding the woman close, would stop, separate himself from the woman by taking a few steps back, and then bend the top of his body downward in a modified bow. This gesture always caused a giggle from the woman.

Charlie's lessons did not end with the two-step. He taught me how to approach a woman, the proper way to ask her to dance, the etiquette of offering a lady a refreshment. Charlie knew the formalities of love, and he gave me the education that I had not received at home.

Near the end of the summer I was still working with Charlie when a lens that I was cutting slipped from my hands and rolled under the bench. This was not uncommon, particularly for someone who was still learning. With Charlie standing at my side, I bent down to get the lens.

Reaching for the lens, I noticed something else under the bench. Bending closer, trying to focus, my nostrils came dangerously close to an uncircumcised part of Charlie.

The incident was so curious that on my final day of work I was moved to ask Charlie about what had happened.

"Charlie," I began, "the other week when I was under the bench, I saw something—"

"A penis?" interjected Charlie.

"Yes, Charlie, a penis."

"Don't worry, Charlie comforted me, "it wasn't mine."

"Charlie," I said, "if you don't mind my inquiring, whose penis was it?"

Charlie thought, and then, moving his hand to the inside of his crotch, gave a tug on his pant leg. I looked down toward his boot and there it was again. But as Charlie had said, it was not his.

The object was an artificial penis that was attached to Charlie's cowboy boot. With Charlie standing straight, no part of the phallus was visible, for his pants covered it. But when he bent his leg or lifted his pant or bowed, the tip would peek out from under his hem. This was the part of Charlie's two-step that I had missed: when bowing to his partner, he would glance downward, making certain that his partner's attention found its way to the bottom of his leg.

On days when I was not having lunch with Charlie I would go upstairs to the fusing room. There, lenses ground with the correction needed for reading were set on top of those used for seeing at a distance; the two lenses were then placed on a conveyor belt and rolled slowly through a brick oven. The oven reached extraordinary temperatures, thereby joining the two lenses into a bifocal. If the conveyor changed speed, or the lenses were jostled or even exploded owing to flaws in the glass, the entire batch of lenses would be ruined. For this reason it was necessary for someone to be in the room at all times watching the oven, and there were very few who could withstand the heat of that room. A cousin of my father's, who also owned an optical factory, worked the fusing room naked.

This room was the province of my grandfather and the men who worked under him. With this, neither my father nor my grandmother interfered. As a young man, my grandfather was in a position to retire. Instead, he returned every day to the fusing room, and did so well into his eighties. He was indistinguishable from the other workers: he wore the same work clothes, worked the same hours, and ate with them.

Some of these men had been in concentration camps, and standing next to the oven, staring into the fire, the numbers on their arms glowed.

Returning from lunch with my grandfather, I was impressed by the difference between the men who worked with my grandfather fusing lenses and those who worked in the surfacing room. The former were easily categorized (central and Eastern Europeans, many of them Jews); the surfacing room was a more puzzling assemblage.

Charlie knew a lot of the people in the plant, and standing in the corner we were able to see everyone on the floor. He would point out details of the people he knew: the deaf and the cripples, the criminals, the alcoholics, the ones who were sexually available, the ones who had been in mental institutions. At first I dismissed this as the imaginings of Charlie, but the longer I worked in the plant, the less likely I was to dismiss his observations; he was a sociologist, albeit one who had a penis strapped to his shoe.

The way that hiring worked in the surfacing room was that Fred Christianson would review applications, select those people he wanted to interview, and then present the ones he had chosen to my father, who would make the final decision. Fred's decisions were based on theories that other employers in Omaha might consider unusual: Fred hired the deaf because they would not be distracted by what was going on around them; obese people were more likely to stay in their seats; men on parole were less likely to leave town. As my brother Harlan has pointed out, if a person whom Fred hired—a cripple, for example—worked out, then every person Fred hired after that would be a cripple until one of them failed to do their job or a flaw was revealed in Fred's theory (the efficiency that was gained by using deaf people, for example, was lost when they used their hands to talk to other deaf people).

As Fred Christianson grew older and his decisions as to hiring became more eccentric, there were certain people in the company who came to the opinion that he was no longer able to handle his job. One of these, an assistant manger, a young man, approached my father to say that the time had come to replace Fred and that he was ready to take on the job. The young man did not, it seemed, care that Fred was standing close enough to overhear the conversation. My father listened politely, looked at Fred, and then turned back to the young man. As Fred tells the story, he saw in my father's eye "a look that meant he was about to punch the kid out, so I grabbed your dad and pulled him away before he struck him."

Fred would not have been able to put his theories into effect without the help of my father. As one of the workers told me, "Word around town as that if you couldn't get a job anywhere else, there was a guy downtown, Nick Rips, that would give you a shot. We were a factory of freaks, but we were loyal to Nick." On more than a few occasions, the police would come to the factory to arrest someone on an outstanding warrant who was happily working away at their job. As they were led off, they had one comfort: the knowledge that no matter what their crimes against the rest of the world, they would be welcomed back into the society that had been assembled by my father. Whatever benefits my father conferred on the workers, he received much in return: the people in his factory strengthened him.

One day early on, Nick Rips looked out over his workers and decided that there was still something missing: blacks. With that, he walked around the factory and to each supervisor gave a very specific instruction: hire blacks. The order was carried out and very quickly blacks and, shortly thereafter, Hispanics, mostly women, became a significant part of the workforce.

The hiring of women was itself unusual: historically, optical shops were closed to women. Nick Rips made certain that women were hired in his factory, and over the years the factory came to be dominated by them. Norman Zevetz, who worked in the factory for over four decades, said that "what was important was not that blacks and women were hired but that your father listened to them. He was curious about their lives. He talked to them and they talked to him."

My father hated sitting in his office. He wanted to be out in the factory, among the workers. But he also worked: if someone was ill or the work was backing up or there was something that needed to be fixed, Father was the one who stepped in. On countless occasions I would see him working the generators or polishers, hand–cutting lenses, or writing up orders; there was a small retail shop on the first floor of the factory, and when time allowed he would sit down there and fit people with glasses.

Before putting lenses into their frames, each lens is examined for imperfections (minute spots that were missed by the polishers, nicks around the edges of the glass, small bubbles inside the lens). If any of these are present, the lens is sent back. Even then it might not be right, and it would have to be sent back again, to be cut and recut, polished and repolished. Every so often a lens would come through that was so clean, so utterly free of everything in this world, that it would vanish and it was in those moments that I came to appreciate the beauty of the invisible.

Excerpt from *Stranger to the Game*

BOB GIBSON AND LONNIE WHEELER

We all noticed a change in my oldest brothers, Josh
and Richard, when they returned from the war. They
never talked about what had happened; I only knew,
from their moods and their attitudes and from what I'd
heard about the experiences of other black soldiers, that
the service had been profoundly disillusioning. Josh, the
oldest, was stationed in India, where many of the locals
actually believed that black people had tails. He would
be walking down the street and Indians would sneak in
behind him trying to get a good look. Richard was with
the Air Corps in Italy, and something there apparently disturbed him deeply. He became angry and with-
drawn. At one point after they were back home, Josh
and Richard fell into a long, impassioned argument,
presumably about the past, and their relationship was
never the same afterwards.

Richard kept to himself and before long moved to
New York. Meanwhile Josh (whose real name was Leroy,
although nobody called him that) completed his work
for an undergraduate degree in history, got a job in a
meatpacking plant, and settled down with the rest of

the family in Omaha, which was to my good fortune because he had always been the central figure in my life—father, coach, teacher, and role model. I could add "pain in the ass," but, while essentially true, that would be grossly ungrateful for all that Josh did—not only for me, but for all the boys in the ghetto. We were all, one way or another, a reflection of Josh.

I can never remember a time when Josh didn't have adult responsibilities. He was fifteen years older than me and became the man of the family after my father, Pack Gibson, died from what we called quick consumption (a form of tuberculosis) in 1935, a few months before I was born as the seventh and final Gibson. From what I'm told, Mother and the other kids were a wreck, and some of the older ones—Beulah and Richard and maybe even Josh himself—were so distraught that they wouldn't even eat. My mother placed a gray wreath on the front door, and to this day my sister Barbara Jean won't buy a Christmas wreath because it reminds her of our father dying. But Josh put his mourning aside and stepped right in to keep us going.

Fortunately he didn't have to earn a lot of money to replace my father's income, because my father didn't have much of an income. My mother, Victoria, worked at Omaha Lace Laundry and cleaned houses and hospitals in her spare time, but my father, who was considerably older, wasn't so lucky. He couldn't find steady work as a cabinetmaker, despite the considerable skill he'd brought to Nebraska from Louisiana (which he had fled to get away from a miserable stepmother), and often covered the rent by doing carpentry work for the landlord. When they first moved north, he and my mother had both held jobs at hotels in Lincoln, but those positions dried up during the Depression and my father caught on with construction crews for the Works Progress Administration in Omaha. That kept him going only temporarily, however, and afterwards he was employed off and on by the city as a janitor. All the while—particularly during the down times—he donated his services to Morningstar Baptist Church, where he was a trustee. Among other projects, he built a pulpit that's still in the church's basement, with his initials carved into it. (Having been named Pack Robert Gibson in my father's honor, my initials were also P. G.—originally. But while I revere the legacy of my father, I couldn't stand his first name and had it changed to Robert as soon as I was on my own.)

My mother's brother, Napoleon Brown—we called him Uncle Son—lived with us after my father died, and helped manage the family. I thoroughly enjoyed the fried chicken he brought home every Saturday night (during the week we ate mostly rice, pinto beans, and the vegetables we grew in the garden), but even so I always thought of Mother as my provider and Josh as my protector. When at the age of three I became deathly sick with asthma or pneumonia—my family seems to disagree on the particulars—Josh was the one who wrapped me in a quilt, carried me to the hospital, and promised to buy me a baseball glove if I got well. According to what a nurse told my mother, as they were about to wheel me into some dark room for treatment, I looked up at the nurse and asked, "Are you going to kill me?" When she said no, I said, "Good. Please don't kill me because my brother Josh told me that if I don't die, he'll buy me a baseball glove." It was a while before I could use the glove, however, because I was weakened by childhood diseases I only faintly remember, including a bone problem called rickets, for which my mother laid me out in the sun in a buggy to strengthen my marrow (despite the efforts of Barbara Jean, who tried her best to pull me out of the buggy so she could play with it).

After Josh earned his degree from Creighton University, he searched all over the city for a job as a teacher and coach. When he was unable to find one, it aggravated the disillusionment he had obtained during the war and prompted him to do several things: He became very angry; he abandoned whatever faith he still had in the American dream; and he organized the neighborhood kids into athletic teams at a recreation center on Lake Street.

By then, we were living at the Logan Fontenelle projects, having moved there after several bad experiences in rented houses on

Maple and Hamilton streets on the north side of the city, including one on Hamilton that was infested with rats after the foundation caved in from snow. We nailed tin cans over holes in the floor to keep the rats out, but they ate through the cans and one of them bit me in the ear while I was sleeping. Another house of ours on Hamilton was haunted, according to Barbara Jean, who said she saw a ghostly image standing next to her once in the bathroom. Another time, as she was getting ready for bed, a strange voice called her name. She told our brother Fred about it, and Fred ordered her to fetch him the baseball bat. She said, "What if it's Jesus? You gonna hit him if it's Jesus?" Fred said, "Yep." That's the way Fred was.

These days people think of housing projects as the urban dregs, representing all that is vulgar and depraved about ghetto life, but to us in 1942, Logan Fontenelle was heaven in Nebraska. It was, at worst, a gilded ghetto. The units were brick, they were new, they were centrally heated—we were accustomed to the house being frigid until we got the fire going in the morning—and best of all, there were ball fields and running tracks just a few steps from our doors. Actually, the track was a sidewalk that rimmed the grassy plaza in the center of the major black section of housing, but to us it was a perfect layout for relay races, long sprints—we had both a 440 circuit and a 220—and barrel-jumping on roller skates. It was no coincidence that, year after year, the best sprinters in Nebraska came out of Logan Fontenelle. In many urban neighborhoods, you had to be mean to survive, but in ours, you had to be *fast*. Speed was the thing that separated the men from the boys at Logan Fontenelle. I could move well enough to hold my own, but even so, I was no match for guys like Leon Chambers, who was about the quickest I ever saw. Mind you, this is coming from a man who played with Lou Brock and watched Gale Sayers grow up. Leon Chambers was the prototype for Gale Sayers. If only he had finished high school, there's no telling what he might have accomplished as an athlete.

The sidewalk was convenient for stretching our legs, but when we really wanted to blow off steam we took to the large field separating the black and white sections of the projects. The field—the famous field—was the place for baseball, football, and interracial fighting. I quarterbacked our little project football team (handing off at opportune moments to Leon Chambers, as you might imagine), but my friends and I had to step aside for the big games on Thanksgiving Day, when the older boys and young men from Logan Fontenelle would take on a team from the black community on the south side of town in the annual Cold Bowl. It was rough-and-tumble, no-holds-barred tackle football with everything but pads. Josh, Richard, and Fred all played for our side, and everybody in the projects turned out to watch. The game generally culminated in a full-scale fistfight.

There was also a basketball court adjacent to the field, and since basketball was my best and most natural sport, my brothers permitted me to play with them. The five Gibson boys—Josh, Richard, Fred, David, and I—would often challenge all comers. With Josh throwing his weight around under the basket and me dishing off and shooting behind my brothers' screens, we were rarely, if ever, beaten. When the courts were covered with snow or the basketballs were too cold to bounce, we moved the games to Josh's gymnasium or the smaller one at the project recreation center, which was located on the edge of the white housing section.

Actually, there were two rec centers in the projects—both of them separate from Josh's on Lake Street, which later became the local YMCA. One, which was for arts and crafts and academic tutoring, was where the girls and college-bound boys hung out. My friend Rodney Wead dragged me there quite a bit. But my hangout was the rec center at Twenty-second and Clark run by Marty Thomas, which, in addition to basketball, offered table tennis and a wild gymnasium game we called box hockey. Occasionally, when the sun was down and the balls were quiet, Marty would bring in crawdads that he had caught and cook up stew for about a half dozen of us. Some of our best nights revolved around Marty's crawdad stew and a Joe Louis fight on the radio.

Marty attracted enough boys to the center to operate a fast-pitch softball league, and Josh tapped into the same talent pool for basketball and later baseball teams that he organized. We didn't think much of it at the time, but in retrospect it seems curious that our group of jocks included white boys like Dick Mackie and Glenn Sullivan, who lived on the other side of the projects. Both of those guys were superb athletes, and I suspect now that Marty and Josh recruited them into our crowd on the premise that they would get to compete alongside some of the best young ballplayers in Omaha. Not only did Mackie and Sullivan play on our teams, but they also fought at our side when the black kids of Logan Fontenelle rumbled with the white kids on the big field. (I suspect that my strong feelings about discrimination result in part from the fact that our neighborhood and school were always integrated, with a mixture of black, white, Jewish, and even Chinese and Indian. Nearly everybody I know from the neighborhood feels the same way I do in this respect.)

I've heard it said that Josh's misfortune in finding a teaching job turned out to be the best break the boys of North Omaha ever had. But while it's true that occupational frustrations drove him in our direction, it was also obvious that his involvement with me and my friends ran deeper than that. In equal measure, Josh thrived on athletic competition and was completely devoted to kids—especially to me, for whom he felt a personal responsibility. I was ten years old when he returned from the war, and Josh noticed right away that I had begun to fall in with the wrong crowd. Along with the paternal, protective role he had always taken on around me, Josh was the sort of fellow who didn't drink or smoke (when I was twelve or so, I got hold of some tobacco, rolled it into a little pipe I had bought, and hid it in the closet, but Josh found the pipe, popped me in the back of the head, kicked me in the pants, and that was that), and he possessed an almost religious fervor about sports and education. He was headstrong and demanding and rough, but in many ways Josh was the ideal role model. He was also a hell of a coach.

I've always assumed that my interest in sports had a lot to do with Josh being a coach, but as I reflect upon it, I suspect now that Josh's interest in coaching had a lot to do with me being an athlete. For both of us, the commitment is probably traceable to a conversation we had when I was eleven. One day late that summer, Josh sat me down in front of our house for a hard lecture on being a professional man. Traditionally, professionalism was and is a matter of education, but at that moment something new was opening up for black people. It was 1947, and Jackie Robinson had just joined the Brooklyn Dodgers. Suddenly, there was the unexpected possibility of a black man being a professional athlete. Josh explained to me that I had to make a commitment one way or the other, and since I never had much enthusiasm for studying in books, I decided on the spot to be a ballplayer. I didn't know if the sport would be baseball or basketball, but I would play one of them professionally.

I expect, though, that Josh knew which it would be. Until that time, black kids in most cities had generally played softball—as we did for Marty Thomas—rather than baseball. But when Jackie Robinson made the big leagues, we rounded up hardballs, moved the bases back, and began firing overhanded. Josh took a particular interest in the pitching part, and as soon as we made the transition to baseball he took me over to Kellom Elementary, the integrated neighborhood school that I attended, built a pitcher's mound in a corner of the play field, and marked off home plate sixty feet six inches away. He had me throwing there practically every day from March until the first snow.

When we played ballgames, though, Josh usually had me as the catcher or shortstop. I guess he figured it would be a long time before black pitchers would make much of a dent in the big leagues—besides which, I was pretty damn wild back then. There was only one catcher, Rudy Skillman, who could hang onto my fastballs, and it really wasn't worth the trouble because we had two fellows, John Halcomb and Wendell Booth, who could throw strikes and take care of business on the mound.

There was a huge amount of talent on Josh's teams, and it wasn't long before we were proudly representing the new North Side YMCA, which opened on the same site as the rec center with John Butler as director and Josh as program director. Among the teams Josh coached was an adult basketball team, the Y Travellers, which he and my brother Fred played on. The Travellers made the rounds of Nebraska and Iowa playing local all-star teams, and few were their equal. Josh was ruthless when it came to winning—an attitude that I suspect had something to do with his war experience and his inability to find a job commensurate with his qualifications—and when the lead opened up and he really wanted to humiliate the opponent, he would put in his skinny thirteen-year-old brother, the water boy. I was more than happy to shoot it up and not at all self-conscious about the uniform that was several sizes too big for me.

From that time until I signed a professional contract and left home, it seemed that I spent every summer crowded into the back of some big old moving van or another that Josh had rented for the occasion. The youth team I played for—the Monarchs (probably named for the Kansas City Monarchs of the Negro Leagues)—traveled just as much as the Travellers. Josh carried us to places we would never have seen if it hadn't been for baseball—places, in fact, that few people have ever seen, little towns in Nebraska and Missouri and especially Iowa, where I have basically fond memories of the likes of Glenwood, Hamburg, Avoca, Exira, Onawa, Logan, Harlan, Missouri Valley, Shenandoah, Red Oak, Griswold, and Woodbine. It was a world we couldn't see from our front stoops at Logan Fontenelle, and if it seemed strange at times—like the day in Iowa when a young girl asked to rub my skin to see if the color would come off—it was seldom unpleasant. We were as much a curiosity to the country folk as the country life was to us.

I can't remember better times than the ones our youth team would have playing in the outer reaches of Nebraska and Iowa and Missouri. What we were experiencing—for a group of young black kids from the inner city—was an entirely new universe. We hadn't known anything but what we saw in the city—the sidewalks and factories—or heard much of anything but the noise of the streetcars. Now here we were, traveling country roads in the back of a truck, screaming, laughing, and best of all, playing ball. I won't say we were the most welcome visitors in that part of the country, and when the people saw a group of young black kids get out and begin playing ball, there was some abuse. But the best part of it was that once the games started, everything disappeared. I think each community grew to respect each other more, even if they didn't always care for one another.

Whatever we felt about each other, Josh saw to it that we commanded respect. I remember one day in Maryville, Missouri, when, after the game, they lined us up on the curb of the town square for cold watermelons. We're tearing into those watermelons and they're standing back taking pictures of us. We didn't know what was really going on, but Josh sure did. He ordered us to stop and ask for a fork. We'd never in our lives used a fork to eat watermelon, but that was Josh's rule for the road. If somebody offers you watermelon, ask for a fork. That worked fine for everybody except Bob. He thought it was demeaning to be served watermelon in the first place and wouldn't touch any if they brought it out on a silver platter.

—RODNEY WEAD *Gibson's boyhood friend*

Some of those towns were serious about baseball, and as a result our talents were not unappreciated. One of our infielders, Jerry Parks, and I were noticed in Woodbine by a local coach named Red Brummer, who asked us to join the farmboys on his Woodbine Whiz Kids. When we weren't touring with the Monarchs, we hooked up with the Whiz Kids and won a few weekend tournaments. The Monarchs also had the honor of playing the first game in Woodbine's new Midget League park, which was the best in the area. We accepted that as a tribute to our baseball skills.

Not surprisingly, there were times when the locals would stack the deck against us. Josh was always alert to this and had no patience for it whatsoever. He was hell on umpires and anybody else who wouldn't give his team a fair shake. In Griswold there was an umpire with a speech impediment who couldn't bring himself to rule one in our favor and would often change his call in mid-stammer when he realized who was playing. He'd yell, "B-b-b-b-STEERIKe!" The guys on the bench would be holding their sides in laughter—Haskell Lee, who later became a minister, has talked about that umpire for years—but Josh would be furious. In another town he once argued so persistently with the umpire that the ump finally asked him if he would like to take the mask and do it himself. So Josh took the mask, put it on, and squatted behind home plate. With that, the ump threw him out of the game. Other times, if he thought he had a sympathetic crowd, he would pace in front of the stands and say, "Did you see that? Can you believe that?" We were amused by Josh's antics most of the time, but it wasn't so funny when my brother tried to fight the entire park. If he thought we were being treated badly, and especially if the fans were taking part in the abuse, he would walk out to the pitcher's mound and invite the home folks to meet him there. There were a few times when we thought Josh was going to get us killed.

There were also times when I wondered if Josh was going to kill me himself. He was much harder on me than he was on the rednecks from Iowa—no doubt because I had committed myself to becoming a pro ballplayer and Josh wasn't going to let me default on that commitment. The other guys on my team would watch silently after practice when Josh would order me back on the field and hit me vicious ground balls until the sun set. After I took one of his best shots in the eye one day, I ran home crying to my mother. She told me that I didn't have to play for Josh anymore, but of course I wasn't about to quit. Josh might let up for a day or two now and then to get Mother off his back, but after that it was always more of the same.

As much as I hated him sometimes, it was impossible not to admire and believe in Josh, because he led by example. He required no more from any of us than he gave himself and, most important, he was no hypocrite. Josh would have loved to have the opportunity, as I had, to pursue a career in professional sports, and in fact he probably had the talent to pull it off. He was bullishly strong, surprisingly agile, and Lord knows he never backed down from a challenge. But since that avenue was closed to him—the color barriers were not broken in time to help Josh—he did as he told me I would otherwise have to do: He got an education. And don't think the boys on the team didn't notice. I recall one day when Josh was late for baseball practice, and Josh was *never* late for practice. Somebody asked where he was, and I said he was at school. He was attending Creighton, studying for his master's degree. The guys couldn't believe it. After a while, here comes Josh—this snarling, two-hundred-pound, kick-ass coach—carrying a stack of schoolbooks. It made quite an impression.

As a coach, Josh could be questioned—not to his face, of course—about the techniques and strategies he taught, but I never played for a coach or manager, in any sport or at any level, who taught me more about winning than Josh did. At that stage of his life Josh did not have the temperament to accommodate losing. He was hell-bent to win, and pity the man or team or injury or excuse that got in his way. Most of the kids who played for Josh developed the same attitude. Our ability to win far exceeded our ability to hit and throw and field. The Y Monarchs played to win, and we won.

In 1951, when I was fifteen, we became the first black team ever to win a Nebraska state championship. It was an American Legion tournament, although few if any of the teams were sponsored by American Legion posts as they are now. The legion supervised the league and found business sponsors for the teams, all of which, except for ours, had full matching sets of uniforms. There were no merchants willing to buy a whole set of uniforms for a black team, however, so Josh paid some out of his pocket and the Y paid some and local establishments would kick in for about a player each. We took the field with one kid wearing the name of a funeral home on his back, the next a neighborhood tavern, and on down the line. But when the games started, we were sharp. Halcomb and Booth did most of the pitching for the Monarchs, I did the rest (between stints at short-stop and center field and catcher) and hit cleanup, Jerry Parks played the heck out of short and second base, and Rodney Wead gave us a big target at first. The finals were in Hastings, Nebraska, and strangely, I don't remember the triumphant details. I only remember how sick and depressed I felt in those years whenever we lost, which wasn't often. I didn't share all the bitter experiences of Josh's past, but I definitely took on his attitude.

The Nebraska championship qualified us for a regional tournament in Kansas City, Missouri. For reasons that most likely were part economic and part racial, we holed up at a community center in St. Joseph, about fifty miles away, and slept on pool tables. While there we managed to get in some practice on a field that had a little dirt between the rocks, and as Josh was smashing ground balls at me in the manner that he and I so loved, one of them bounced up and put a gash over my eye. I still have the scar. Josh had little sympathy for me, but he did have a Band-Aid, which he stuck on the cut while ordering me back to my position.

We were eliminated early in the Kansas City tournament, but when we arrived home I learned that I was an American Legion all-city selection as a utility player—a distinction that did absolutely nothing for me the next spring at Omaha Technical High school. Blacks didn't play baseball at Tech, despite the fact that we comprised approximately half of the student body. According to school policy, the spring sport for black athletes was track. This was largely the doing of the baseball coach, Ken Kennedy, who apparently hadn't heard of Jackie Robinson, and the track coach, Dutch White, who knew a good thing when he had one.

Kennedy also coached football, where a few blacks were permitted, and he had cut me as a freshman because I stood less than five
feet tall and weighed about ninety pounds. Usually Kennedy picked
his squad by lining up the players on the sideline and having them
roll up their pants legs. He kept the guys with scars, figuring they
were the toughest. But I was eliminated before I even got to show
him my shins. I told Kennedy that I had been playing football all
my life with many of the guys he was keeping and could outrun, out
throw, and out kick most of them. He told me to eat some potatoes
and come back later. Not a chance. By the time I was a senior I had
shot up to about six feet, 175, and Kennedy caught a glimpse of me
tossing and booting around the football one day with my friends.
He came up to me and said he'd get me a uniform, and I essentially
told him what to do with his uniform.

When, in my teenage innocence, I tried out for the baseball team
as a junior, I reasoned naïvely that my all-city status ought to count
for something—that, and the fact that the Monarchs had pounded the crap out of the summer team that most of the varsity guys
played for. But Kennedy informed me he couldn't accommodate me
on the team because I had reported a day late, and it wasn't until
years later—in fact, during my induction party at the Hall of Fame,
when another Tech coach gave me the real poop—that I found out
about the school policy.

Like all of the other blacks who were shut out of baseball, I turned
to Dutch White's track team, which was the best in the state. I wasn't
quite fast enough to sprint for Tech—although I suspect I could
have run any race I wanted for any other school in Nebraska—but
I manned a leg on the sprint relay team that claimed the city title,
won a few broad jumps, and set the Omaha indoor high-jump record at five-eleven.

Finally, in my senior year—by which time I'd already been offered a contract by the Kansas City Monarchs—we got a new baseball coach, Tom Murphy, and I was allowed to participate. I pitched
some and played the outfield. Jerry Parks also made the team as a

shortstop, and together we broke the color line on Omaha Tech's baseball team. Socially it was no big deal, since we commonly played with white guys in the neighborhood and in the small towns of Iowa and Nebraska, and the ballplaying benefits proved to be mutual. There was no state championship in high school baseball, but in the Intercity tournament (so called because the league included two schools from Council Bluffs, Iowa, across the Missouri River from Omaha) I was called on to pitch the semifinal game against Omaha North. I threw strikes that day and North managed only a scratch single in the sixth. That put us in the finals, also against North, and we beat them again for the championship. As a result, I made all-city as an all-purpose player. It was more meaningful to me, however, that as a switch-hitter I finished second among the city's batting leaders with an average of .368.

Since pitching was only secondary to me at the time—and all I could really do on the mound was throw hard—I assumed that my future lay somewhere in the outfield, perhaps, or maybe third base or even catcher. Or basketball. Basketball was easily my best sport, and the one for which I received the most recognition in high school.

Tech's basketball coach was an energetic young guy named Neal Mosser who, much like Josh, made everything else secondary to winning. He was my kind of coach, and his kind of player was one who could play. On that basis I was in. So were Jerry Parks and several of my friends from the projects, including the white boys who played with us at the rec center—Dick Mackie, an excellent left-handed shooter, and Glenn Sullivan, another lefty who shot even better than Mackie. I started at guard as a junior and, feeding Mackie and Sullivan, averaged only six points a game for a team that was ranked second in the city and third in the state. Our season came to an abrupt end early in the state tournament, however, when we were upset by Fremont.

I was certain that my senior year was going to be our year. Sullivan was gone, but we had so much talent returning that Mackie started only occasionally. Among my friends from the projects, Jerry Parks was a crackerjack point guard and Artie Sanders played a nifty game at center. I was one of the smallest guys on the team, but since I could jump I played small forward, from which spot I could rebound and score and maneuver. Although we didn't win the Intercity League—things being as they were, Tech had a lot of difficulty on the road—we clobbered the teams that were at the top, Creighton Prep and Abraham Lincoln, and considered ourselves easily the equal of any team in the state.

Our chance to prove that came at the state tournament in Lincoln, and Mosser had us ready. He put his heart into his job and as a result was an extremely excitable coach, well known for screaming at referees and jumping up and down in front of the bench. One time he was so upset during a game that he threw himself chest-down onto the floor. Like Josh, his conduct stemmed, in large part, from the fact that our team often got screwed. Mosser knew that he offended a lot of people by starting so many black players, but he didn't give a damn. When we were called to take our places in the University of Nebraska gym to play our state semifinal game against Fremont, he courageously sent five black players onto the floor. That had never happened before, and there was stone silence in the arena as we were announced. I'll never forget that eerie feeling.

The evening grew increasingly peculiar as it wore on. Fremont was a scrappy team but very small and not particularly gifted. Its strategy was to stall with the ball, which made sense. Nothing else made sense that night, however. As slow as the action was, somehow the referees managed to foul out four of our starters in the first half. I was the only one remaining to start the second half, and I was gone a couple of minutes later. When it was over, we had lost by a point, 40–39. I cried in the locker room afterwards, unable to cope with the reality that we had been cheated and there wasn't a thing we could do about it. I believe it was the last time I ever shed tears over a ballgame.

I gained a small measure of consolation when I was a unanimous choice for the all-city team, having averaged seventeen points and involved myself quite a bit with the rebounding and ball handling. I still have the clipping from the *Omaha World-Herald* when it announced the all-city team, saying, "The most spectacular [of the all-city players] is Gibson. He's the boy with springs in his toes and basketball magic in his fingertips." Strangely—Omaha politics being what they were—I made all-state in the Lincoln paper but not in the *World-Herald*.

After the season, I played some AAU basketball for Offutt Air Force Base, just outside Omaha, and the Kitlow Institute, a correspondence school in the southwest Nebraska town of Alma where I averaged twenty-five points. My objective was to make a name for myself and catch the attention of Branch McCracken, the coach of Indiana University's national championship team. Coach Mosser wrote McCracken on my behalf, and then I waited. Finally the reply arrived: "Your request for an athletic scholarship for Robert Gibson has been denied because we already have filled our quota of Negroes." The quota was apparently one per class—or perhaps two on the whole team, it was hard to tell. The Hoosiers already had a black fellow a year ahead of me from New Jersey named Wally Choice, who turned out to be their leading scorer as a senior, and in my class—in my place, as I saw it—there was a guard from Indianapolis, Hallie Bryant, who started as an upperclassman and later played for the Harlem Globetrotters. They were good ballplayers, but that didn't change my opinion about the situation. I remember watching Bryant play on television over the next few years and thinking to myself, "They got the wrong Negro."

When they played in Omaha, the Negro League teams used to park their old multicolored Greyhounds on the street in front of my friend Rodney Wead's house, which of course wasn't far from mine. Rodney would rush me over there, and we would gawk at the guys as they stepped off the bus to walk to the rooming house a block and a half away (the street in front of it was too narrow to park on) or to find some supper or occasionally to practice at the same field we used on Twenty-second Street. The players were all alike to me, but Rodney read up on them and would get carried away when he spotted Sam Jethroe or Luke Easter or Ernie Banks. He followed them around and got their autographs and somehow managed to be the batboy when Easter's team played in Omaha or across the river in Council Bluffs.

It might have been because of Jackie Robinson that I wasn't especially interested in the Negro Leagues. Jackie had played with the Kansas City Monarchs, but as soon as he made the big leagues, the Negro Leagues seemed to me to be a moot point. Besides that, I wasn't especially interested in watching someone else play ball. Whereas a guy like Rodney had to keep his mind busy, I had to keep my hands busy.

That was part of the reason why I seemed like a mama's boy. (Actually, many of my friends were mama's boys, too, as attested by the fact that, in the ghetto tradition of "playing the dozens," we called each other by our mother's names. I was Victoria, Rodney was Daisy, and so on.) Mother was good with her hands, and by copying her I learned to mend my own clothes and cook and fix things around the house. Because I had been so ill when I was young, I also slept with my mother for several years and became her pet, more or less. She had much more patience with me than my brothers and sisters did, and they all tired of hearing her tell them to "leave my baby alone."

Robert was always into something or bothering somebody. Josh had been a big track star in high school and he had a box full of medals. One day, Robert was trying to get a ride on another kid's bicycle and ended up trading the kid all of Josh's medals. Another time, he was playing with Richard's model airplanes and set them on fire by lighting a match to a tray of glue. Robert and his friends used to make go-carts out of wheels and orange crates, and once, when he didn't have any wheels handy, he took them off a buggy I played with—the same one Mother had laid him in for sun treatments when he was smaller. He also used my roller skates to make a scooter.

Robert was always getting into some kind of trouble. When he was about three, he followed the rest of us to school and then couldn't find his way home. Mother finally called the police. After that, she had to chain him up in the yard to prevent him from running off. Nothing could stop him, though. Once he ran off and fell into Carter's Lake and had to be pulled out. Robert just wouldn't sit still. Josh and Uncle Son used to offer him dimes if he would stay in one place for five minutes, but he couldn't do it. Apparently, he was the same way in school. He was always bringing home notes from the teachers about throwing paper wads or pulling some poor girl's hair. Mother would find the notes hidden in Robert's shoe. He was a pest, is what he was. If you sat still, Robert was going to bother you. We would all get so mad. We'd say to Mother, "Why don't you give him a whipping?" She'd say, "I don't have to. Every one of you has beat him already." He would always go to her for sympathy. I can remember him still sitting on Mother's lap and crying when he was twelve years old.

—BARBARA JEAN GIBSON STEVENS

That's not to say that Mother wouldn't spank me. She packed a wallop and she packed it often. When I was thirteen, she was still spanking me, but I figured I was too old for it by then and one time I just laughed. I said, "You can't hurt me." With that, she grabbed my head and pushed it through the Sheetrock.

I suppose I gave her ample reason to discipline me from time to time. Like all little brothers, I liked to hang around with my big brothers. Josh would never lead me astray, but Fred wasn't quite so fatherly and his buddies were even less concerned about the example they set. They weren't big-time troublemakers but delighted in profitable mischief. For example, street vendors used to make their way through the projects selling ice cream, milk, and tamales. Stealing from the ice cream guy was a tricky proposition because he could tell something was missing by the amount of steam coming up from the dry ice; so we would stick our treats under the truck until he drove off. The tamale vendor was nearly blind, but that didn't make him an easy mark—he could still feel things pretty accurately. He sold three tamales for a dime, and our hustle was to fool him with a penny. There were silver pennies back then, but he could distinguish them from dimes by feeling the edges, so we would crimp the edge of a penny with a pair of pliers to make it feel like a dime and walk off chomping on three tamales. We didn't bother with the milk guy—although, now that I think about it, we could have used some milk to go with the doughnuts we stole. On Lake Street, not far from the projects, there was a bakery that sat on a steep incline. The baker worked in the basement, which, because of the hill, had a window just off from and a little below the sidewalk. Fred and his friends would stand a few steps up the hill, then dangle me by the ankles upside down over the window of the doughnut shop. When the baker took a sheet of doughnuts out of the oven, he would place it on a rack right in front of the window. My job was to reach in and take the sheet off the rack when he turned away, then hand it to Fred or somebody. The doughnuts were great, but the best part was seeing the look on the baker's face when he discovered them missing. Around the fourth tray or so, he'd stop and look around and scratch his head. I don't think he ever figured it out.

For all of our petty crime, we never got into any serious trouble with the police—primarily because we could always hear their cars coming from a couple of blocks away. The police cars all had the same sort of standard transmission, and we recognized the sound of the cops down-shifting when they took off. On top of that, their unmarked cars all had license plates beginning with 420.

Ironically, Fred did get arrested several times in later years when he was doing nothing more than walking home from work late at night. Every time, he'd say to the officers, "You know I've been working," and every time, they threw him in jail anyway. I was never harassed by the cops in that manner, but I did spend part of a day in jail when I was about seven years old. My friends and I were making a clubhouse and knew where there was a keg of rusty old nails in an abandoned barn at the end of an alley. We managed to get ourselves spotted taking the nails. Most of us ran off, but one boy, Donald Moore, was picked up and told on everybody else. I had sprinted straight home and jumped in bed, which is what I always did when I was scared, and while I was under the covers there was a knock at the door. The policeman took me in and locked me up for a couple of hours.

Donald Moore, in fact, made my life miserable more than once. He was a little older and meaner than Rodney and me and used to chase us both home from school. He would give us a head start and tell us that he would beat us up if he caught us. He never caught us, but it got to be tiresome after a while and I happened to mention it to Barbara Jean, who's about three years older than me. Barbara Jean told us to run past a certain location the next day, and when Donald came by the same way she stepped forward and beat the crap out of him. Donald never bothered me after that.

There was an even tougher kid, though, named Tony King, who was the neighborhood bully. He threatened me a lot and one day got me cornered by the pool table in the recreation center. I had no choice but to fight him, and to my surprise I came out of it unscathed. I was so scared that I pounded the guy into the floor. I never had to fight after that. (Years later, Tony King was found dead in an alley in Chicago.)

Fighting was fairly routine around the projects, and if I didn't participate in many fights, I was seldom far from one. Fred and his cronies often found themselves in the mood for a scrap, and when the urge hit them they simply walked over to a redneck bar at Twentieth and Charles, the opposite side of the neighborhood. I'd always be right behind them, but when they went inside I stayed out. All they had to do was order a beer, and fists were flying. Now and then, somebody would come crashing through a window and land at my feet. It always amazed me that by the next day Fred's crowd and the rednecks would be walking to and from school together as if nothing had happened. It seemed like it was their *duty* to beat on each other from time to time—to at least give off the appearance of mutual hate—and once the duty had been fulfilled, things could get back to normal for a while.

The worst and scariest fight I ever saw was at a football game between Creighton Prep and Boys Town High. That was always one of the biggest games of the year and people came from all over town to watch. It was a mean-spirited rivalry because Creighton Prep was a well-heeled private Jesuit school and Boys Town had a lot of homeless and black kids. When I was thirteen or so, I was watching the game from outside a fence on a hill beyond one of the end zones. A lot of people were milling around, including a couple of ex-marines who were apparently spoiling for a fight. Making sure they had an audience of black guys, one of the marines announced, "I can beat the shit out of any nigger I've ever seen." Naturally, a circle of people quickly gathered, and I saw a guy named Raymond Manuel, who happened to be standing right next to me, take a handkerchief out of his pocket and wrap it around his hand. Without saying a word, he stepped through the crowd, walked up to the marine, and with one punch knocked the guy out cold. The marine never saw the fight that ensued. Before long, the whole stadium was involved, inside and outside the fence. It was black against white, and it was ugly. There were people hanging from the fence, hooked by their shirts to the wrought-iron spikes at the top.

At another high school game, Omaha South, an integrated team, was upsetting a mostly white team in the third quarter when what seemed like the entire student body of the white school came over to the other side and provoked a major melee that left me cold and frightened. There were fistfights all through the bleachers and spilling down onto the sidelines. The game was called when the police arrived in force.

I give Josh credit for the fact that the violence of the neighborhood never really touched me or many of his athletes. Years later, after I had achieved some success in baseball, I made periodic visits to the state penitentiary and nearly always saw somebody I knew from school or the projects. Generally, though, they weren't Josh's kids. His athletes weren't choirboys, but for the most part we vented our aggressiveness—and there was plenty of it to go around—on those who would try to beat us or cheat us.

There are other neighborhoods in America that have produced impressive lists of athletes, and maybe some have been more prolific than the north side of Omaha. Oakland and Los Angeles and Cincinnati and Mobile have turned out numerous major-leaguers, for instance; but I have a hard time believing that any community as small and isolated as the Logan Fontenelle housing projects can match us for quantity and quality and diversity of athletes. I was the first of Josh's protégés to hit the big time, but not long after I made it in baseball, Bob Boozer turned up with the Cincinnati Royals of the NBA. Around that time, Gale Sayers set pro football on its ear by zigzagging down the field for the Chicago Bears; some still think he's the greatest running back ever. Few people realize that Gale's brother, Roger, was a world-class runner. Then came Marlin Briscoe, who with the Denver Broncos was one of the first black quarterbacks in the NFL; Ron Boone, who set a consecutive-games record while playing for several teams in the American Basketball Association and NBA; and Nebraska's Heisman Trophy winner, Johnny Rodgers—all disciples of Josh Gibson and alumni of the North Side YMCA.

As a kid, my universe revolved around the Y and the rec center. Aside from fighting on the big field, footracing around the sidewalk, and hanging out by the clubs and shops of Twenty-fourth Street, there wasn't much in the way of diversions in my neighborhood. Only one family in the projects had a television, and the rest of us watched cartoons and cowboy movies through their window. Some of us shined shoes downtown, but there weren't enough shoes to go around. So we were content to spend entire days in the gym.

The project rec center was more convenient for us than the Y, and I took full advantage of that fact. It closed from five to seven in the evening, but Marty Thomas knew that I loved basketball and he would let me in during those hours to shoot around by myself. I'd invent all sorts of crazy, impossible shots, then pull them out in the next Tech game.

I also got plenty of practice—and plenty of elbows from Josh—on the concrete floor of the Y (which also had a low ceiling that forced me to develop a flat jump shot). The only difficulty in utilizing the Y was finding a safe way to negotiate the ten blocks between there and the projects. The unwritten rule was never to cross over to the white side of the neighborhood, so we walked straight down Twenty-second Street to Lake, steering two blocks clear of the roughest corner in town at Twenty-fourth and Lake. The danger resided in the fact that our mothers usually gave us a few pennies for something to eat, and everybody knew it. Our strategy was to lie low and swing by the bakery for orange juice and day-old doughnuts. We generally managed to avoid trouble, and the only real scare I received along the route occurred when I was walking alone at about five o'clock one morning, on my way to meet up with the rest of the team for an out-of-town baseball game. On Twenty-second Street, a few blocks from the Y, a car full of rednecks pulled up alongside me. I tried not to pay any attention, but one of the guys inside rolled down the window and said, "Hey, we need some good old black poontang. You know where we can get some?" I kept walking and said, "Follow me." My plan was to lead them straight to the Y, where a small army of my friends would be waiting to kick their asses. Unfortunately, the good old boys got bored and turned off before we reached the party.

We could usually find Josh at the Y, where, if he wasn't conducting a practice of some sort, he was doling out lectures in his deep, gruff voice, imparting homespun lessons in growing up while nervously weaving rubber bands between his meaty fingers. As a coach, Josh was part social worker, which, in fact, he officially became much later, specializing in counseling single mothers. (Rodney Wead also—not coincidentally—gravitated toward the field of social work and remains in it to this day.) Among the social services Josh performed for me was setting me up, more or less, with my first wife. He had married his secretary, who happened to have an attractive niece named Charline who visited often at the Y. I was in my element there, which was fortunate because I was not generally comfortable in the company of girls and my encounters with them often didn't develop as I'd hoped.

Probably my first serious flirtation occurred when I was about twelve. There was a particular girl from school who I thought was pretty special, and I managed to meet up with her once at the back door of her house. She was standing with her heel against the wall, as girls do, and we were getting along nicely until suddenly she broke wind. I couldn't believe it. I guess I had imagined that girls didn't do that sort of thing. Anyway, with no further ado I took off running home because I couldn't wait to tell my friends. There was no way I could date the girl after that. I wouldn't have been able to look at her without laughing.

Things went a little smoother with Charline, whom I met the summer after high school and started going steady with almost immediately. We had no immediate plans, however, because I had no idea what I'd be doing over the next few years. I bided my time playing for a city league baseball team sponsored by the Chicago Bar, all the while depressed over being rejected by Indiana and second-guessing myself over passing up the offer from the Kansas City Monarchs. I was also being tempted by the St. Louis Cardinals, who had a Triple-A farm team in Omaha and whose local scout, Runt Marr, had been in contact with me for several years. Professional scouts were fairly commonplace around Omaha because, in addition to the Cardinals, the city hosted the College World Series every year, and I'd talked informally with representatives from several teams, including the Dodgers and Yankees. Marr seemed to be the scout most genuinely interested, however, and the only one who offered me a contract—such as it was—after high school. I wanted to accept it, but Josh said no. He still supported the idea of being a professional athlete, but since the immediate prospects were slim, he also insisted that I go to college. The problem was, I couldn't pay for it, and the colleges weren't beating a path to my door with scholarships. It was incumbent upon Josh to make something happen.

A few weeks before school was to start, I was shooting baskets at the Y when Duce Belford walked in. He was the athletic director and baseball coach at Creighton University, which was located only a few blocks from the projects, but he was there mainly to talk to me about the Blue Jays' basketball program. It was coached by a fellow named Subby Salerno, and I didn't know much about it because nobody I knew had anything to do with Creighton basketball; the team consisted mostly of workmanlike white boys from the private schools. Josh was a little more familiar with Creighton since he had earned his bachelor's and master's degrees there, and he was acquainted with Belford well enough to put in a good word for his kid brother—which explained why the athletic director approached me instead of the basketball coach. I don't know if Belford accepted Josh's word at face value or whether he or Salerno had seen me play, but that didn't matter. Nor did it matter that I wasn't Catholic. What mattered was that he was offering me a full athletic scholarship—a chance to get an education and play college basketball at the same time.

I shook hands with Belford, thanked Josh, and kissed my mother.

Excerpts from "Prairie Homeboys"

KENNETH LINCOLN

> In my book a pioneer is a man who turned all the
> grass upside down, strung bob-wire over the dust that
> was left, poisoned the water and cut down the trees,
> killed the Indian who owned the land, and called it
> progress. If I had my way, the land here would be like
> God made it, and none of you sons of bitches would
> be here at all.
>
> —CHARLES RUSSELL TO THE GREAT FALLS,
>   MONTANA, BOOSTER CLUB, 1923

The "West" in America is not so much a place, it seems
to me, as *going* somewhere, just out of reach. Our West
began on the Eastern seaboard, naturally so, backed
away to the Alleghenies, sloughed down the Ohio and
bottomed out across the Mississippi, then skyed across
the Great American Desert and up against the Rockies.
This last century the West then layered across the Great
Basin and southern deserts, crowhopped the Sierras,

and lapped the Pacific surf. Since the mirage of the "West" receded "out there," down where the sun set, the frontier was soon associated with time as motion. This progressive sense of motion translated into unlimited growth, unfenced expansion, and Manifest Destiny. Our frontier history came to mean a continentally destined westering. So Western man is always on the go. We are not quite grown-up, but new and growing—the bigger, the better. Ours was, and still is, a young dream of paradise.

Small Midwest towns, where the rangeland survives in all its rawness, instill the old rough values, the tight biases of an American heartland. Here the American male may be most traditional, most toughened, most threatened. Frontier culture still pits cowboys, pioneers, and migrant fundamentalists against severe weather, unforgiving odds, and timeless tribes of natives.

Men and women hunker down and struggle to hang on. They see themselves homestead-stubborn. The men feel threatened by feminism. Was my mother, Dad snickered, *a wimmin's libber?* These pioneers are weather-blunted on the oblivion edge of the Great American Desert, a thousand miles from urban centers. In the 1930s at Pine Ridge Reservation, north of my hometown, John Neihardt went looking for a Sioux warrior to complete his plains epic. It was no accident that he found Nick Black Elk, second cousin to Crazy Horse and Catholic catechist, a healing *wicasa waken.* The purblind old Lakota, a "man holy," not an Achilles figure, was expecting him.

Out West, the personal roots and work of America's frontiersman are hardwon. The red-line through these lives, cowboys to Indians, is rugged individualism with a dash of spit. *I won't paint pretty pictures,* says Robert Penn, a Lakota artist in Omaha today. *I'm nobody's dancing bear.*

Prairie-shadowed and horizon-obsessed, western men tend to run away, to drive right over what doesn't get out of the way, or to reach for a weapon. The hired gun goes back a long ways, from Achilles in *The Iliad,* to William the Conqueror, down to Han Solo in *Star Wars*. Free will and heroic individualism score the violence of star-spangled anthems. In fact and fantasy, George Custer to the Marlboro Man, our godly gunslinging has pitted light-skinned peoples against dark, imperialist West against colonial East, citizen against savage, industrial competition against tribal cooperation. The world can no longer afford this story.

> I was young and I thought I was tough and I knew it was
> beautiful and I was a little bit crazy but hadn't
> noticed it yet.
>
> —NORMAN MACLEAN

First hunt, first drink, first kill seed narratives of "male ritual," Corporal Pat Hoy says in *Instinct for Survival*, a personal story of soldiering, from a world war through Vietnam. Add to that three more life rituals—first work, first sex, first failure. Here's my story:

[I was] born in western Texas into the Second World War, as the Allies were losing. When it was over, and our side won, as it seemed, my father took us back to the Midwest. We settled into the house where he and his father were born, in Bayard, Nebraska—a village of fifteen hundred farmers along the North Platte Valley, founded by pioneers trekking westward. Bayard edged toward the Wyoming prairie where the grasses ended and the great deserts began. Over the century, many frontiersman wintered in the green valley run-off and cut their western pilgrimage short. My father's grandfather, a cousin to the Abe Lincoln line, came west from Wisconsin, and his son married a Whitman. My mother's people, on the other side, traced back through the Maryland Bradfords and Sumners of Boston. Yet family pedigrees thinned when immigrants buckled down in the shortgrass West.

My grandfather and great-grandfather built a white clapboard house with green shutters and roof shingles. The screened front porch was for cooling off in the evenings. The backstairs led up to the women's kitchen and down to the basement where winter provisions and the men's things were stored—saws, axes, hammers, pliers, screw drivers, anvils, shotguns, rifles, fishing rods and reels. The furnace coalroom was dark, and gunny-sacked potatoes sent out white fibrous tubers to find the light. It was a cellar of dreamy fear. A rough-hewn workbench bordered the south wall, and mountainous jars of preserves—tomato, peach, onion, apple, strawberry, rhubarb, corn, and beans—were lined along the north wall. My great-grandfather's dandelion wine and salted carp were stacked in mason jars on the top shelf, out of reach.

An old elm stood over the yard in back. I loved to climb into its top branches and look down—my brother squatting in a puddle making mudballs, my mother hanging out sheets, our dog Rex asleep in his kennel, our goose Bubbles slopping in her shelter. Mrs. Bristol to the north was making gooseberry pie; Grandmother Heil next door was chasing down a chicken and chopping off its head. The wings kept flapping and the legs running, headless, spurting blood around the melons in her garden. Pink and lavender hollyhocks rustled by the driveway. It was a time of waking to early light, running wild through the sandhill pastures, and going to sleep with the chirruping of crickets.

We lived eight years with my father's grandparents, who had helped raise him when he was orphaned. Robert Lincoln and Ida Tunks were stern, turn-of-the-century homesteaders, old-fashioned Methodists, Scottish-English and German-American. I called him Grampa, and he called me Kenny Bob, or just "son." He wore thick-soled black shoes that tied up over his ankles. On Sunday Grampa put on a shiny black pair of the same lace-up shoes. I remember Grandma Lincoln's aproned shadow in the kitchen, the yeast-heavy smells of home-baked bread, the starched rustle of her skirts. Her face is a shadow of murmurs.

In those days of great-grandparents and family ghosts, my father always seemed to be working. His own father had been dead from the flu epidemic twenty years before. My earliest memories are of ditching corn rows with my father's grandfather, the caulky smell of alkali becoming mud, bringing irrigated water to the roots—and of his crusty temper, blue-eyed patriarchy, and bentwood pipe. His name, Robert, became my middle name.

As Great-Grampa sat in an over-stuffed chair and smoked, I dreamed of shortgrass and cedar burning far across the prairie, a distant place of gnarled roots and fisted authority. Robert Lincoln ran the house, he kept order, he gardened bare-knuckled. After Ida died, he ate burned roast beef and mashed potatoes with us on Sunday after church; my brother and I kept our mouths shut. Grampa's plate was where the talk stopped and patriarchal authority started.

And there along the North Platte River, under the obelisk of Chimney Rock, I went hunting at the age of nine with the men. We woke in the dark and stumbled into the freezing late fall rain, the men shouldering decoys and slugging whiskey and loading shotguns. I carried a single-barrel four-ten that could kill a man. Keep the muzzle down, they warned, or pointed to the sky.

We drove in winter silence to the river. The backseat ride made me nauseous, the cold knifed my fingers. The smell of whiskeyed coffee gagged me. Was this how it felt to be a man? The gun barrel was blue. We buried ourselves in a makeshift duck blind, a hole of dead reeds and broken cottonwoods, and waited for dawn.

"Be ready, Kenny Bob," my Uncle Jack said with a wink, "and don't shoot until you smell duck breath."

They came with a rush of wings, and the men blasted away, and a few feathered bodies fell, and it was over. We slogged back with sacks of wild fowl.

"Now you know," my father said.

I was too young—didn't know where to aim, hadn't even pulled the trigger. I went home disconsolate, wondering what all this killing was about. No one asked me to dress the dead birds.

I found out more about killing a few years later, when Pat Green took me pheasant hunting, and I shot a cottontail, and its eyes glazed over. The blood stained my hands warm and sticky, smelling raw. Then I shot a ring-necked pheasant, skittering down a corn row, and had to wring its neck clean off. I cleaned the bird, and ate the parts my mother cooked, and went to bed feeling sick of the whole thing, but afraid to say so.

Fishing in Red Horse Creek, I felt the tug of the undercurrent, the draw of the eddy on my sinkered leader. The cattail reeds stank of frogspawn and stale wet feathers. I knew the plunge of a brown trout as it hit the hook and panicked. I learned to slit it end for end, gut it with two fingers, and cook the flesh over an open fire. A burlap sack of bullhead, a washtub of bluegill, plastic bags of crappies, aluminum-foiled bass and northern pike. In these early days, the men knew no game limits. The watery hauls fed us through the summers. In the fall the women preserved fruits and vegetables in the cellar. We bought sides of beef and froze waterfowl and fish in a walk-in meat locker. The rime cold sucked my nostrils together until I thought I couldn't breathe. My brother stuck his tongue on a spigot and couldn't get it off. These were postwar economies, frontier carryovers, working-class thrifts. It was the last of a survival economy from the Depression, a blue-collar shadow of western frugality. And everyone assumed it was the only way to live.

My first job was sacking beans at the elevator where my father worked with his childhood pal, Harold. Shrouded in field dust, we cleaned beans, sorted them, gunnysacked them, and shipped them away by railroad and truck. The ache of eight hours' work hardened my back and dulled my brain. Grip burlap, yank bar, lean in, pull up, sew shut, heave a hundred pounds onto the dolly, stack five bags, trundle a quarter ton into a boxcar tomb, dump dutifully, go back for another load. A work ethic, of sorts. *You can do it, son.* At day's end we stopped by the vfw for beers, and the men bought me Squirt. The work paid more than I'd ever held in my hand—two dollars a day—saved to buy football cleats.

My first drink was homebrew, bootlegged by high school boys, drunk quickly before the sediment rose and darkened the fetid yeast. I tore off my shirt, pounded my buddies, shouted obscenities, and ended up running through a beet field in the night, crazy with the booze thrill, charging the dark.

"Screw the hogs and whores! Fuck the mud!" It was a purgative binge better forgotten, a mindless swilling that older men parsed over a lifetime. *Blowing out the cobwebs*, guys called it.

What sticks in a boy's gut that needs such release? What drives men to deaden themselves for life with pain killers? I looked to my father with those questions, felt his toxic rebuff, and watched him drain his own self-respect with each shot of whiskey.

In the Elks Club basement, I stood up and challenged him to stop drinking.

"I drink because I *want* to drink" Dad snapped over a pool table, "it's my own business." He lit a cigarette, sighted down his cue at the eight ball, and kept shooting. We didn't talk anymore about it.

By thirteen, my friends were hanging around the whorehouse in Indian Town. A Black man from Denver driving a white Cadillac curated the Pick-a-Rib shanty: jukebox, two linoleum-covered tables, a sixty-watt light bulb hanging from the ceiling. Tacked on the wall, a calendar with busty women leaning against tractor harrows. We danced with Sioux girls only a few years older than ourselves and drank two-bit whiskey out of teacups; but we were shooed away by ten o'clock, when the townsmen came in and shouldered the girls to the back rooms.

I'd stayed virginal through high school. Besides a rough gentleman's code in our small town, there was church decency in my upbringing, and I was taught to value a woman's honor. On the road the rough code won out. The end of my freshman college year in California, driving home with Oklahoma boys in a red Oldsmobile, we stopped at a moonlight ranch in Winnemucca, Nevada.

"What are you, some gutless shit?" my Tulsa friend razzed. Riding shotgun, it seemed I had no choice: dickless boy or real man? A gate opened in the chain link fence, the dogs stayed leashed, we went ahead. The girls lined up against the wall, their dime-store night-ies loose, bra straps hanging. Five bucks a pop. I was last to get the situation, last to choose, left with a scowling brunette and a lanky thirty-something redhead. I took the redhead who struck me as less hardened. She drew me to bed with professional tenderness, guided me into her body, and told me when my time was up.

"You're not in college here, kid." I paid out my innocence and was left wondering, again.

I fell in love my senior year, got married that spring to a Stanford "dolly," and we went to an Indiana graduate school together in the English department, then moved to Los Angeles for our first jobs. Things went bad from there—or got better, depending on your perspective.

First big failure: after seven years I had a broken marriage, a run-away mother, an abandoned child. My wife said she hadn't loved me for years, thought me *disgusting* but didn't say why. I'm still puzzling that one. Something in my stomach crazed like rotten ice on an old pond, and I went numb. I've spent several decades trying to crawl out of a romantic drainpipe. I felt I'd lost everything—a marriage, a home, a wife, and, in the separation, an infant whose birth redefined my life.

I dreamed of strange people in those days. Ghostly women coming to my windows. Friends turning away. Relatives seeming not to know me. Undercurrents heaved beneath the surface of things, little understood, menacing. Then one late evening I woke to a dream of clasping my wife's hand. She had a nervous way of picking her cuticles, and holding her hand always made me feel tense. There we were, reaching across space, and she began to rise above me. There was nothing around us but dull grey mist. Beneath her, I felt my weight dragging on her arm, and then realized, to my horror, that our daughter, Rachel, hung between us, crying. She was being pulled apart. I let go. And woke in a cold sweat.

Four months into our separation, Ann told me to go to her mother's house in Berkeley and get my daughter. So turning thirty in Los

Angeles, I found myself the single parent of a child in diapers, still drinking from a bottle.

"Daddy," my three-year-old asked, "why don't we live with Mommy now?"

How does a man explain *irreconcilable differences* to a toddler? "We'll . . . we'll all be happier living this way, pumpkin," I stumbled through an answer. "Mommy needs her own place for now. We love you. You'll be with both of us now, one at a time." But eventually her mother decided to break off all contact, with no explanations.

I wasn't taught mothering as a postwar redneck; learning to bend didn't come easily. It opened me up to remake myself with this child—pondering a woman's humbling by the home fire, a man's numbing at the office. And I began questioning our choices, our patterns, our genders. Errant Adam and Eve, westering child, loss and regain, revisions.

What was this male stuff all about? Freezing your ass off in the river cold, killing small animals, busting your balls in the dirt, going nuts with cheap beer, rutting sex with no heart in it—just because the other guys did. Failed marriages and directionless children as the norm? Ninety-two percent of single parents then were women. I didn't get it, questioned my role, thought twice about American men and women—then began a long course in male reeducation.

At thirty, I turned to my own life with a baby daughter and asked some hard questions. The heaviness a man drags to the office and home at night had to be lifted. That fear of intimacy in my gut needed to be softened. Ours was a lesson in starting over—grounding myself in a child's vulnerability, getting to know my own adult losses and going on, listening to her needs and staying clear. Where was I headed? Nowhere, mister, without your daughter. I was going to learn to grow from loss.

Divorce before thirty tapped a gut-wrenching failure, my first acute sense of defeat. I felt clubbed, rejected, and betrayed—partly by my own masculinity. Marriages were supposed to last a lifetime where I grew up. Even though my parents were ill-matched, deeply unhappy with each other, they stayed together half a century; both their parents married for life. Small towns do that to couples. But here I was with a baby, alone and adrift in Los Angeles.

So, again, what shaped my American manhood? I puzzle, looking back. What built and betrayed my male identity, then needed redesigning? We need better myths than toughing it out on the frontier. Making a home and raising a child was a start for me.

In due time, masculinity was lightened by what parents find outside themselves—a release into the daily lives of others, gossiping, cleaning, caretaking, cooking, driving, waiting, playing, dreaming. Rachel was strong-willed. I learned not to force her cooperation but to coax her desire. Circumstances improvised a grandmotherly axiom, strangely enough, that my wife had cherished: *you can't squeeze blood from a stone.* I learned a thing or two from asking, not demanding: men can be tender. Men can give in without giving up, bend without having to bend others to their will. Men can lose gracefully, without failing.

To be a man is not conquest, mothering taught me. Maybe it's more consent. *I Olwis Wot to Be Wtith You I Love You and I allwos Will + Love Rae.* My daughter's valentine on a pink, rough-cut heart triggered something deep in me. Being strong is not always gain, but steady giving. However I look at it, this ideal has given me back my life with grace, in humility and no small amount of humor.

My life is yet a *find-out*, as an elder medicine man put it, still brokering the frontier, translating cultures, cowboys to Indians, academia to the people—a teacher for some thirty years. And it still troubles me, this western macho stuff. It wakes me up late at night, thinking about war, and drunk fathers, and sad mothers, and mute children, and blood on my hands—and women distant in fear, unloved, locked up in Nevada ranches for passing men. We need alternatives, new men. . . .

South of the tracks where I was raised lived Sioux families, poor as dirt, dispossessed of the earth that was once their homeland. The good ol' frontier boys saw them as "blanket-ass Injuns, nary a pot to piss in." They were the poorest of the poor, living off-reservation in canvas war tents, jobless, undereducated, malnourished, rotgut-addicted, embittered against whites. Yet these *native* Americans, or Lakota *allies*, gave me a sense of belonging that seemed rare among blue-eyed boys. All they had was themselves, and they cared for their own, for better or worse. When I crossed the tracks, and stayed on to listen, work, and learn, they cared for me.

"Uncle Ken's here," the kids sing out when I come to the back screen door of the Indian Center. In Alliance there still lives a Lakota man in his early sixties, who runs the American Indian Center. He has a contagious smile, dark skin and hair, and a spark in his brown eyes. He is my adopted brother Mark.

Non-Indians don't really understand the significance of a *hunka*, or brother ceremony, for the Sioux. It means you are family for life, an adoption as literal as state legalization, though more binding since it is a spiritual tie. The bond is unquestioned and unqualified, as with my blooded brothers. It involves extended kinship into the Sioux community and culture. This means that we would place our lives on the line for the other—and all our resources as well. For thirty years Mark and I have spoken of each other as brothers, and we mean it.

Mark is my *other* brother, that is, shadowed. The rednecks in my hometown never got it, never quite understood why I went south of the tracks to hang out with Indians. My father resented it to his death. To my thinking, Mark represented a dark man who came back from the dead, a warrior who fought, bled, and stumbled as an addict, then pulled himself out of the sewer. My father was buffered in whitebread America. He could drink himself stupid in the sumpholes of weekend WASP warriors—the VFW, the American Legion, the Elks Club, the Eagles Club, the Country Club. Mark couldn't even buy a drink in King's Korner Bar until 1964, let alone join a private men's club to closet his alcoholism. He was lethally drunk in the alleys of my hometown. At the bottom, he came to see the devastation to his own Indian people, then he stopped. Others in Alliance didn't, whether Indian or white.

My other brother was an alternative model for my father—a decade younger than my dad, thirteen years older than me. He had worked with "Link" at the bean elevator, and there was measurable distance between them. The Buckskin Curtain threw up a solid wall, as far as Dad was concerned. Indians fell one step lower than his own self-esteem, giving him abject measure of white superiority.

Mark saw my interest in the Indian world as a chance to educate White America. We talked for years on end about the cultural differences, visited many other Sioux in south Alliance and the Dakotas to hear their stories, and traveled from Pine Ridge, to Wounded Knee, to Rosebud, and across the state. The Nebraska Humanities Commission sponsored our travel and dialogue one spring—an example of Indian-White collaboration. In a declared year of ethnic "reconciliation," we seemed to be an alternative to fraternal wars across the west over a century. It was one step in a long trek home, for both pioneers and Native Americans.

"Damn, Ken! Things have sure changed around here," Mark often says.

The surest sign of Mark's brotherhood rests in his voice. When we trade stories, tell tales, open up, and laugh hard—every time I go back—his voice speaks clearly as summer wind in shortgrass. He likes to talk, likes people. And our conversations convince us that a brother is listening, that a man cares with a man's strength, reacting to what he hears.

"Remember, Ken, this here is your *tióte*, your home roots," my brother Mark says when I return to Alliance. "You have a big brother here, a home-place and family."

The Lakota traditionally speak of "sending a voice," singing and praying and confiding in the spirit world—for strength of heart, clarity of sight, depth of understanding, honesty of feeling. Mark sends me that voice, hears me out as a brother, and counts as family, no less than my other brothers. A bear's guardian spirit connects us.

An Indian Candidate for Public Office

MARK MONROE

When I returned to Alliance in November 1968 after
being in Hot Springs, I was sober, and things seemed
so different to me. It was the first time I'd been sober
with my family for a long, long time. Getting adjusted
to being back home was hard at first, but I was so happy
and so proud of myself and my family that it seems as
though I wanted to begin my life all over again. After
thinking about what I'd gone through and how I'd re-
covered, it gave me kind of a momentum, you might
say, to really do something.

Emma told me that during the spring or summer
of 1968, they put her on welfare because I was drawing
very little in compensation pay for my Army disabili-
ty. My wife was a very proud person, and she did not
want to become a welfare recipient; I think it kind of
took some of her pride away, and mine, too. But I was
so happy to be sober again that I just accepted it, and
we continued to stay on welfare as long as I still was not
in good enough physical shape to get a job. Deep inside
me I was really wishing that they would cut the checks
off. I don't think it amounted to much money, but it
was just the idea of it.

At that time Community Action was a very important part of Alliance. It was the federal program that worked with low-income people. One day I noticed an advertisement in the paper saying that the Community Action program needed a center director, so I went uptown and applied for the job. This must have been in December, maybe a week and a half or two weeks after I got home. Before this I had looked around to see if I could find some type of job that was suitable for me. I couldn't do too much work because I wasn't quite strong enough yet. They told me at the center that they would be interviewing people who applied sometime in January. So I signed up.

In the meantime, whenever I'd go to town, I felt so ashamed that I'd done something really terrible in my life by becoming an alcoholic and this gutter-type person. A lot of my true friends, both white and Indian people included, were very happy to see me and see that I was sober. However, there were many Indian people who wouldn't even talk to me. The Indian people saw me sober, and they would immediately tell me some of the things I had done when I was drunk. They were just mad that I was sobered up and would not accept me back as a friend. So it was hard for me to go around town and hard for me to talk to them, as ashamed as I was of what I had done. But I was so proud of my sobriety that I just said to myself, I'm not going to drink any more, and I don't care what happens to me. I'm going to stay sober, stable, and maintain my family life.

One day, as I was walking back from the Community Action Center, which was probably a mile or mile and a half away from where we lived, I saw this poster stating there was going to be a city election for police magistrate. I knew the present one. Her name was Mrs. Nell Johnstone, and she had been in office for twenty-five years. She was a college graduate and a very important person in Alliance. Her father was one of the old founders of Alliance, and Mrs. Johnstone had the reputation of being a fair judge. I had gone before her at least three or four times during my drinking days. She always asked me if I was guilty or not guilty, and I'd plead guilty, so she'd give me a fifteen-dollar fine. I knew that she was fair, but she did not want to do anything for alcoholic people.

I remember back one morning when I woke up in the city jail on a Sunday and there were twenty-seven people in jail in a very small twenty-by-twenty foot room. They were all Indian people. The city of Alliance had a trash system where the truck with three to four Indian prisoners behind it would pick up the garbage barrels and throw them into the trash truck, and two more guys would throw them back out to be refilled. Even though Mrs. Johnstone knew these things and that she had a large number of Indian alcoholics in jail, she never made any attempt to try to rehabilitate them. It was just a day-to-day job she had of fining Indian people, giving them a place to work, and getting the city of Alliance labor free of charge. When I saw this election poster, right away, I felt that maybe if I were to be elected, I would be in a better position to help a lot of alcoholics, Indian and white alike. All of them needed some type of recovery program built for them.

I really was thinking seriously about this, so I went home that afternoon and thought about it that night and finally decided to run for the office of police magistrate. However, I was kind of scared, too, because this would be the first time in northwest Nebraska, and probably the entire state, that an Indian had run for an elected office. I knew also that it would be very hard to be accepted in Alliance as a political candidate. But I talked it over with Emma that night and told her that the next day I would go to the city hall and file a petition for the office of police magistrate. Emma looked at me as though she thought I was crazy. It was kind of an unheard-of thing to do, and the more I thought about it, the more I thought it was crazy, too. We discussed it further, and she told me to go ahead and continue to apply for jobs and to file for office, too. So, with her support, I knew I wanted to try.

I didn't go into politics just for personal reasons or personal gain. I really wanted to become the police magistrate so that I could work for the recovery of alcoholics. I knew how hard it was going to be in Alliance. I went to the city clerk's office and told the city clerk I wanted to file as a candidate for police magistrate. The lady said that to qualify to be on the ballot I had to be a registered voter and a resident of the city for six months. So that day I registered to vote. Emma also registered. After I registered I went back to the city clerk's office and filed as a candidate for police magistrate. The clerk gave me a petition and told me that I had to have 300 registered voters sign this petition and to bring the petition back to her. She would check and see if the people were valid voters. If they were, she would notarize the petition, and my name would be placed on the ballot. I knew some people in Alliance, but I didn't think I knew 300 registered voters. That night the *Alliance Times-Herald* reported that Mark Monroe had filed for the office of police magistrate, and this news certainly upset our Alliance citizens. The editor or publisher of our paper made a big story of it, and it sounded like a "Ripley's Believe It or Not" type of thing. In the long run, it may have helped me. The same day that I got the petition, I called a few of my friends and asked them if they'd sign it. They did, and I began to get signatures by going from house to house. These were all white people, and 150 of them signed.

Every Indian I asked couldn't sign, however, because he wasn't registered to vote. So I went to my mother-in-law's place and to all of my Indian friends' homes and asked them, "Aren't you guys registered to vote?" I talked to all the people and told them I had gone down and registered to vote. "I'm running for police magistrate," I said, "and I want you guys to vote for me and get me elected." So all my Indian friends started questioning me, and I think some were kind of scared to go to the county clerk's office to get registered. My mother-in-law and father-in-law and my mother and father went there with them. In about four or five days after all this work, I must have gotten at least ninety people registered to vote for the first time in their lives.

About two or three days before the time limit was on my petition, I still needed forty-five or fifty more signatures. The media got hold of the story, and they followed up on what I was doing. This helped me. It gave me a lot of leeway, such as going into the police station.

I knew that the city jail always had ten of our local winos in there and that none of them were registered to vote, either. That morning there were twelve guys in jail, so I asked the chief of police if I could go talk to them, and he said to go ahead. I went in, talked, and asked them if they were registered to vote. They said, "What's that? What do we do?" I told them I was going to run for the lady's job of police magistrate who had put them in there. "I'm running against her," I said, "and I need registered voters. If I can get you up to the county clerk's office and have you registered, would you do it?" They all said, yes, they would register and vote for me.

The next morning I took five guys up to the county clerk's office from the city jail with the chief of police's permission. He kind of supported me and liked the fact that an Indian was finally doing something. When I think back to that morning, I always remember Stanley Standing Soldier, who was a very good friend of mine and one of my former drinking partners, a gutter-type wino. Stanley was in the Navy, and he was a very intelligent person, but he was hooked on wine. Stanley never became physically violent or mentally ill. He was one of the winos who is still drinking today. He was a very comical type of guy, always joking and raising heck with somebody.

When I took the five guys up to the county clerk's office, Stanley was the first in line. He signed his name and put down everything but an address. The county clerk looked at it, and she said, "Mr. Standing Soldier, what is your address because I've got to go by the address to decide what ward you should vote in?" He looked at her and said, "My address is the Alliance City Jail." The county clerk said, "No, you've got to have an address." Stanley looked at me. He was the type of guy who lived in a park or in abandoned cars, anywhere he could find a place to drink. So he didn't have an address. Stanley said he had been in jail twenty times a year and spent all his time in there. The jail was some place to eat and some place to sleep. The police needed someone to work free of charge on the garbage truck.

The county clerk looked at me and said, "Mark, is this guy for real?" I said, "You bet." Stanley had lived in Alliance ever since I could remember. He came here in 1941, the same time my mother and dad did, but he didn't have an address. However, he was and is a resident of Alliance. The county clerk couldn't believe it. She said, "I didn't know people like Stanley existed here. I thought everybody had an address." Very hesitantly, she took down Stanley Standing Soldier's address as the Alliance City Jail.

I think what was happening now was that the city of Alliance and its problem with Indian alcoholism was finally coming into focus. Some of the people in Alliance didn't even know we had that many alcoholics who didn't have a residence and couldn't give a street number address and who didn't have any place to live. I'm glad this happened because I found out later on that members of the news media were following me around town to find out whether I was putting out enough effort and initiative to get on the ballot. A lot of people were watching me closely.

I worked all day and clear into the night sometimes, trying to get the still-needed names on this petition of mine. I was still short and had only a couple of days left to get it in. One night, I attended a couple of AA meetings in Alliance, and I took my petition along with me. The AA meeting was full of rich white people who didn't want anything to do with an Indian. So when I went in and asked some of the members to sign the petition, they absolutely wouldn't do it.

I still needed some signatures on my petition, and I thought at this time maybe I'd exhausted all my supply of names and people that I knew. What I did next was to go into a bar. I knew all these guys were drinking, and I knew the bartender. The people who were there all seemed to like me. I asked the bartender or the owner if I could give a little speech. He quieted everybody down, and then I told them, "My name is Mark Monroe, and I filed for police magistrate. I want to get on the ballot, and I need your signature on my petition if you are registered." So, in King's Corner Bar, people just came up to me saying, "Mark, you really want to get that old lady out of there?" They were really talking bad about Mrs. Johnstone. I told them I did, and a lot of them signed.

So I went from bar to bar in Alliance until I had my petition filled with 375 signatures. I wanted to get on that ballot so badly that sometimes I worked clear up until the bars closed. I wanted to get more than 300 signatures, at least 400 if possible, in case some of the names were rejected. In this two-week period I worked so hard and I knew I was still weak, but just the fact that I had a chance and had the support of these people who signed their names and were registered made me very happy. I was very proud of my mother and father, my mother-in-law and father-in-law, who finally were going to vote, and all these guys from the city jail.

A lot of people made fun of me, and a lot of them supported me, and a lot ran me into the ground thinking Indians shouldn't do this kind of thing. "It's unheard of—What are you going to do when you get in there? You don't have enough education, and you aren't qualified for this job." These were the comments I heard. But I did get ninety or more Indian people registered to vote. I'm pretty proud of that fact. This was the first time the city of Alliance had Indian people come to the county clerk's office to register to vote. Our *Alliance Times-Herald* and our radio in Alliance (we didn't have a TV station at that time), these two news media covered all I had done. They even mentioned my taking American Indians from the jail and registering them with city jail as their address. Everybody was waiting to see if I could get three hundred registered voters' names and be on the ballot.

In the end, I got nearly four hundred signatures, and a lot of Indian people registered for the first time. People were voicing their concerns in the *Alliance Times-Herald*'s "Rumblings" column. They would say that an Indian is running for public office—congratulate him and support him. In a two-week period I made a big step forward for our Indian people, and I didn't know that this kind of support existed. I could look in Emma's eyes and know she was very proud that I even tried. My children were elated. There were so many positive things coming out of this experience, and it was something that I should have done years ago. That's the way I was feeling at that time.

It was on Friday evening. My petition was due at five o'clock when the city clerk's office closed. I walked up there with this petition, and when I went into her office, reporters from our radio station and the *Alliance Times-Herald* were there, standing around waiting for me to make this deadline. At this point in my life, I was beginning to understand politics and how to fight back against the opposition. Even though I had my petition ready that morning, I didn't want to go down there and just give it to them. Instead, I knew the longer I waited, the more newsworthy it would be. This was what I wanted, to be on the news. I was getting smart. So I waited.

I think I waited until about a quarter to five. It was very shortly before the office closed. I went up to the city clerk and said, "Here's my petition; will you accept it?" And she had to get a notary public and sign in exactly the time I entered my petition. When I did this, the news reporter started asking me questions right away. I told him right then and there that I was running for the office of police magistrate for these reasons, and when I had told the public, they were happy to sign my petition. The night I filed my petition, I got the news coverage that really helped me later in my campaign for the police magistrate's office. The city clerk told me that Monday morning they would have to go through all the names and verify that they were all registered voters. She told me that by Monday or Tuesday I would be notified whether I would be on the ballot for election or not.

That weekend, I think, was one of the busiest weekends I ever had. A lot of people who didn't believe that an Indian person could ever do this—because nothing like this ever happened before—called and told us how happy they were. A lot of my Indian friends came over to our house to congratulate me and my family, because everybody knew what Emma had gone through during this drinking period of mine, and I think they were very happy and proud of my family and me.

Someone knocked at the door, and there was old John Anderson standing there, one of the most respected members in our community. I was very surprised. As the county attorney he had helped put me into Fort Meade many years ago, and he had now gone into private practice. He had always been a pretty good buddy of mine. John asked me how I was and how I was doing, and he seemed very happy that I was sober. It had been a long time since John had seen me that way. Evidently, he had been reading the paper and following what I had been trying to do. We sat there drinking a cup of coffee, and he asked me if I knew what to do as a police magistrate, if I knew what the job involves and some of the court procedure and the laws that you follow. I told him, "Hell, no, I don't know nothing about it, but I want to learn."

He said there was a lot involved. Every afternoon from now on, he said, at three o'clock I should come to his home, and he would teach me some of the things that a police magistrate would have to do according to law. He said the way he saw things, I stood a pretty good chance of getting elected, and he wanted me to go into that office knowing the job. This really surprised me. I didn't think that my filing for public office would ever create this kind of awareness or attention from people like John Anderson. I told John I wanted to run and to tell me where he lived, and I'd be over there at three o'clock. After that, I always made my time clear at three o'clock so I'd go to John's home from three to five-thirty or six every evening for the rest of the time until the election.

John started teaching me the things that a judge had to know and some of the things that a judge had to do. One of the things that I did not know was that Mrs. Johnstone was a police magistrate and also the county judge, too. She held both of her courts in the same building. John told me, "Mark, if you win the police magistrate job, you'll have to tell Mrs. Johnstone to move her county job into the county building. This is perfectly right; if you win the judgeship, you have the right to do this." Without John Anderson's help, if I'd won the election, I would have been very afraid and maybe even run out of office. But John did this for me, and I've always been grateful for that man, because he did help me, and I did learn a lot about city and county laws.

Newspapers across the whole state took our *Times-Herald* stories and printed them, so my campaign became statewide news. I didn't ever think that my being on the ballot would create the type of concern and awareness that it did or the quarrels it caused among the white people. Some of them were supporting me, and others weren't. It was just a really controversial thing here in Alliance.

Monday evening the city clerk called me to her office. I went down there, and they verified pretty near every one of the signatures I had on my petition. The media was there again and told the story. The newspaper printed, "Monroe will appear on the ballot as a candidate for police magistrate." It went on to tell some of my life history as an American Indian and that I was the first American Indian ever to file for public office. It created so much news here in Alliance that at times I was kind of afraid to go around. Sometimes during the night, we'd get crank phone calls from people who'd call us all kinds of names. For a while it became very dangerous for my children. Terry, Daryl, and Connie were going to school at that time, and some white parents didn't like the idea that I was running. It caused a lot of fights between the children. Practically every morning after I found out I was going to be on the ballot, our sidewalk would be covered with eggs, and on the front of our house they'd hang dirty signs on the walls and scrawl more stuff over our front steps. I saw things like this happen on TV and thought it was a hardship for my family, but it was something we had to go through.

One day Mrs. Lewis, a very close friend living across the street from us, called me up and asked if she could send a very good friend of hers over to meet me, and I told her I would talk to him. This was probably in February or March of 1969. Kenneth Lincoln came to our door and introduced himself to me. He had lived here in Alliance most of his life, and I had read about Ken in the paper quite often. He was a good athlete and a good golfer. Ken was really a nice appearing man, very well educated, and very interested in my running for police magistrate. After we talked for quite some time, I was really surprised that someone like Ken was so interested in my electioneering, you might say. But Ken started writing articles in the paper for me, and my election really seemed to be going well. He helped me all the way through the campaign, and I think he was kind of surprised that I didn't win because everything seemed to be going good for us.

The primary election was held in early May, and I did lose, but some of the things that happened to me in that interim period were really comical. Ken did a lot of writing about how it was the first time that an Indian ever ran for public office. He said people should support the fact that a Native American was running for police magistrate.

Ken wrote a letter to the editor of the *Alliance Times-Herald* that was published a few days before the election. He said he thought there were some important steps for Alliance to take if it wanted to help its Indian population, starting with electing me as a police magistrate. There should be a ward for Indian patients at St. Joseph's Hospital, and Indians should be allowed to serve on our local police force. The high school had to graduate Indian students, which it had never done before, and there needed to be an Indian counselor appointed to the school board. He wanted to show that it was possible for people of different races to get along in Alliance. The community would be strengthened by this kind of effort.

When I first filed for public office, there were two other people running for the police magistrate job: Mrs. Johnstone and a man who used to work at the meat market where we shopped. But during the time that Ken was doing all the writing and I was getting very popular in Alliance, this man suddenly disappeared, and I started to ask around town what happened to him. Someone told me he became so frustrated over running for police magistrate, since I had also entered the picture as a candidate, that it must have gotten to him. I was told he was sent to a mental institution. With Ken's help, with the attorney's help, and with a lot of friends in town backing me, we were getting a lot of good publicity. I never spent a dime for promotion, but I had more publicity than the other candidates.

During this time I was also invited to the Elks Club to speak at a symposium that was held for the candidates. When I was told about being invited to go there to give my views about the job and about the police magistrate's office, I was very surprised because at that time Indian people weren't even allowed in the Elks Club. It's still that way today. When the man approached me about speaking there, I told him right away that I could not go into the Elks Club because I'm an Indian, and the Elks charter says that it's for Caucasian people only. He didn't know that the Elks didn't allow Indian people into their club, but he said he'd make arrangements to have me allowed in. But I didn't feel comfortable in that situation and didn't want to go into that racist club. I also thought it could be dangerous. When Ken found out about this, he supported me, but he said I'd better go and present my views. Finally, I made up my mind that I would go. I think the only reason they had that symposium was to picture me in a negative light.

Everybody had to wear ties and suits to make a good appearance. But I didn't have any suitable clothes. On the day of the symposium I met a friend of mine uptown. His name was Larry Lassick, and he was a social welfare director at that time. He asked me how I was going to dress. I told him, "I'll just have to go in my shirt and the way I dress normally because I don't have anything better to wear." Well, he wanted me to have a tie and look good. That afternoon he took me and bought me a shirt, tie, sweater, and new pants. A lot of people went out of their way and did a lot for me during this time, because probably they wanted to see an Indian win and, if he was elected, just what he would do when he got into office.

That night I did go to the Elks Club, was admitted, and was treated very nicely. Everybody there seemed to be pretty decent. I knew if I didn't appear, this would go against me in the election. I'm glad I did because after what happened at the Elks Club, I drew a lot of votes. I changed a lot of peoples' minds, particularly the ones who were rich and who were the establishment in Alliance. We had three men who were moderators for the program. I was told I would speak with Mrs. Johnstone. Then they would ask questions first of Mrs. Johnstone, then of me.

She answered a lot of questions. Some asked how much her salary was, but Mrs. Johnstone didn't want to tell anybody that, so she said, "Well, I make less than the dogcatcher here in Alliance." Unfortunately for her, the dogcatcher or animal control officer was sitting right in the front row, and he stood right up and cussed her out. He said, "Don't you ever compare your job to mine. I work hard." He told her off, and it really made her look bad. Mrs. Johnstone had been in office for twenty-five years, but she sure didn't present herself well that night. She wouldn't answer very many of the questions that were given to her from the audience either. She was very prim and proper, and with her college education, she knew that I didn't stand much of a chance against her, so she didn't put up too much of a fight.

When it came my time for questions, I was really nervous. I knew that a lot of people in the crowd of maybe 100 or 150 people were all white, rich, establishment people, and I thought they were going to really rake me over the coals. When I got up, I introduced myself. "My name is Mark Monroe. I have lived in Alliance since 1941. I am an alcoholic, but I haven't had a drink for six months." This is what the attorney told me to say about my being an alcoholic. I think the reason for that was, he told me, "Well, how many people in the audience can say they haven't had a drink for six months?" He said probably none of them could answer that, but my saying so would get over the fact that I was an alcoholic who just got out of the treatment center. It would stop a lot of people from asking more questions about it. Well, it did. Some people clapped for me who were probably alcoholics or had drinking problems. It made me feel good.

One of the questions was about my education. I told them that

I had nine years of formal education and that what else I know I learned through experience in life. Another guy asked about my qualifications for running for public office, for the police magistrate's job. I told him my qualifications were that I had been in front of Mrs. Johnstone as prisoner and the only thing she ever said was, "Are you guilty, or not guilty?" Usually I was guilty, so I'd plead guilty, and the only thing she ever did was to fine me fifteen dollars, and, I said, *I can do that.* I told the man I thought my qualification was that I could do the job. I don't know whether this made a lot of people mad or not because nobody said a word for a long, long time. Finally, one man got up and started clapping for me. In comparison with Mrs. Johnstone, I was speaking the truth and telling people what I wanted to do and that I would do something about it. This really fouled up Mrs. Johnstone's image right then and there.

I told them also, being an Indian alcoholic, I would work with Indian alcoholics and try to promote programs to help sober them up. I said this had never been done before. In the twenty-five years that Mrs. Johnstone had been magistrate, no attempt had ever been made to work with Indian or non-Indian alcoholics. It was just the swinging-door type of thing where you go in, get fined, and if you can't pay your fine, you go to work with the city trash truck. No attempt was ever made to help these people. We, at that time, had the highest arrest record for intoxication anywhere in the state of Nebraska. I told them that after I fined a man and sentenced him, I would try to do something for him. This seemed to please the crowd very much. Some of the people who I was very afraid might do me a lot of harm stood up and started clapping. Because I was speaking the honest truth, it probably brought me a lot of votes.

At that time, I was getting statistics on how many Indian alcoholics went through city jail. At one time, there were 150 different men who had gone before Mrs. Johnstone, and practically every one of them was an Indian. Stanley Standing Soldier had been in jail twenty times in one year. I got these statistics from the county clerk's office. I also told the crowd at the Elks about Stanley. I said, "Now, here is a man who has been in jail twenty times, and he's never been offered any type of recovery program. It has been just an ongoing type of swinging-door thing for him, and he's the kind of man I want to do something for. After I fined him, sentenced him, I would try to rehabilitate him because right now all we're doing is just playing games with this guy."

Everything seemed to be going real well. After the crowd in the Elks Club started supporting me, I found out I could talk a lot better than I thought and could get my viewpoints across. I think that after what Mrs. Johnstone tried to do and what she said, the crowd became very negative toward her. They didn't want to ask her any more questions. She represented the institution type of people we had here in town, and she didn't want to change. She didn't want to do anything progressive. After the symposium was over, I answered every question that was given to me the best I could and honestly. I think I made a lot of friends in the Elks Club that night. I was asked by some of the people to become a member of the club. But with my own feelings so strong, I politely turned them down. I simply said, "No, I don't want to be a member of the Elks Club, but I thank you very much for letting me speak at your symposium." And that was it. I came out of there feeling happy just over the fact that I had gone and spoken to them.

The next day Mr. Kemper, the editor or publisher of our local paper, wrote a big story about the event, but he didn't report that the crowd accepted me well and cheered me on. He has died since then, but his son runs the *Alliance Times-Herald* now, and we still have the very same thing. He is an establishment person, and whatever he doesn't like, he won't print in the paper. Of course, a lot of people listen to him. Even though I got my points across positively and truthfully, it still didn't sound right when it came out in the paper. This made Ken mad because he was at that symposium, too, and heard everything that was said. He knew about the people supporting me. So Ken started writing editorials in the paper again, and some of the editorials that he wrote kind of made Mr. Kemper look bad. Anyway, as far as I was concerned, I was feeling good about the election.

At this time Emma was working for Dr. Goding, a dentist here in town. She worked for his wife as a housekeeper, and Mrs. Goding really liked Emma. Fact is, they were very close friends. I was told that two or three days after Ken started writing, Dr. and Mrs. Goding were having supper at one of our local restaurants. Mr. Kemper was also there and started making remarks about me and my candidacy in a very loud, coarse voice. So Dr. Goding got up from his table and went to Mr. Kemper's and told him to keep his mouth shut. He said that I had done a lot of things that need praise instead of running me down. I guess Mr. Kemper was a fighter, too, and they had an argument in the restaurant over my running for public office.

I was told later on that this was happening in the Elks Club, in the American Legion, all the veterans' clubs—that people were taking up sides for me, and there were rumors of other fistfights. I really didn't know what to think at this point. I seemed to be causing a lot of good and bad publicity. The only good thing that came out of it was that people were taking an interest. They were seeing the point of view of a Native American.

Sometimes I felt sorry I had decided to run for office, but with a lot of encouragement from Ken and from Mr. Anderson, the attorney, and the welfare officer, Larry Lassick, I just kept going. I thought I was creating a lot of hatred and division in Alliance, and it kind of made me feel bad. However, I continued going from bar to bar, where I'd talk to people and tell them what I was going to do. I was invited to several ladies' clubs to talk to them, too. I think my appearance at a lot of these places just changed a lot of peoples' minds. For many of them, their image of an American Indian in Alliance was the "dirty, lazy, drunk" stereotype. A lot of these people were really surprised when I'd show up in good clothes, sober, and they gave me a lot of moral support so I was able to get my views across to them.

As I mentioned, I had also applied for the job as director of our Community Action Center. I knew I could do it because even though I'd had only nine years of formal education, I was good at bookkeeping. Sometimes in February or March, they interviewed me for the job. There was one other Indian who applied, Carl Janis, who had come from South Dakota. He was a college graduate and had had a lot of experience in directing on the reservation. I thought that Carl would probably get the job because he had more experience than I did.

When I went for the interview, I told them about my being an alcoholic, of course, but I didn't have to tell them about running for city election because it was something everyone knew and was talking about in Alliance. The man who was doing the hiring called me up one afternoon and said that I did not get the job, but the only reason I was turned down was because Mr. Janis had more education. He was very nice about it, so I accepted it.

About the same time, I was contacted by Mark Goldfuss, a VISTA worker. He called me about a job opening with the Panhandle Mental Health Center in Scottsbluff. He wanted me to apply for it because the job was working with Indian alcoholics and Indian mental patients. So I did, and I talked to the mental health representative who seemed to be very interested in me. I was on my way again.

After Mr. Carl Janis got the job at the Community Action Center, I used to go there quite often at night. I knew Community Action was good for the city of Alliance because it represented the low-income and minority people. Almost all of them were Indian. I knew after staying around the center that we needed more than just giving people food and clothing. It was the center that hired people for mainstream programs now that it was part of the Comprehensive Employment and Training Act (CETA). But I knew something else had to be added. I talked with Mr. Janis one time and said, "Let's start an Indian committee and try and get some of our rights, some of our views across to the white population here in Alliance. We need to find out why they are sending us to jail, why they are not trying to help us recover, and why there is so much racism here." He agreed and promised to support me in any way he could.

That evening I went home and wrote some kind of speech to present to people. What we were going to do was call upon the mayor, the city councilmen, the judges, the chief of police, the social services office director, and anybody who was in some kind of position in Alliance to help the American Indian. What I wrote down was an American Indian Committee philosophy. We would read this to people we invited to our meetings and question them as to why American Indians weren't receiving the recognition and the care that they deserved. I wrote that night, "We have organized an American Indian Committee. A committee of non-violence. We have no wish to violate the laws of city or state. We have no ideas of revenge. We simply want to know our rights and what could be done when these rights are violated. We feel that many of them have been violated and would like very much to have an explanation. We think that working as a group will be more effective in solving our problems."

I took my statement to Mr. Janis, and he was really happy about it. At the first meeting that we had, I was in complete control because nobody but Indian people were allowed to attend. We probably drew 125 of them. Everyone who came told me that I should have been the director of the Community Action program. I didn't like that because I didn't want to create a division between Mr. Janis and myself; I thought he was well qualified for the job and that was the way we should keep it.

During this meeting of the Indian people, I was elected chairman of the American Indian Committee. We also elected a vice-chairman and secretary. I conducted all the meetings and was the person who went out to make the invitations for public servants to attend. The first man I contacted was Glenn Fiebig, a former FBI man. He had retired in Alliance and was hired by the county as the county attorney. The county attorney was the person who would always do his best to get an Indian convicted no matter what the charge was.

He was anti-Indian, you might say. However, he was the first person on the list to attend our American Indian Committee meeting. Soon as Mr. Fiebig came into our group session with about a hundred Indian people there, we questioned him to see if we could do something about his convicting so many of our people.

Well, when Mr. Fiebig came into our room, it must have looked kind of dangerous to him. The first remark he made was, "I'm not afraid of Indian people." Everybody in the room started laughing at him. He was so uneasy. I went up to the door and told him that he was welcome at the meeting and that it shouldn't last more than a couple of hours. I made him feel at ease. We sat him down, and a lot of people started asking him questions. Some of the people were mad at him, and this was the only chance they ever had in their lives to question somebody like Mr. Fiebig. I think a lot of the questions were completely out of line and were very derogatory toward him, but I kind of fielded the questions. Whenever someone would ask an embarrassing, derogatory one, I'd stop it, and we'd go on from there. Mr. Fiebig didn't give too many explanations because he was the law in the county, and I don't think we did anything to influence any decisions he was going to make. But it turned out to be a real good session.

I believe that forming the American Indian Committee in 1969 was very effective. As a committee of people representing the American Indian in Alliance, we got a lot of recognition, and a lot of people heard about our concerns. I think we gained a lot of respect in the community, too. In our philosophy, we were not militant or planning on any revenge. All we wanted to do was to be heard, and to be recognized. I think we accomplished that. We did call about every director of every organization in Alliance. We also worked and called many of the people from the school system, like the superintendent of schools, the principals of the local elementary schools, and the junior and senior high schools. At that time, American Indian children were having a lot of problems, but after we got some of these administrators to attend our meeting, things seemed to change a lot. I think what was happening in Alliance was that the American Indian was finally being recognized as a human being. Most people thought of us as second-class citizens. But when we, as parents, spoke up for our children, it seemed to draw a lot of attention, and things got done.

To give an example: One night during the same election that I was running for police magistrate, there were about four or five people running for the school board. At this meeting the five candidates were presented: Dr. Richard Jaggers, Mrs. Ray Fulton, Kenneth Dobby Lee, Jack Moldern, Terry Shannon. Most of them entered into the question-and-answer discussion that followed Mr. Johnson's report. Now, Mr. Johnson was working for the local school board. He had a master's degree in sociology from the University of Wyoming and had been working in the area since early on in the 1968–69 school year. Mr. Johnson warned that Alliance was a potential racial hot spot, that red (Indian) militants were coming in calling for Red Power. He declared that problems in schoolchildren should be identified in grade school, and that when they were identified at this early age, they could be corrected.

Mr. Johnson refused to attend our meetings, but he had the nerve to report to the school board about us. So the very same day that this story came out in the paper, we got together and gave a statement to a reporter from the *Times-Herald*.

What we said was, "The Alliance American Indian Committee has read the article in the Wednesday's *Times-Herald* concerning the report of an individual to the school board in regard to racial problems in Alliance. This person is totally misinformed as to the attitude of the American Indian citizens of Alliance. The statement that red militants are coming into town calling for Red Power is characteristic of his charges. We, as Indian people, know of no such red militancy. The individual in question is not considered a knowledgeable reference by Indian people. He has neither attended any meetings of the Alliance American Indian Committee, nor has he discussed its policies with its officers. In order to explain our organization to the public, we, hereby, publish our statement of philosophy concerning the formation of our organization." And we restated our philosophy and signed our names: "the American Indian Committee, Mark Monroe, Chairman, Members James Schmidt, Edward Flood, Carl Janis, and Carol Janis."

The day that our reply came out in the paper, Mr. Johnson was removed from his position, and I was told that he was fired because he had falsely called the American Indians "red militants." Mr. Johnson and the school board were very fearful that we, as a committee, would bring suit against them for making statements that were completely untrue. The part I really liked about it was that the county attorney, the chief of police, the welfare director, the sheriff, and everybody we had called to our meeting supported us. We commanded a lot of respect. I didn't like the idea of Mr. Johnson losing his job, but I think it was his fault.

With my running for public office and making speeches for a number of organizations who would call our committee and ask for me, a lot of good things began to happen. The rapport between whites and Indians improved and made Alliance so much more livable for us. Our Indian children began to attend school, and the arrest record for Indian people went down quite a bit during this period. During my campaign I told people that I would ask the city council not to use Indian people who were arrested for being drunk as workers on the trash trucks. The American Indian Committee also wanted this practice stopped. Alliance got thousands and thousands of dollars per year from drunk Indian people. Word got around to the police and Mrs. Johnstone that they better not arrest Indian people unless they had a valid reason to do so.

We were gaining respect, recognition. Because of the American Indian Committee, Indian people were working together. I felt very proud of the fact that I had organized this committee, and our members were very proud, too, because, for once, we were getting something done. The American Indian Committee was still operating out of the Community Action Center in the spring of 1969.

Everything was working real well, but of course, we still had a lot of flack coming from the community about why an Indian was running for public office.

During the campaign, we had a local Indian businessman by the name of Mr. Tyndall, who came to me and to the committee offering assistance. He runs Tyndall's Plumbing. Mr. Tyndall used to be a white man. Although he was Indian, he never did socialize with Indian people, and I think a lot of times he was probably ashamed that he was an Indian. But he put me on the air on radio and wrote up several articles about having an Indian candidate for police magistrate. I think my campaign really brought about a lot of Indian awareness in Alliance.

My campaign was still going well at this time. I continued to go to the attorney's home to learn the laws and how to be a police magistrate. I met a lot of important people in Alliance, and I learned a lot. Ken left Alliance sometime in March 1969 with his wife and his daughter, Rachel, who was probably about five or six months old. After Ken left, I kind of felt bad and got scared all over again. However, I continued with the election, which wouldn't be held until May fifth. Sometimes at night I would think to myself, what if I did win? Things like that sometimes scared me. I don't really know what I would have done if I had won the police magistrate's position then. I wonder if I would have been a good judge, and if I would have been able to handle it. A lot of times when I think back about that time and how I recuperated from alcoholism and the years at Fort Meade, I'm glad these things happened to me. They made me a better person and better able to work with people. I think what I did by filing for police magistrate and forming the American Indian Committee was helpful. It got Indian people recognized, and recognition was the most important thing we accomplished. To have white people think good of us instead of always stereotyping us was a big step forward.

Weighed Down by Buckskin

DELPHINE RED SHIRT

In August in Nebraska all the farmers and ranchers come into town for the county fair. There is a parade on Main Street and a rodeo and carnival at the county fairgrounds. The fairgrounds sit at the edge of town, at the eastern end next to the cornfields where the paved road ends and the gravel roads begin. The rodeo is the main event at the fair. A small carnival traveling through provides entertainment for everyone. The usual Ferris wheel, rides, and sideshows accompany the carnival. One year a carnival brought a hippopotamus in a trailer, and people paid a quarter to see it open its wide jaws. I remember my mother standing on the narrow step, peeking into the trailer and then falling back when the hippopotamus opened its mouth.

I also remember one August, during the month we call "Wasut'ų Wi," or "the moon the chokecherry ripens," the temperature was about ninety degrees. I stood behind the drugstore on Main Street. My mother left me there to wait while she checked on the progress of the parade. I was supposed to be in the parade as part of an Indian dance group, but we were late and the parade had already started. Mom-mah left me on the sidewalk, and I stood next to where she left my buckskin dress in a bag. My hair, neatly combed into two long braids, fell down my back. My braids were tied securely close to my ears with two beaded hair ties decorated with feathers. When I moved, the bright feathers fluttered lightly like cotton candy.

I wore a boy's white T-shirt, jeans, buckskin leggings, and a pair of beaded moccasins. My cheeks were brushed with rouge, and I wore a beaded headband across my small forehead. I felt hot and sweaty. I had seen my father select the bolt of buckskin at the arts and crafts store on the reservation. He had bought another outfit for me at the same time he bought the buckskin. In the old days he would have had to kill an elk to make a dress for me. They said it took one whole elk for a small girl's dress. He also bought two "fancy dance" boys' costumes for my older brother. The other outfit I owned was not buckskin but was made of dark blue, blanket-like material. It felt lighter and easier to wear. It had several bands of bright red-and-white ribbon sewn around the collar, hem, and cuffs. It was my favorite dress. It had small ivory-colored shells or simulated elk's teeth all up and down the front, about seven rows each of eight or nine teeth. It had matching leggings, and I wore the same moccasins I wore with my buckskin dress. I preferred the blue blanket dress to the buckskin one, especially in August when the high temperatures and dry weather meant that everything was covered by a light powder of fine, dry dust.

The day I stood on the sidewalk behind the drugstore, I held an ice cream cone in my right hand, a double scoop of chocolate chip that came from the counter at the soda fountain. In all the years we ordered ice cream from that drugstore, we never sat at the counter. We usually ordered and then took our purchases with us, out the door to our side of town. That day as I stood quietly licking my beloved treat, a little white girl, a "wašicu," looked at me standing in my boy's white T-shirt, jeans, and headband and said, "Look Mom, a little Indian boy." I continued to lick my cone that was melting in the heat and quietly watched her. I thought it preposterous that she would call me an "Indian boy," but I did not challenge her assertion. I just waited for her to go away so that I could eat my ice cream cone in peace.

In those days we did not converse with the wašicu. We were too self-conscious in our use of English, and they were too self-conscious to speak to a Lakota. The only people who spoke to us were the storekeepers, and they raised their voices an octave as if we were hard of hearing. "How are you doing?" they would yell, not waiting for a answer "Okay," my mother would yell back. "Tośke . . . ma nųḣ cą kecį se ce," she would add. "Does he think I am deaf?" Mom-mah loved to make side comments in Lakota when she spoke to the merchants on Main Street. "How much do you want for that?" she would ask, pointing to an object for sale. "Four dollars," the merchant would say, or "maza ską topa," meaning "four of the white metal," which signified money or dollars. Mom-mah would say under her breath, "Zigzica na śice eyaś," which meant, "It is flimsy and poorly made. Why ask that much for it?" My mother would then walk away, and the merchant might say, "I'll tell you what. I'll give it to you for two and a half bucks." "I'll take it," my mother would say, money in hand. I do not remember any real conversations between us and them, only an exchange of money and goods. The money was worth far more than the cheap goods we bought at premium prices. It was in this place that I learned to grow quiet and to watch the wašicu with distrustful eyes—the way the storekeeper watched me when I entered his store on Main Street.

When I put on my buckskin, my bright beads, and my moccasins, suddenly the wašicu shed his distrust and paid me quarters to pose with me for photographs. I know how Sitting Bull must have felt when they wanted to pose with him. I saw my pictures from those days, a somber-faced little girl in buckskin and feathers, my forehead wrinkled in a hot frown. I was not a smiler; smiles did not become me. I was a frowner from the beginning. I frowned in more pictures than I can remember so that by the age of thirty my forehead should have resembled a plowed field with neat, even-spaced rows of deep frowns acquired over a lifetime of practice.

I wore my buckskin dress at the age of seven, even when I did not want to wear it. When I put it on for the county fair in August, it felt hot and heavy. My whole outfit consisted of the buckskin dress, buckskin leggings, beaded moccasins, a beaded headband, beaded hair ties with bright-colored feathers, and a long bone necklace that covered my entire chest. The bone necklace I wore was actually simulated bone. It made a lot of noise when I moved, so I did not move much. It sounded like rocks rattling in a cardboard box, and when I felt hot and uncomfortable, the noise irritated me. I felt too weighed down when I was dressed in my full buckskin outfit—heavy and painfully self-conscious.

I danced the traditional women's dance, which required that I stand in one spot and move my knees up and down to the rhythm of the drum. I could dance in a circle in the spot I stood, but once I planted myself I did not move. If I did move, I walked in a direction opposite the men, tiptoeing and jerking my knees to the beat of the drum. We all danced in a circle—men, women, and children. The men and boys danced in one direction in a circle to the right, and the women and girls danced in the other direction in a circle to the left. Women danced on the outside, enclosing the men in the inner circle. The role of women was to be on the outside, as spectator, even while dancing. We watched our men who watched themselves dancing.

My brother's two outfits were different from the traditional outfits in that they were more feathery and showy. My older brother wore his outfit less self-consciously. He danced tall and proud, his light skin glistening in the heat. He looked slender and light in his outfit. He wore four sets of round feather bustles, one on his upper back, one on his lower back, and two smaller ones on his shoulders. He wore a headgear called a roach that was made out of porcupine hair. He also wore a beaded headband with three small mirrors fastened to it, one on the front and two small ones fastened to each side. These small mirrors caught the reflection of the bright sun and flashed back brilliant light when he moved his head.

He wore beaded cuffs and a beaded belt over a loincloth. He wore shaggy leg gear with bells tied at the ankles and beaded moccasins. He lifted his legs high, dancing lightly, and deliberately moving sometimes like a bird spreading its wings and twirling in time to the rhythm of the drum. When I see a hawk or eagle circling lazily in the sky, I remember my brother spreading his thin arms wide in a circle as he danced around and around. His only limitation was the drum. When it stopped, he too had to stop at the last beat or the other dancers would give a loud cry of dismay and the older men would say he missed it. "Naśna. Hą-ų . . . hą-ų," they would say, meaning, "He missed it. Too bad, too bad." My brother was easily embarrassed and wanted to please the adults around him. He tried never to miss a beat. He could keep perfect rhythm to the drum. Being six years older than I was, he seemed much more capable.

I felt no joy in my dancing. I did not look forward to the heat and dust at the county fair. I could not say, "Wawaci kte śni," which means "Dance-I-prefer-not-to." Even the songs sung for us to dance to were meaningless. For me, it all came down to spectator versus me. I did not want to perform, to dance in my heavy buckskin dress in the dusty heat, to dance to the small sound of the drum. The drum competed with the loud sounds of the livestock at the rodeo. When I look back on those days, I know what Mom-mah meant when she would say to us, "Wacį t'ąka ye," which literally meant, "Enlarge your thoughts" or "Be patient" or "Show endurance." As a child, I tried to be that way, to endure in a long-suffering way, as only a child knows how to do when asked to do something against her will.

I danced with other men and women. We were all given payment in the form of free beef. We had to appear at the appointed time and place in the center of the rodeo arena where I had seen the "Heyok'a," or rodeo "clown," run and hide in a wooden barrel. The clown ran and hid there to try to distract the massive bull that the riders rode in the rodeo. When the rider was thrown from the bull, the Heyok'a ran into the arena frantically waving red flags and diving into the barrel, which the bull then attacked with a fury. Those times I stood in the arena, small and boiling under the dress, I felt the bull's rage. My insignificance enraged me. I was all buckskin dress, feathers, and regalia, fluttering in the heat. I was shriveling under that dress. And there was no barrel for me to dive into.

I stopped dancing when my buckskin and elk's teeth dress burned in a house fire. At least I stopped doing the kind of dancing I had done for the county fair and rodeo. I danced with my cousins and friends at summer powwows on the reservation where I no longer worried about the spectators, because they were my relatives, my "tiośpaye," my extended family. We called our powwows "wacipi," or "that place where they danced." At those dances we flung long cloth shawls upon our backs, over T-shirts and jeans. These shawls are called "śina kaswpi," "śina" meaning "shawl" and "kaswpi" referring to the long "fringes" decorating the cloth shawl. We wore our hair long and loose down our backs. Our faces expressionless, we danced in a line of twos, side by side with a partner. The older girls were usually in the front, the younger girls behind them. We danced as the men—my uncles and cousins dressed in bells and feathers, and usually in full regalia—danced in the opposite direction. The spectators would later tease us. They said that we danced with only one thing on our minds—boys. We danced intermittently, spending our time at the powwows looking at which-boys-stood-where and which-girls-were-with-which-boys. In our attraction to boys, we resembled the moths that flew around the high outdoor lights that lit the pine-covered dance arbor at night. We were like the "wanaǧi t'a kim mela," the "ghost butterfly," which is what we call the common moth.

The dancing on those summer nights, when the crickets sang by the creek and the lightning bugs flickered like dancing "wanaǧi," or "spirits along the water," was a natural part of me. On those cool evenings, the śina kaswpi on my shoulders felt right, and I danced unhurried and relaxed while the spectators sat in folding chairs around the pine arbor.

I wore moccasins, and my feet felt light upon the grass where the wacipi were held. I listened to the drummers so sure in their song. I listened to the bells ringing as my male relatives danced. I watched how the old women danced, swinging their śinas back and forth rhythmically. That was how I danced those nights when the announcer at the powwow called out, "Hokahe, hokahe, wacipi yo, wacipi yo, wacipi yo," which means, "Strengthen your hearts, be strong, dance, dance, dance."

Excerpt from "From Pine Ridge to Paris"

JOE STARITA

Freshwater streams spill through deep ravines, creek bottoms layered in groves of cottonwood, elm, ash and oak. Thickets of plum and chokecherry fan out from the banks, packed tightly against a rutted dirt road. High above, the dense green forest fades to steep cliffs ringed in ponderosa pine. Beyond the canyon walls, in rolling swells of native grass and pine, a succession of sloping hills are pockmarked with old log cabins, windmills, rusty pumps and broken-down corrals. The hills gradually climb all the way to the top, past an occasional tipi or a sweat lodge draped in canvas, until they reach the immense, flat plateau overlooking miles of unbroken prairie. Halfway across the plateau, wagon ruts cut through knee-high grass to the wooden church and loop west toward a small cemetery on the hill.

Rugged, remote, isolated, the Yellow Bear Camp was home to traditional Lakota who did not know how to give up the old ways. It is where the people had hidden Chief Dull Knife after the escape from Fort Robinson in 1879, and where George Dull Knife heard the big guns firing along Wounded Knee Creek eleven years later.

During much of the decade of the 1890s the Pine Ridge Reservation became a cultural, emotional and psychological wasteland, a place where the dead Ghost Dancers symbolized the end of the Lakota's world. Traditional families who survived, who had endured years of fighting, fleeing, forced removal and a desultory succession of reservation homes, eventually found their way to Yellow Bear. After wild game gave way to sacks of flour and sides of beef elsewhere, Yellow Bear families still hunted deer, rabbit, and wild turkey, and fished the streams for trout. Throughout its harsh terrain, canvas tipis took longer to become log walls, and schools were slower to gain a foothold. At close-knit family gatherings, children and adults spoke Lakota. Horses were valued more than cattle, the medicine men more than priests. In summer, back in the hills, it was not unusual to hear the eagle-bone whistles of the forbidden Sun Dance.

For the families who lived here, who had made their homes in the tangle of the hill country, there remained a lifelong attachment to its powerful landscape, to the memories of what life had been like when they were trying to make the transition from one century to the next. Many were related, had lived in the old communal way, in the tightly woven extended families of the tribe. At the top, in the small cemetery on the plateau, lies Chief Yellow Bear. And the army scout Joshua Wolf Soldier. Albert Has No Horse and Albert Trouble in Front. William Plenty Arrows and Abraham Conquering Bear. George and Mary Dull Knife.

Between the winter of 1879 and the summer of 1973, four generations of Dull Knifes came to Yellow Bear. The old man chief had come to hide, to heal after the escape from the barracks. His son, George Dull Knife, returned to rest up between Wild West Shows. Guy Dull Knife Sr. was born and raised in the camp, and came home to it from the trenches of World War I. A fourth later found comfort in the solitude of the pines after Vietnam.

In the early photographs taken in the years after Wounded Knee, George Dull Knife appears as a man of striking features. He is tall with broad shoulders and thick chest, coal-black hair framing a

finely chiseled face: high, wide cheekbones, intense dark eyes and a
set jaw. In one, there is the long, neatly parted hair, an eagle feather,
a blanket, and moccasins. In another, short cropped hair, a buffalo
robe coat, trousers, and leather shoes.

"My grandfather lived until 1955," said Guy Dull Knife Jr. "He was
born the year before the Custer fight and died two years after the
Korean War. So he had seen a lot during his eighty years. He was fifteen at the time of the massacre and for a long time afterward, he
said a lot of the people on Pine Ridge didn't really care what happened to them anymore. A lot of them gave up. They didn't want to
really do anything. Especially the men. They didn't care about farming or ranching or working or doing anything. There was a lot of
drinking and just sitting around.

"During this time, my grandfather said it was the women who
really kept things going, who kept the families together and just
kind of took over. They were the strong ones while a lot of the men
were weak, had more or less given up. They couldn't find anything
to do that made sense to them anymore, so they quit. For a lot of
the people, the years following Wounded Knee were the worst they
had ever known.

"I think he was always kind of glad that the Wild West Show
came along when it did. It was a hard life in many ways and after he
got married and had a family, it was very hard on them, but at least
it gave him something to do at a time when there wasn't a lot of op-
tions. It gave him something to do and it brought in some money
that helped his family survive until things got better."

Through friends at the Yellow Bear Camp, George Dull Knife first
met recruiters with Buffalo Bill Cody's Wild West Show in 1892. Off
and on for the next fifteen years, he was a part of the large troupe
of entertainers who reenacted the buffalo hunt, dramatic battles
and heroic rescues in arenas throughout the eastern United States
and Europe. For many Lakota who went on Wild West tours, the
show life was often harsh. They were afraid and homesick and sick
in other ways. Some died en route during the long Atlantic cross-

ings; others died in Europe, buried in foreign soil far removed from their native lands. A few became addicted to alcohol and had to be sent back. George Dull Knife was seventeen when he went away for the first time. He was tall, sturdy, healthy, and he was lucky. Over the years, he stayed healthy, earned some money and sent much of it home to help his people in the Yellow Bear Camp. Eventually, he became an interpreter for Cody, and for the rest of his life, like many other Lakota, he spoke well of the unusual man whose relationship with the Indian had always been a complicated one.

By the time he died in 1917 William F. Cody, as much as anyone, had come to define the American West. Born in Iowa and raised in Kansas, he had scouted in Oklahoma and Montana, hunted in the Dakotas, ranched in Nebraska, and retired to Wyoming, living out his last days in Colorado. Along the way his numerous avocations mirrored a time and place, a way of life, that embodied many of the romantic myths and legends of an era. As a teenager, he had gone on a gold rush to Pike's Peak, ferried messages from a freighting company to Fort Leavenworth, and ridden for the Pony Express. As a young man he got in on the tail end of the Civil War, worked as a contract hunter for the Union Pacific Railroad, and served as army chief of scouts in warfare against the plains tribes. At his death a few weeks before his seventy-first birthday, Cody could include among his friends and acquaintances Custer; Sitting Bull; Red Cloud; Wild Bill Hickok; Calamity Jane; Annie Oakley; Frederic Remington; Charles Russell; generals Sherman, Sheridan, Crook, and Miles; governors; presidents; counts and countesses; and the Prince of Wales and Queen Victoria of England.

The transformation from frontiersman to showman had begun years earlier. While serving as chief of scouts for General Philip Sheridan's Fifth U.S. Cavalry in 1869, the twenty-three-year-old Cody met a young writer, Edward Zane Carroll Judson, who was fascinated by the roving hunter and army scout. Writing under the name Ned Buntline, Judson began to churn out a succession of dime novels, each casting Cody as the stuff of legend—bold, fear-less, flamboyant, a prolific killer of buffalo and Indians, the rugged new hero of the American West. The dime novels became enor-mously popular among East Coast readers starved for western adventure, a readership that soon began to link Cody's name to its romantic image of what life was like in the great lands west of the Mississippi.

In 1872 Cody cashed in on his newfound fame and starred with Wild Bill Hickok in a Buntline play—*The Scouts of the Plains*—that opened in Chicago to good reviews. Off and on for the next eleven years, he toured with the play throughout the eastern United States, returning frequently to the West between engagements. By 1882 Cody had settled on a four-thousand-acre ranch in North Platte, Nebraska, and in response to the pleas of townsfolk that year, he agreed to stage a Fourth of July celebration. Credited by some as the beginning of the modern American rodeo, the Fourth of July bash was a huge success, and it gave Cody an idea.

On May 17, 1883, what would become known as Buffalo Bill's Wild West Show officially opened in Omaha. More than eight thousand spectators watched that afternoon as Cody, dressed in embroidered buckskin and gleaming black boots, rode into the packed arena on a white stallion. Behind him followed a procession of painted Indian chiefs, mounted warriors, a buffalo herd, horses, cowboys, trick-shooting specialists, and a shining coach from the old Deadwood Stage Line. Entering to the music of a twenty-piece band, the troupe soon launched into a series of well-rehearsed performances: a Pony Express ride, an assault on the Deadwood stagecoach, an Indian at-tack on a settler's cabin, and the finale—a boisterous, thundering buffalo chase around the sold-out arena. The crowd loved it. The next day an enthusiastic press corps gave the performance rave re-views, and for the next thirty years, it would become the staple for a succession of American and European Wild West Shows.

To make good on a promise that his show was the genuine ar-ticle, Cody needed real Indians, and for three decades, he found them on Pine Ridge and nearby reservations. For the first seven years, the show included Indian performers recruited from tribes of Pawnee, Arapahoe, Cheyenne, Crow, and Sioux. However, age-old rivalries among the tribes eventually created too many problems, and by 1891 Cody decided to draw exclusively from the Sioux, primarily the Oglala. Among his troupe that year were Short Bull and Kicking Bear, the Ghost Dance leaders; and Corporal Paul Weinert, the Seventh Cavalry gunner who had manned the Hotchkiss cannon at Wounded Knee. Each Indian performer received a contract, guaranteeing that he would be well treated, fully supported while away, and returned home in good health. The contracts also stated that a portion of each Indian's monthly salary, usually twenty-five dollars, would be sent back to the reservation.

In Wild West Shows at home and abroad, the Sioux became crowd favorites. Cody, with his fringed buckskin, black boots, white stallion, trademark goatee, and flowing locks, had long symbolized the American West, and now his Indian performers did, too. They had been the classic Plains Indian. In the cities of the United States and Europe, it was their culture—feathered, nomadic warriors living in tipis, hunting the buffalo, fighting settlers and the cavalry—that was represented on thousands of colorful posters, flyers, and handbills promoting the arrival of Buffalo Bill's Wild West Show. Eventually, the image of the Sioux Indian would find its way onto stamps and coins, calendars, dolls, coffee mugs, and plates—an image that twentieth century western novelists and Hollywood filmmakers incorporated into scores of books and movies, until for many, it was the Sioux who had come to symbolize all Indians. Cody's Wild West Show had set it in motion, had initiated the creation, marketing, and distribution of a powerful American subculture, a genre steeped in romantic stereotypes and mythic heroes. What began in Omaha soon spread east, then overseas—and it never really stopped.

In the beginning Cody had earned a name for his proficiency at killing the animal the Lakota needed to survive. As a contract hunter for the Union Pacific Railroad, he claimed to have shot and killed more than four thousand buffalo in less than nine months, sixty-nine in one eight-hour stretch. Later, he had served as a scout in the army's campaign to rid the plains of hostile Indian bands. On July 17, 1876, three weeks after the Little Bighorn, his cavalry command intercepted a band of Cheyenne at War Bonnet Creek, Nebraska. During the battle, Cody is said to have killed Chief Yellow Hand, a deed later reenacted in many Wild West performances. When the Ghost Dance troubles began, it was Cody whom General Miles had chosen to arrest Sitting Bull. A few weeks later he rode with the army during the days of unrest following Wounded Knee.

George Dull Knife liked Buffalo Bill Cody. When the Lakota were strangers in foreign lands across the water, homesick and out of sorts, Cody did not forget his Indian guests. He took good care of them, often leaving his comfortable hotel to sleep in their camps. He made sure they had enough to eat, took them on sightseeing tours throughout Europe, and gave them parting gifts—small things that the others had forgotten, that George Dull Knife would remember. Over time, the young Lakota and the middle-aged showman became friends. It was a friendship that lasted until Cody's death in 1917, the year before George's oldest boy went off to war in the white man's army.

In a large black trunk at the family home in Loveland, Colorado, are some of the mementos of the Wild West days. On top, there is the faded pair of black binoculars, scratched and dented, and the inscription *La Dauphine—Paris*, a gift from Cody to George Dull Knife.

Of the many stories Guy Dull Knife Jr. heard as a small boy growing up on the Pine Ridge Reservation in the early 1950s, some of the ones he remembered best were the stories his grandfather used to tell about the years he traveled with the Wild West Show. The boy was fascinated by the large black trunk and he spent hours rummaging through its contents, looking at the mementos and keepsakes the family had gathered from one generation to the next. Inside, he found the binoculars and an old dusty pistol, nickel-plated, with a pearl handle and leather holster. After the last show of the season one year, Cody had given the pistol to his grandfather, and the boy used to take an oily rag and buff it and polish it until he could see his face on the barrel. At the bottom of the trunk, he found a bundle of photographs tied together with a rawhide thong and he saw that there were a few very old ones of his grandfather and the showman. In one, Cody wore fringed buckskin and his grandfather had an eagle feather in his hair. Another was taken in Paris, in front of the Eiffel Tower. His grandfather and the other Indians were wrapped in blankets, huddled together, looking at the camera with blank expressions.

Later, long after George Dull Knife had died, when the grandson was in Vietnam, sitting by his father's bed in the nursing home, or driving alone through the Dakota Badlands, he would think back on the photographs and the stories he had heard and he would try to imagine what it must have been like to be a young Lakota from the Yellow Bear Camp walking the streets of Paris and London at the turn of the century. During the years that his grandfather was away it was forbidden to talk like an Indian, dance like an Indian, and worship like an Indian on the Pine Ridge Reservation. But off the reservation, in foreign lands five thousands miles from the Yellow Bear Camp, European royalty and commoners paid good money to sit in the stands and watch the American natives, to see the dances, war bonnets, and fast ponies, to hear their singing, chanting, and battle cries.

Of all the things he found in the trunk as a small boy, Guy Jr. had liked the photographs best—was fascinated by them—and so he would ask his grandfather a lot of questions. In the early years of the 1950s, he and his parents would occasionally drive to the Yellow Bear Camp to visit his grandparents in their old log home. During the winter months sometimes, George Dull Knife would put on a heavy coat, wrap himself in a blanket and sit in the kitchen by the wood-burning stove, his grandson on his lap, telling stories that made the boy laugh out loud.

"One year when they were in England, they had the day off and so Cody decided to take some of the Indians to a kind of fair or circus that was playing in the same general area where the Wild West Show was. All the Indians were dressed up in their native clothing and they were walking around, and pretty soon, they came to a part of the fair that had some rides. They didn't know what they were and Cody asked if they'd like to try one. They said sure, so they got their tickets and they entered it one by one.

"Inside, the ride was completely covered with mirrors—on the ceiling, on the floor, on all of the walls. My grandfather said they had never seen anything like this, and before long, they were all doing their war dances and watching themselves in the mirrors and laughing out loud at the strange box, when the room suddenly started to move. It moved slowly at first, but after a while, it began to spin faster and faster, until they weren't sure what was going on or what they should do about it. One of the men started to move around the room to try and find the door, but nobody could stand up and pretty soon, the room really began to spin and then everyone started to panic. Some of them began to get sick and a few others started to sing their death songs. Finally, the room began to slow down and then it stopped. When they got outside, everyone was sick. Grandpa said it was the last time any of the Sioux ever went on a carnival ride.

"Another time, they were at a different fair or carnival, and when they passed by a tent, a man ran up to them and began talking real fast and pointing to the tent behind him. There was a picture of a giant ape on a board outside the tent and one of the Indians asked Cody what the man was saying. He told the interpreter and the interpreter told the Indians that the man was offering twenty dollars to anyone who could wrestle his ape to the ground. The Indians got together and talked it over and one of them told Cody he wanted to try it. Grandpa said Buffalo Bill got really upset. He told the interpreter to tell the man that the ape was called an orangutan and that it was really strong and he might end up getting hurt. But the man would not change his mind, so Buffalo Bill gave up and everyone walked inside the tent.

"The man told the Indian to step into a ring where the ape was sitting down. All the other Indians formed a circle around the ape, and before he stepped forward, the man did a little war dance and sang his battle songs. When he stepped to the center of the ring, the ape suddenly jumped up and sprang on him and threw him to the ground like he was a toy. Well, the Indian was really afraid then, and when the ape started to try and rip off his breechcloth, the man jumped into the ring and broke it up. By now, all the Sioux were laughing really hard at their friend. Grandpa said they teased him for the rest of the trip. When they got back to Yellow Bear, they told him they were going to tell everybody on Pine Ridge about the ape who counted coup on the great Sioux warrior."

For many Lakota, a tour with the Wild West Show lasted a long time, from a year or eighteen months to as long as two or three years. When they left the rough hill country of Yellow Bear, some did not know they would cross an ocean, heading for distant lands they had never heard of. They were usually paid monthly, the amount depending on their status in the tribe, their job description and previous show experience. One year, when 125 Indians traveled with the show, 72 were Pine Ridge Lakota. Their monthly salaries ranged from $75 for Rocky Bear, an early and longtime favorite of Cody's; to $60 for the interpreter John Shangreau; $35 for Bear Foot and Sam Last Horse; $25 for Thomas Kills in Winter and William Feather on Head; to $10 for Her Holy Blanket, Good Dog, and Looks Back. From Yellow Bear, George Dull Knife and the other Lakota from Pine Ridge often rode horses or buckboards to the rail station in Gordon, Nebraska. From Gordon, they took a train east to New York, where they were transported by ship across the Atlantic, two-week journeys that many of the Indians never forgot.

"Grandpa always said that the ocean crossings were the worst part of the Wild West Show," said Guy Dull Knife Jr. "The Indians had lived on the plains and they had never seen anything like the ocean. It terrified them. Some of the Indians aboard the ship never made it across. Some of them were in bad shape before they left New York. They were depressed and lonely and the shock of crossing the ocean was more than their systems could take. Their nerves went bad. Some of them had diseases and they got seasick and they couldn't stop vomiting. They had always been on land and they couldn't adapt to the water. Some of them died and so there were some burials at sea. Others got sick and died overseas and they were buried in many different places, in England, France, Holland, and Belgium."

On March 31, 1887, the first Wild West Show to play overseas left New York for London. Aboard the *State of Nebraska* that day were 138 soldiers and cowboys, 97 Indians, 180 horses, 18 buffalo, 10 elk, 10 mules, 5 Texas steers, 4 donkeys, and 2 deer. Annie Oakley was a featured attraction, and Red Shirt, an Oglala subchief from Pine Ridge, led the contingent of Lakota, Cheyenne, Kiowa, and Pawnee. A week out to sea, an intense storm battered the ship for forty-eight hours, pitching it between huge swells and setting off a fear and panic among many of the crew. Many became violently sick and some of the Indians began to sing their death songs. Badly stricken himself, Cody went from cabin to cabin, talking to the Indians, asking them to stay calm, saying the storm would pass. It eventually did and the ship arrived safely in London on April 14.

It was not unusual, the grandfather had said, for Cody to do whatever he could to help them when they were alone and afraid. The Indians did not forget, and told their friends and families back home; and over time, they came to trust him. One spring, after the show had closed out a long European run, the troupe set sail for New York from Hull, England. The day before, the Oglala holy man Black Elk and three Lakota friends, all members of the show, had gotten lost and so they missed the boat. Stranded and homesick, they eventually signed on with a smaller, rival Wild West show and traveled through England, Germany, Italy, and France, trying to save enough money to get back to Pine Ridge. In France Black Elk became ill and was cared for by a French family in Paris. A year later, Cody returned to France and Black Elk rejoined the show. When Cody asked if he wanted to stay or return home, Black Elk said he had been away for more than two years, that he missed his people and he wished to go back. A few nights later, Cody held a large feast in Black Elk's honor. Afterward, he gave him ninety dollars cash and a ticket for a ship sailing to New York the next morning.

In another year, in the summer, Sitting Bull traveled with the show for four months, sharing top billing with Annie Oakley. Throughout the tour, Cody let him sit out the mock battles between cowboys and Indians. Instead, the Hunkpapa holy man was introduced individually, a spotlight following him into the arena. That year, the tour played before packed houses in more than forty U.S. and Canadian cities. When Sitting Bull was introduced, the American crowds frequently booed. In Canada they cheered. By the end he was astonished at the number of whites he saw in the East and the poverty he found there, often giving away his show money to the ragged horde of children who followed him around. "The white man knows how to make everything," He told Oakley, "but he does not know how to distribute it." Sitting Bull and Cody became friends, and when the tour ended, the showman gave the Lakota leader two gifts. One was a white sombrero, the other a gray horse trained to dance at the sound of gunfire. On the morning Sitting Bull died, during the first burst of gunfire outside his cabin along the Grand River, the horse sat down and pawed the ground. It is said that some of the dead chief's shaken followers believed it was doing the Ghost Dance.

When the Lakota first arrived in England, George Dull Knife told his grandson, many could not adjust to British food. Hearty meat-eaters all their lives, they found it difficult to get by on plates filled with a lot of vegetables and little meat, meat they had never eaten before. One year, shortly after checking into an expensive London hotel, a large group of hungry Lakota were summoned to the dining room. Many of the younger men arrived at the table in native dress, painted faces, and feathered hair. Soon, white-gloved waiters brought in platters of mutton and vegetables for their American Indian guests. "The meat was cut into small pieces and served with potatoes and other vegetables and some greens," Luther Standing Bear, an Oglala from Pine Ridge, later recalled. "We cared nothing for the greens. All we wanted was meat, and plenty of it. So we would take the meat off the platter and hand the platter back to the waiter with the potatoes and other things still on it."

On one occasion, Cody tried to bridge the cultural distance between host and guest. "Buffalo Bill apparently took a group of Sioux to some kind of a polishing class in London. My grandfather said there was an instructor at the class who was trying to teach the Indians which forks they should use while eating and how to properly pull back a chair at the dinner table for a woman to sit on. Some of the Indians at that time had never eaten with a fork and they thought the whole thing was pretty funny. For a while, after they got back to Pine Ridge, they used to tease each other. They would say they saw so-and-so eating with his meat fork when he should have been using his salad fork.

"Another time, I don't know exactly how this happened, but they all ended up going to see the Pope. When they got there, the Pope wouldn't see them. Grandpa said he told the Sioux to come back again when they had found a different way of communicating with the Great Spirit."

Of the many Wild West performances abroad, the highlight of each season often became the shows that were staged for royalty. On May 9, 1887, more than twenty-eight thousand came to London's Earl's Court to witness Cody's first European show. Fascinated by what had happened in their former colonies, London newspapers primed the event for weeks in advance. On April 25, while British and American workers readied the large stage grounds, William

Gladstone, Britain's most powerful politician, visited the Wild West campground and met Cody, who introduced him to Chief Red Shirt. Not long afterward the Prince of Wales, his wife, their three children and a small group of French and German aristocrats arrived at the cold and rainy camp. The prince asked Red Shirt if the persistent cold bothered him. It was nothing, Red Shirt assured him, compared to the cold of his Dakota homeland. Before leaving the prince gave the Lakota a box of his favorite cigars. A few nights later the actor Sir Henry Irving invited Red Shirt and a group of Lakota to see his production of Goethe's *Faust* at the Lyceum Theater. Seated in private boxes at the posh theater, the Indians watched the performance, with Irving playing Mephistopheles. A newspaper review said the Lakota seemed "greatly scared at its horror." Afterward Red Shirt said it had all seemed like a big dream.

On June 20, the day before Queen Victoria's Golden Jubilee, celebrating her fifty years on the throne, the Wild West troupe gave a special command performance. Before the show Cody had worked out some changes for the Deadwood stage rescue scene. Inside the coach were the kings of Belgium, Denmark, Greece, and Saxony; and the Prince of Wales. As Queen Victoria and the crown heads of Europe looked on, the Cody-driven stage survived an Indian attack, its royal guests eventually making it back to the safety of their private boxes.

George Dull Knife often told his grandson the story of another performance before European royalty. It was the small boy's favorite and he had asked to hear it again and again. After their first trip abroad Cody knew the Lakota did not like the taste of beef, pork, and mutton. In later years, before leaving for Europe, he arranged to bring along a few extra head of buffalo so the Indians would have a fresh supply of the meat they craved. The rest were used for the chase scene, which became the crowd favorite for many Europeans.

"When they were preparing for a show in Spain one time, a member of the Spanish royalty came to the camp to look at the buffalo," said the grandson. "He had heard of the buffalo, but he had never actually seen one and he kept coming to the campgrounds every-day to look at them. Finally, after a week or so, he came up to Cody and challenged him to a special match between his prized bull and one of Cody's buffalo. He told Cody that these strange, hairy crea-tures he had brought from America were no match for his Spanish bull. Cody tried to explain to him that he was sure he had a fine bull, but that it was a domestic bull. The buffalo, Cody told him, were wild animals and they would tear his bull to pieces. But the Spanish man paid no attention to Cody and he kept bugging him about it until finally, my grandfather said, Cody came to the Indians one day and asked them what he should do. The Indians all said, 'Hao, Hao, Hao—do it,' and so a match was set up between the bull and the buffalo.

"On the day of the match, there was a lot of people in the stadi-um and the Spanish bull, a large white bull, was all decked out in colorful flags and pennants. Cody had brought several big buffalo bulls with him, but he and the Indians chose a younger, smaller, and faster one for the match. When the match began, the Spanish bull charged and hit the buffalo flush on the side, rolling him across the stadium floor. After a while, the buffalo got up and when he did, he went wild. He was a lot faster and he charged the bull furiously, over and over, until he finally got the exhausted bull down on the ground and then ripped him open with his horns.

"The bull did not live very long after it was all over; the Spanish man came down from the stands. He was really mad. He told Cody that the bull was very expensive, that he had spent a lot of money feeding and grooming and caring for the bull and that he had come from a long line of champion bulls. Cody let him talk and then he told him that he had tried to warn him, but that he hadn't listened and so it was more his fault than Cody's. In the end the Spanish man gave the dead bull to Cody and Cody gave it to the Indians. That night they butchered it in the camp and had a big feast."

When they traveled overseas the Indians all lived together.

Shortly after arriving in England, France, Germany, Italy, or Spain, their camps soon began to resemble the camps they had always lived in on the plains. A village of tipis clustered in traditional fashion emerged near the show grounds. Inside the tipis animal-hide parfleches contained native clothing, and many had packed their favorite catlinite pipes in beaded deerskin bags. Sometimes Indian men were allowed to bring their families, and children ran through the villages abroad as they had always done. There were usually a number of campfires burning and in the close-knit Indian village, the occasional smell of fresh buffalo roasting on a spit drew the people together. While women tended the fire and beaded inside the tipis, the men sat in small groups smoking and talking, relaxing between shows. The Lakota were introduced to dominos during the trips abroad and many became fascinated with the new game. Clustered on the ground, whooping and hollering, occasionally making wagers on the outcome, they would sit in circles and play the game for hours.

Despite royal visits, frequent dinner invitations, and the general social swirl of European cities, Cody often preferred life in the Indian camp. He liked the nightlife, liked to drink, and liked the parties, but after a while, George Dull Knife said, Cody wanted to be with his own kind of people, people who had lived in the American West. "One afternoon, Grandpa said, they all went to a fancy bar in Paris. By the end of the day, Cody was really loaded. He had his six-shooter on, and at one point, he pulled out his gun and emptied it in the ceiling. The French people in the bar dove under the tables and everyone started to panic. When the gun was empty, he put it away, finished his drink and they all left. That night, instead of sleeping in a nice hotel where some of the others were staying, Cody slept with the Indians in a tent back at their campgrounds. My grandfather said it was something that he often did. He would spend a night or two in the hotel and then show up with his bedroll back in the Sioux camp.

"In one of those years when my grandfather was with the show, they had all been gone a long time, about a year and a half, and all the Indians were really homesick. They got back to New York and then they took a long train ride, three or four days, before they arrived in Gordon. Some of their relatives were waiting for them at the train station and there was a lot of crying and hugging, but instead of everyone breaking up and going home right away, Buffalo Bill insisted on throwing a big party for all the Sioux. He wanted to thank them for their work in the show, so he had some of his people slaughter eight or ten head of cattle, and there was a couple of barrels of cognac, and I guess they had quite a going-away party. My grandmother had come in with some of the others from the Yellow Bear Camp to meet the train. She had never heard of cognac before and I guess she got pretty drunk that night. From what I heard, she never touched the stuff again.

"When the tours ended the Indians were always happy. They missed their home and their people and they couldn't wait to get back. But Grandpa said Cody always seemed a little sad. He would talk about resting up for a little while and then he would see them again in the spring or the fall or whenever they would be leaving Pine Ridge to start another season."

In the Time of the Buffalo

ALAN BOYE

On the flat divide ten miles north of Beaver Creek are
a series of sharp canyons dipping abruptly northward
to the Republican River and the border of Nebraska.
In October 1878, with the hope of finding fresh horses
and the memory of the bounty of this area, the weary
Cheyennes climbed down those canyons into the great
buffalo land.

With no imagination it could be buffalo land
yet. I have crossed the Republican and am north of
Benkelman, Nebraska, where the prairie rolls as far as
the eye can travel. It is shortgrass prairie: big patches
of golden-white tips throwing sheets of light across the
darker shades of other grasses, silver-green sage not yet
in bloom, the sandy edges of countless rolling hills thick
in forests of yucca, until with distance the jumble of
grassy hills flattens to a single vast horizon, its enor-
mousness only dwarfed by the immeasurable sky, the
ceaseless wind.

I hike along the major creek of this part of the county, the route the Cheyennes followed as they headed for
a camp on Frenchman River. The Frenchman River was

a familiar place for the Cheyennes to camp, for often they had come here for buffalo. Now, however, they had been running for twenty-three days; they had traveled 450 miles mostly on foot, eating what little they could find on the once buffalo-carpeted prairie. They stopped only for a day on the Frenchman.

In the morning warriors reported seeing troops nearby, so the Cheyennes split up into small groups. Some moved twenty miles further to a small river whose very name foretold the disaster that by then was spelling the end of the old ways of life. Flowing through the heart of what had once been the richest buffalo grounds on the continent, the Stinking Water Creek had been named for the thousands of buffalo carcasses left to rot on its banks by non-Indian hunters.

With the demise of the buffalo, Indian culture on the plains changed forever. A new life would have to be shaped where once the buffalo had held the center. From the sacredness of the buffalo hat to the practicality of the buffalo chip, Cheyenne culture, like that of all Plains Indians, had evolved from a long association with the bison.

The Cheyenne tribe is made up of the descendants of two ancient tribes. Perhaps as late as 1700 the Cheyennes lived in more permanent villages further east, near the Mississippi River in present-day Minnesota, cultivating fields and occasionally venturing out in search of buffalo. Around 1700 the Cheyennes joined together with another tribe in that region, the Suhtais, who spoke a similar language, to form a single tribe. While there were distinctions in language, custom, and heritage, enough similarities existed that the two groups easily melded together. With the arrival of the horse, the Cheyennes moved further west to occupy the great buffalo lands of the higher plains. The distinction between Suhtais and Cheyennes is still a matter of tribal discussion, and most Cheyenne families are aware of variations in vocabulary as well as the lineage of their own ancestors. The current division of Southern and Northern Cheyenne tribes is more an arbitrary result of geography rather than a cultural distinction; in the 1830s they had broken into northern and southern bands for convenience of trading and hunting. All Cheyennes were to be kept on a southern reservation until some, like those who escaped north with Dull Knife and Little Wolf, gained a reservation in the land they preferred.

When the Suhtais and the Cheyennes came together, tribal stories were reconciled to incorporate the two traditions. Each tribe believed the power and mystery of the Great Spirit was embodied in a sacred object. A group of four sacred arrows—called the medicine arrows—were given to the Cheyennes by the cultural hero Sweet Medicine to protect the tribe and bring them strength. For the Suhtais a powerful covenant—a sacred buffalo hat—was the incarnate object of the Most Powerful One. Both objects were always in the care of selected individuals whose job it was to see to their safety and to ensure their proper handling.

Inside a special crescent-shaped sack trimmed on all sides with buffalo tails, the Sacred Hat remained hidden almost all of the time. On the most special of occasions or to bring good luck in a battle, the hat was removed from the bag. The thick fur of a cow buffalo served as the main covering of the sacred hat, and spectacular, shining blue beads adorned the sides. Slender, long horns came from the sides, and each horn was decorated with a pattern of red geometric shapes. On those rare occasions when the hat was taken out to renew the people's power, or to bring blessings on a great hunt, or in times of tribal crisis, it was placed on a bed of buffalo chips and adorned with sprigs of sage.

Objects from the buffalo also played an important role in the Cheyenne version of the Sun Dance, a midsummer ritual that has been practiced continuously for centuries by the Cheyennes and other Plains tribes. In the old days the individual dancer, who had found himself in a dangerous situation, or who was threatened by something, or who wanted success at some great endeavor, promised to make a sacrifice by performing a special dance in the sun. While some of the cultural aspects of the ceremony have vanished, the buffalo remains an important spiritual aspect in the modern continuation of the Sun Dance.

Such devout respect also was evident as the Cheyennes prepared for a buffalo hunt. Medicine men were consulted, dreams were discussed, and rituals to lure the beast toward hunters' weapons were performed.

Often small parties of hunters would spread out in search of buffalo. If a large herd was located, signals were sent back to the main camp and final preparations were made. Before the arrival of the horse, Indians often would surround a herd, hoping a shift in the wind would not give them away. Slowly those participating in the surround would move in, trying to form a human fence around the herd so that those men most skilled in the use of the lance or arrow could kill a number of beasts. Likewise, this method was used to drive a herd into a box canyon, or over a cliff, or—in winter—into deep snowdrifts or onto thin ice, where the weight of the huge beasts would cause them to fall into the water and thus become easy marks for a hunter's arrow. Other times the Cheyennes used a combination of wooden and human fences to impound the creatures in a natural or manmade trap. Another method was to set prairie fires to drive the buffalo toward waiting hunters. This method was always at risk, of going awry. Some fires set for hunting changed direction or raced off across the prairies for miles.

When the horse arrived, its value in hunting the buffalo was so great that virtually overnight it took a prime place in Plains Indian culture. At first the horse was used in the surround, where its speed and agility made it ideal in herding buffalo. As Indians became more proficient and skilled with horses, the buffalo hunt became a contest that matched the skill of a horse and rider against a twelve-hundred-pound bison. It is no wonder that the Plains Indians quickly became some of the world's foremost equestrians, and the Cheyennes, it is commonly agreed, were the foremost horsemen of the plains. Quickly the horse became the most valuable commodity in the tribal culture, and the number and quality of a man's horses was a mark of his wealth. More and better horses meant more buffalo, which meant that a man not only could afford a large family but also required additional wives in order to tan and prepare the hides and meat.

Meat from a crudely field-butchered buffalo was wrapped in its hide and loaded onto a horse for transport back to camp, but if the kill was large, or close enough to the camp, the people came to the kill site for butchering and returning to the camp for preparation of the meat. Strips an inch thick were dried in the air and sun into jerky; bits of chokecherry might be pounded into the strips to give the jerky a different taste. Pemmican was made by pounding jerky into long strips with a rock, placing it into leather bags about the size of grocery sack, and then pouring hot fat into the bag. It was then sealed, pounded flat, and stored. The contents, which were considered a delicacy, remained edible for years. Such bags of pemmican were often cached under specially marked rocks as insurance against hard and lean times, or stored away for the winter months. While pemmican provided a reliable long-term food supply, fresh meat was prepared in all manners, and the Cheyennes ate it raw or barely warmed, made it into thick stews and soups, or roasted it over a fire of glowing hot buffalo chips.

Occasionally a great deal was wasted, as in mass kills or when whole animals could not be butchered on the spot or dragged back to camp, but generally Indians used most parts of the buffalo. The Cheyennes used the hide for tipis, clothing, and tools; they used the hair as rope and ornamentation; the horns were glued together to make superior bows, used as spoons and ladles, arrow tips, and cups, or ground into medicines and potions; the bones were worked into versatile tools and weapons; the marrow was eaten, or it was dried and used as sponges and paint brushes. Occasionally the teeth were used for ornamentation on special dresses, while the sinew was prepared as sewing thread and bowstring. Parts of the buffalo were ideal waterproof containers, and stomachs, bladders, and scrotums were useful ready-made pouches. In winter children used the beasts' ribs as runners for sleds, and year round they used them as sticks for games or whittled them into whistles, dice, or drums.

The lowly buffalo chip was renowned as a source of fuel. First off, the properly sun-dried chip is nearly odorless and, when burned, gives off a faint incense-like smell of cinnamon and citrus in a nearly invisible smoke. The chips can be broken up into small slivers, which serve as kindling, and then larger and larger pieces can be added to the fire. They do not flame up as wood, but rather glow red much like charcoal. They give off a strong, constant heat without flaming up to sear the cooking meat. They continue to glow for a long time from the center of a nearly pure white ash. In the morning a buffalo chip campfire is nothing but a pile of white ash, still retaining the shape of the original chips.

The bison was so integral to the life, culture, and health of the Cheyennes and the other Plains Indians that it is easy to see why some military leaders for the U.S. government understood that the best way to eliminate the Indian was to eliminate the buffalo. When the demand for buffalo hides and meat reached its peak, the most shrewd military strategists saw ultimate victory over the Indians.

Grazing buffalo might give the impression of being clumsy and slow, but the animal is an excellent runner, capable of outlasting even a relay team of horses. When in a hurry, the buffalo gallops much like a horse, each leg pounding the earth in succession; but for fastest speeds the gallop gives way to a uniquely powerful, bounding leap. The bison throws out its skinny hind legs until they are well beyond the front feet, and then it leaps forward, all four legs suspended in air. At full speed of thirty-five to forty miles per hour, the leaping rear legs fly up high on either side of the huge head, a bluish-purple tongue wagging from an open mouth.

A tightly packed herd of these running beasts can flatten anything in its path, leveling fence posts and trees six inches in diameter. In his unmatched masterpiece on the animal, *The Time of the Buffalo*, Tom McHugh describes a stampeding herd:

[The lead animals,] alarmed by some disturbance, dash off in headlong flight. . . . Following by the others is virtually automatic. . . . At the beginning of a stampede, the buffalo rush headlong into a tight bunch, massing together with a herding instinct so powerful that the group can seldom be divided. This same stubborn tendency to bunch thwarts ranchers attempting to drive a buffalo herd onto a different range. No matter what technique—pushing with a line of men, chasing with jeeps, or encircling with horsemen—the task is so difficult that many drives end in failure. Sooner or later one buffalo manages to outmaneuver its pursuers and squeeze through a minor break in the line, whereupon the rest of the animals quickly slip through the opening like so many links in a chain, and the drive falls apart.

On a trip across the plains in 1862 a group of travelers were stunned one morning to see an enormous stampede of these bounding beasts. The herd was at least ten miles wide. For well over an hour the ground was a seemingly solid mass of buffalo as they raced past the observers.

Reports like these seemed exaggerated to people who had not witnessed the enormous numbers for themselves, but the vast quantities were truly beyond measure. One traveler on the Santa Fe Trail took three days to pass through a single herd. The entire horizon was "so thickly covered with these noble animals" that he could not see the bare ground. He calculated the herd to cover 1,350 square miles, an area roughly the size of Rhode Island.

Clearly, it would take more than hunting parties to wipe out these numbers. It would take more than tourists shooting from trains, more than Sioux and Cheyennes and Arapahoes and Pawnees and dozens of other Plains civilizations. Motivated by greed and inspired by money to find ever more efficient means of slaughter, it would take a few hundred professional buffalo hunters a handful of years to bring the buffalo nearly to extinction.

New breakthroughs in the tanning process, combined with an increased demand for the flexible, tough hide of the bison, spurred the initial wave of non-Indian hunters. The market-economy demand for hides brought on by railroad expansionism and the need to feed the populations of growing frontier towns resulted in staggering numbers of bison kills. As late as the Civil War the bison herd was estimated to be as large as fifty million, but by the early 1870s the methodical slaughter by professional hunters was well underway. During the 1873–74 season the Santa Fe Railroad alone shipped 459,453 hides. As many as four million were killed in a three-year period ending in 1875. The slaughter was so widespread and wasteful that pioneers let their hogs roam the prairies in order to feast on the buffalo meat left behind by the hide hunters. The decimation of the buffalo was so complete that in 1883 the discovery of a single hidden herd of twelve hundred near present-day Bison, South Dakota, was so monumental that it made international news.

The annihilation of the bison coincided with an increased demand for beef cattle. As the railroads pushed west, new towns along the routes served as shipping terminals to send beef east to a growing population. Nearly wild herds of cattle, fattened on grasses so recently vacated by the demise of the bison, were driven northward to savage railroad towns like Dodge and Oglala by gangs of rough-edged cowboys. Dull Knife and Little Wolf's route paralleled—and sometimes followed—the Western Cattle Trail north through Kansas, to the Nebraska border, and across the buffalo land. Remnants of the cattle trail can still be seen near the Frenchman and Stinking Water Rivers.

By the time the Northern Cheyennes were crossing the buffalo land between the Frenchman, the Stinking Water, and the Platte, news of Colonel William Lewis's death at the Punished Woman and stories of the brutal deaths of the pioneers in Rawlins and Decatur Counties was everywhere. The full might of the U.S. Department of War turned to stopping the Indians. From Texas to the Dakotas, from the Missouri to the Rockies, troops moved across the Great

Plains like chess pieces trying to stop the three hundred Cheyennes. Many feared the Cheyennes' actions would cause widespread revolt among other Indians being held in the newly developed reservation system. Others worried that Oglala Sioux under Red Cloud would flee their new South Dakota reservation. As in Indian Territory, rations were short on the Oglala reservation. Thousands of troops moved into positions along the Nebraska–South Dakota border. Rumors of a general Sioux uprising were rampant.

Because of those fears a band of Oglalas was nearly wiped out in October. Traveling from the Missouri to the White Clay River, the Oglala panicked when they came upon 250 soldiers along the South Dakota border. They didn't believe the story of the Cheyenne outbreak and believed, instead, that the soldiers were after them for having left the Missouri. The soldiers faced the Oglala, and the Indians took cover. The chiefs had trouble holding the people together; the soldiers called for reinforcements. A group of chiefs and officers met all night long to prevent fighting and to talk over the confusion. After the tension eased in the morning, the Sioux moved off in one direction and the soldiers in another. One tragedy was averted, but far greater bloodshed awaited the border area.

By the first of October Captain Mauck moved through the buffalo land south of the Platte with his heavily armed troops. Mauck had recently been transferred from elsewhere in the West to this place so troubled by the Cheyennes. He now was in charge of five companies of infantry and thirty-five cavalrymen—over three hundred men—completely outfitted with two weeks' rations. He was confident that he would stop the Cheyennes before they reached the Union Pacific railroad tracks at the Platte, one hundred miles to the north. Meanwhile, to the south, Captain Vance with seventy field infantrymen and twenty-five cavalrymen was moving across the headwaters of the Little Beaver and toward the Republican. Another one hundred troops under Major Dallas were on the lower Republican, headed west. Orders were for the three groups to converge at the Republican and to engage the Cheyennes.

It was 9 a.m., October 2, when the Cheyennes crossed the Republican River five miles east of the forks and moved north to the one-day camp at the Frenchman River. That day a rancher on the Republican named Connor lost forty-five horses, two mules, and about eighty-five cattle killed; a neighbor named Wilson lost twenty-seven horses. The Webster spread on the Stinking Water lost about twenty-five head of horses and seven or ten head of cattle killed. In total the Cheyennes captured sixty-four horses from local ranchers, and although the body of a slain rancher was found some weeks later, after crossing into Nebraska there was no more bloodbath.

They now had restocked the horses lost at Punished Woman and had as many as 250. They could move much more rapidly. According to two Cheyennes, Wild Hog and Crow, it was when they camped at the Frenchman River, and Cheyenne scouts saw the troops in the distance, that the band split up into numerous smaller bands and moved north. Besides confusing their pursuers, splitting into smaller bands was effective because the organization of the U.S. military made it nearly impossible for troops to scatter into small units to follow every trail.

Racing northward toward the Platte across the now nearly lifeless buffalo land, the Cheyennes hoped to avoid another head-to-head confrontation like Punished Woman. The new supply of fresh horses made their travel swift, although the cries of the wounded and sorrow for the lost ones resounded with every hoofbeat.

All around me are the tall spires of soapweed yucca, which thrust skyward from a bouquet of dagger-thin leaves. The massive taproot of the soapweed yucca is a foot-thick appendage that slams five feet deep into the earth.

There are at least 720 species of tubular plants growing without cultivation on the prairies of western Nebraska. Of these an astounding 670 are native species in a land that to some appears to be nothing but a monotonous carpet of grass. The golden-white flags throwing sheets of light across the darker green near the yucca are the seed tips of buffalo grass, the dominant species, unique because it grows in mats and not isolated bunches, and because it produces both male and female plants. The taller male plant is responsible for these one-sided spikes I see everywhere before me.

While the climax bunchgrass community remains largely unchanged for a long period of time, other areas change in composition from year to year. Often the reason for the fluctuation is soil disturbance. In the time of the buffalo these plants thrived in the wallows where bison rolled dust onto their hides. These days, after the soil has been disturbed by erosion from cattle, wind, or human activity, a hearty, fast-growing group of grasses and plants known appropriately as the pioneer plants establish themselves. Blowout grass, a plant typical of this community, sends out slender shoots in all directions, stabilizing the soil. It can be buried under wind-blown sand and still survive, but eventually gives way to other species that take hold of the soil it has helped to stabilize. While these plants grow quickly and can produce a lot of seeds, they cannot tolerate competition from other plants and so disappear once their rapid growth has stabilized the shifting soil.

Blooms are everywhere around me in this land of the buffalo: the bold white flowers of sand cherries pepper the hills; purple fireworks of lacy-leafed asters grace the ground, while amid grass and daisies, milkweed and flowering cacti, I nearly fail to notice the slender poles of the delicate palespike's bluish-white flowers. I follow a dirt path alongside the coolness of the wet creek bottom and pass a thick, dense thicket of Arkansas rose. I smell the sweetness of the bloom just before I see its pink flowers opening in the sunlight. In the tiny valley are thickets of wild plums, framed by an abundance of leadplant, prominent because of its hairy blue flowers. Near the ground where cattle have kept the grass cropped close to the earth, bush morning glory forms a spray of white flowers. By fall it will dry up, break off at ground level, and roll away in the autumn wind like a tumbleweed, scattering its seeds across the entire length of the creek bed.

At the center of the small valley is a wet meadow where taller grass and more flowers are blooming. A few trees are here: cottonwood and ash, box elder, and hackberry. Out here trees survive only near water; seldom does one thrive on the dry uplands. Stands of cottonwood and ash sometimes can get a few acres in size, but the ground below such small woods usually is barren as a result of the cattle that have congregated in the shade. It is not clear how trees found their way into these drylands. Whether or not human attempts to control prairie fires contributed to their growth, they have established themselves in these wet lowlands and in the fields now long abandoned.

Although we have killed off the buffalo, tried and failed to plant our crops, and finally sent our cattle out onto these plains, grass steadfastly resists our repeated attempts to leave a mark on the prairies. Grass covers the bloody pools left from battles with Indians, and it masks the horrors of lynchings, suicides, and deaths in fiery gun battles; grass hides the shame of the surrender of pioneers, and it grows through the concrete slabs of the hundreds of nuclear missile silos that are scattered over the land of the buffalo. Over and over it wins battles fought only by us, yet we continue to rage against it: the mushroom blast of death and horror in downtown Oklahoma City was created with a bomb made of fertilizer. The dust of its deathly destruction now enriches the soil where a grass-covered memorial will be built.

In their time the buffalo were so numerous, the grassland so vast, that men thought nothing could ever change. Although I have walked for miles without seeing much change to this landscape, I have as much chance of looking into the inch-long, pear-shaped iris of a buffalo's eye as I do of seeing one of the giant tortoises whose petrified bones are often unburied by the perpetual wind of this lonely land. In this time the tortoises were countless. The tortoise, the buffalo, the human: all so numerous in their time on this sea of wind-whipped waves of grass.

Excerpt from *Magpie Rising: Sketches from the Great Plains*

MERRILL GILFILLAN

The thought of certain lives can lead one to break two-by-fours.

North and a little west of Red Cloud, Nebraska, on the rolling Republican–Little Blue divide, there stands an empty farmhouse preserved as the fictional home of Tony Shimerda/Cuzak in Willa Cather's *My Ántonia*. When the weather has been wet the farmstead is a half-mile walk down a greasy gumbo road from the nearest all-weather. It is a good way to approach the place. From behind the dense shelter belt a chunky white frame house slowly emerges. Remnants of March snow hang in the roof angles. Then a big tin barn behind it; a shed or two. Closer, the barnyard has a recently abandoned look, a preserved look. A superannuated farm truck moulders under a tree.

There is a complete, precarious stillness about the place, a curious silence beyond the chatter and bicker of house sparrows in shrubs down by the barn and ponds. Day-old coon tracks skirt the leafless windrow. An old fruit tree stump, cut off four feet above the ground, is busy with new growth. Fifty feet from the house the cellar door juts from the earth—the cellar door leading to barrels of pickled watermelon rind in the novel, the door that pours forth Ántonia's brood in a sun-drenched *moment fixe.*

The gray day seeps and slops. The layers of the place, the fact/ fiction relationship, the play between the fictitious Ántonia and the Pavelka girl, her prototype who lived here, broke the tall-grass sod—all this makes for an evasive, almost eerie suspension. The lines of a life, as on a palm. The luminous, slow-moving spot of a life, the land it stands upon, and the artful act that crystallizes it into stories of the great complex ecology.

What leavens Willa Cather's prairie books is the elementary unmistakable secret of all books that send one to the two-by-fours: Behind the fiction there is the actual referent, a detail-studded ballast from a real and long-absorbed world. The light on the sandbars of the Republican River. The roll of the red-grass landscape. It is an imagination of heightening and arranging a given world rather than one of aggressive invention. Its eyes are soft but sharply focused. It picks up small things and turns them slowly in the hand. Bee-bush and rose mallow; ruts of old roadways. The colors are primary and fast.

So we are given a human life incandescent in its arc, an Ántonia of heartbreak and blossom, or the fated lovers beneath an apple tree in *O Pioneers!* And the galvanic thoughts of their various actual vectors are nearly matched in intensity by thoughts of the warm gifted eye that saw it all and chose it, and the cool lean prose that set it down amid the manifold flows and currents of the daily species. Here at this house the process and the spark of it all are nearly tangible. A human life and a sharp pencil. The sharper the pencil the finer the line, the sparer the accompaniment, the higher the solo parts. And the life stands out then, as the act of noticing stands out, in its passion and cartilage through the fine tracery of its line.

We circle the house, leaving soggy footprints in the spotty snow, shading the eyes against the window glass to peer in the empty rooms. A small stairway; the kitchen and its pump. Fragrant ghosts of Tony's spiced plum kolaches.

Earlier today we had circled and peeked in the same restless, hungry way through the lace curtains of the Cather childhood home in Red Cloud. Tomorrow we will do likewise at the wind-blasted concrete-block Mari Sandoz Museum farther west, near her birthplace in the Sandhill solitude: a handful of dusty personal items, a strange unidentified naked manikin, Mari's large wall map of Manhattan far from her Hudson Street apartment, a few sharp pencils.

Layers and echoes and the still farmhouse of a Bohemian family fictive as unicorns, carved out of the Republican valley and blown off the palm of the hand like cottonwood fluff. And "that is happiness, to be dissolved into something complete and great." And this raw day of the ankle-deep mud the Hastings, Nebraska, phonebook is full of Pavelkas.

Driving northwest from Red Cloud it is possible to cross the Platte River (known in the early 1800s as the Nebraska, its roughening valley to the west called the Coasts of Nebraska, as in *côtes*) at about the same moment one crosses the ninety-ninth meridian, that hypothetical divider of East from West representing the continually wavering, wandering moisture line that separates prairie from plain—during the drought of the 1930s it crept one hundred miles eastward.

Biologically, the plains have usually been viewed as a sort of negative space, divisive space defining and enforcing the continent's east-west speciation. Eastern flora/fauna mingle with the western in ragged overlap as the former creep up the river valleys in their farthest extensions. Climbing north from the Platte and west from the ninety-ninth, there are distinctions on the human level as well. This is the ascent from the *hither* to the *yon*, from farm to ranch, tillage to herding. The change is one of attitude and mentality; almost of viscosity. From the massively irrigated, utterly possessed Platte valley one climbs through Custer County to the Loup divide through an unrelenting, musical progression of rises and falls, ascending steadily into the open and the roofless, to the great Sargasso of the plains, the Sandhills.

Of all the geographical pockets on the continent, the Sandhills and their sheer rippling extent hang in the mind like clouds seen from a plane above. Their twenty thousand square miles comprise the largest sand dune area in the western hemisphere. They remain the "greatest unbroken grassland in North America." They are among the great cattle producing regions in the world. As pure wilderness—in the sense of untrammeled and self-willed space—the Sandhills hold their own against any mountain terrain.

Lying between the Platte and the Niobrara Rivers, the hills were formed thousands of years back when mighty winds from the north stirred ancient river beds and piled their sands into long parallel dunes. Big ones extend 10 miles and loom 350 feet high. The dunes are stabilized by thrifty bunchgrasses, but within the system there is continual change as wind and other disturbances to the fragile surface alter the lay of the dunes. The result is a rolling, billowing, delicate landscape unique in the west. Approaching from Broken Bow, or Gordon, or Ogallala, once you top the first real hill and drop into this utterly different topography with its more complicated spatials, something closes behind you and the earth feels possible and receptive again.

From high points you see them ripple away, the hills, mile upon mile, muscular yet gentle, supple but spartan. Wind-rumpled, pocked and dimpled. Dream mountains. It is a reassuring spaciousness (the Sandhill population density must rival outer Nevada's) surrounding the elemental rhythm of the ranches as one moves from water-wealthy hay meadows resting close upon the Ogallala Aquifer to yucca-dotted grazing reaches. It is a place one can drive happily in circles for days.

The hills also muster some of the harshest living conditions in the world. The wind is a constant and in winter brings slashing blizzards and a mineral cold. Summers, it can whip fires for miles through the dry grasses; you can smell a Black Hills blaze way down in Cherry County, Nebraska.

From a friend's cottonwood-shaded ranch house north of Hyannis

I hike north over the first range of hills. George, the bull-chested tireless black mutt, comes along. It's a midsummer day; the going is slow in the sand. Sharp-tailed grouse flush off as we get higher in the yucca and rosehips, or are suddenly there cackling and coasting over a rise. Upwind half a mile three mule deer stare and ease off into the dunes. In a small blow-out—one of those cups of vegetationless sand common in the hills—an unexpected resident stops everything to crane at me: a box turtle, one of many I would see that day, all of them plowing their way across blowouts. As I kneel beside him I picture him reaching out for a rosehip in astounding slow motion, grasping it just right in his beak.

Coyotes yap and whine regularly even though it's midmorning by now. There is a cutoff distance to which George the tireless is carefully attuned. If the coyote is within that range George is off like a shot toward it across a meadow and over a rise at least a half mile distant. Thirty seconds later he reappears and races back to me, never slackening the only pace he knows. If another coyote cuts loose in the other direction ten seconds later George is off again without a thought. Now and then he pauses to work a cactus needle out of his foot, but in general his energy and sense of limits are boundless and staggering.

From the top of a good hill I watch valley, range, valley roll away, receding infinitely like the images in a barber's mirrors. This part of Cherry County is within the "lake country" and nearly each valley is graced with a chain of long narrow lakes from three to six feet deep. I can see four lakes in two different valleys to the north. This sweet water drew men of the Dismal River culture centuries ago. This morning's breakfast was built around a platter of fried Sandhill bullheads and a pile of biscuits to wash down the bones.

To the untrained eye all these valleys look the same. Early mustangers in the hills were forced to haul in tall poles from the Dismal to place atop certain hills as landmarks. George and I descend on a slalom angle to the nearest lake. Bullrushes grow thick along the shore; on the far side I find a muddy little beach covered with duck droppings and scattered feathers. Cicadas drone and marsh wrens rattle from the rushes. I am as alone as I have been in a long, long time. The noon is hot and the deerflies and "greenheads" are biting with a vengeance. There is no human sign visible or audible, save a fenceline trailing up and over the hills nearby. The heat, the expansive silence, and the cluttered mud on that shore, stirred by a lethargic intermittent breeze, concoct a primeval feeling. I sit there amid the duck scat for half an hour, then strip down and wade in for a Neolithic splash and swim.

To swim alone, completely alone in the middle of many hectares, is a luxuriant thing. Maxim Gorky wrote five interesting pages on "Man's Behavior When Alone." Chekhov stubbornly pursuing a sunbeam with his hat. Tolstoy whispering confidentially to a lizard on a wall—men for whom solitude was a rare circumstance. In the Sandhills it is sometimes the dominant commodity.

On another trip to Cherry County we stopped to visit a friend of the family, an eighty-year-old bachelor rancher living alone a mile off a tertiary half-road in a place that throbbed with that open-ended, one-way silence of isolation. We found him sitting at the kitchen table mending his leather work gloves with an awl and cobbler's needle, mending the gloves he would need to mend his fences. His house dated from the 1960s; the original homestead stood a few yards away. He had framed arrowheads and photos of nieces on the walls. There was a huge television in one corner. He rose to the sudden occasion of company by reeling off old stories and Sandhill jokes laced with family references and national politicians. It was all in the vein of a child's piano recital, somehow, in its pure desire to please.

Outside he showed us the old thick-walled sod home where he was born and reared. It stands full of junk and raccoon droppings. And then we all shook hands and said goodbye. There was an almost audible clicking off of the social in the man's carriage and eyes. It was a small Sandhills epiphany. I glanced back as we pulled away and saw him walking, a bit stiffly, even formally, back inside, alone again, for how many days?

George and I while away three hours by the lake, working the rushes for a clear view of the wrens, slapping greenheads, and taking occasional dips. We are visited by several dazzling red damselflies; I should collect one for a still-life painter. Now and then a night hawk dives and roars overhead, that most ethereal, unplaceable sound from above that never fails to excite and baffle the dog. A trio of white pelicans flies with great dignity across the far end of the lake. It's time to dress and pack up and head over the hills. As we climb away south, the light is just changing, fading toward sundown, and a summer moon is low on the hills. Away down below, young night herons flop along shore in that reduced golden glow—the delicate remix of two celestial lights—and a huge solitary Angus bull stands chewing his cud in knee-high grass to the west end of the valley.

The Sandhills are as private as the Ozarks. Children frequently commute sixty miles a day to school, or board in town during the week. As is typical of areas where human company is valued for its scarcity, news travels fast, people know one another for fifty miles in all directions, and their recall of events past is phenomenal. Around the dinner table or sipping whiskey in the bunk house, they reach back and pull them in with casual dexterity.

"I worked for him in the hayfields in 1929."

"I never got to North Platte till '54."

"We were at a rodeo up in White River in '47."

"I bought that mower in the spring of '68."

Regarding the infamous blizzard of 1949, I heard a rancher recite the full name of the man who drove the National Guard bulldozer that finally showed up days after to clear the ranch road, how they saw the blinking lights moving slowly toward them down the valley, the name of the man who sat beside him, who he had married, when, and the name of the boy who drove the fuel truck following behind.

When the railroad pushed west from Broken Bow into the hills, someone among the crew was a Massachusetts man with a good eye.

Moving through the dunes he aptly named a village Hyannis. There is also a Whitman, and farther south in Nebraska, a Wellfleet. With the railroad providing a ready outlet the cattle business boomed in the Sandhills and big-time ranchers prospered. Many bought shady town homes in Hyannis and retired there. In 1931 the Omaha *World-Herald* called Hyannis (present population 360) "the richest town in America." In 1947 the *Saturday Evening Post* described it as the "Sand Hills Paradise," "the town with 13 millionaires."

Today, coal trains lumber east through the village twice or three times an hour carrying low-sulfur coal from Wyoming. They lumber by the spot where Teddy Roosevelt stopped for a tailgate moment during one of his campaigns, past the local fur buyer with his ancient trailer full of dried coyote hides, past the millionaires' modest frame homes. But when I stroll along those tracks or follow them east or west on Highway 2, I find myself thinking of a different Sandhills visitor.

In mid-1943 Fort Robinson, an old military installation northwest of the hills near the South Dakota line, was designated a POW camp, one of several in Nebraska; one of many in the heartland. All the western camps were under the supervision of the largest facility near Atlanta, Nebraska, south of the Platte. The Atlanta camp processed some ten thousand German prisoners during its two-year existence. Prisoners from the North African theater, mostly—Rommel's men, arriving on slow trains from the east coast, destined for casual farm labor and irrigation work in the surrounding countryside.

Fort Rob was a smaller satellite, processing only fifteen hundred men during the late war. It was a typical camp with three compounds within a barbed wire stockade, guard towers, and machine guns. All this within yards of the log jail where Crazy Horse was killed in 1877 and the stockades where Dull Knife's Cheyennes were held and later shot down escaping one freezing January night. Nights in the mid-'40s you might have heard *biergarten* tuba tunes drifting from the compounds to the Red Cloud bluffs.

In the spring of 1945 one German soldier simply walked away

from a work detail and hopped a freight on the Burlington line. It carried him south from Crawford to Alliance, then east through the heart of the Sandhills: Ellsworth, Hyannis, Thedford, and southeast through Grand Island. After dark the man detrained in York, Nebraska. His priorities were admirable. He cavalierly entered a joint called "Buddy's" and even more cavalierly ordered *eine bier*. Back at Fort Rob the next day, he explained he wanted to see America; especially Omaha.

Now, at least once each trip to the Sandhills, at some heady point on the highway when the big spaces reopen in the head and the heart, I think of that man and his day through these hills many Americans don't know exist. Some of the Nebraska POWs returned to the state to farm after the war. Maybe the escapee is here somewhere, taking it easy in Omaha or rocking away on a Sandhills porch by now. Either way, I see him forty years ago crouched in the door of an empty freight car lumbering through the hills, peeking out full of adrenalin-spiked wonder.

Excerpt from "Tending to Ruin"

JACK TODD

Home. Pop's easy chair up close to the furnace so he can fry his back while his feet freeze. Leaner and meaner and crazier than ever, seventy-three years old now and still working fourteen-hour days seven days a week training his horses. My mother gone straight from raising us to caring for a neighbor's kids, with more time now for her Chekhov and Tolstoy and Balzac and scratchy opera recordings on the old turntable, a woman ground down by decades of poverty, finding her salvation in books and children.

They're a strange couple, Jack Carney Todd and Maxine Marguerite Morgan. He quit school after second grade and had to move his lips when he read, running his finger under every line. She made it through tenth grade before her mother died and left her an orphan with two younger brothers to care for—but she never stopped reading and learning. He comes back from the corrals and tracks horse manure through the house, and she looks up from reading Chekhov and screams at him as she has every day for forty years to take his boots off outside, and he goes right on through to the bathroom at the back pretending he doesn't hear, stomps through the house again on his way out, kisses her on the neck and grabs a feel and goes back to the horses. When he's gone, she mops up his footprints and returns to her book.

He was on the downhill slope as a boxer when he picked her up in 1929, a thirty-one-year-old veteran of more ring wars than he could remember, riding a motorcycle with a sidecar over the bridge between Scottsbluff and Gering, offering a ride to a pretty young pedestrian. She was nineteen, the daughter of a marriage that got her mother booted out of the house of Squier Jones, one of the wealthiest ranchers in Wyoming. Velma Jones had married a no-good bronc rider named Frank Morgan, who left her with two kids—Maxine and her younger brother Kenny. Another marriage to a salesman who died young left Velma with another son, Jimmy Wilson. Velma was always frail, so much of the work of looking after Kenny and Jimmy fell to Maxine, even though she had a crippled left arm from a tumble into a fireplace at the age of three.

Pop came to Nebraska as a fourteen-year-old with five brothers and three sisters, the boys sent ahead from southeast Missouri to drive a hundred head of cattle across two states in 1912, while the women followed behind in wagons with the family patriarch, old W. T. Todd, a powerful, athletic man who could still hold a broomstick in both hands and jump over it when he was seventy years old. With four older brothers, Pop came out of the crib fighting and never really stopped—the Todd brothers always ready to fight at the blink of a crossed eye. They settled first in the sandhills ranch country up in northern Nebraska, and every Fourth of July the Todd brothers would go in to fight the town of Ainsworth. People would come from miles around to see the brawl, the Todd boys against all comers, Pop fighting the first of a lifetime of battles as a scrawny fourteen-year-old. If you asked him then or at any age how it was going he would say, "I'm a-fightin' 'em," and he was.

They were married in Denver in the summer of 1929, made a go of it on a homestead west of Scottsbluff through the early years of the Depression. When his brothers started working in the defense plants in Oregon at the beginning of World War II, they sold the homestead and headed west. In a bar in Wyoming, Pop met a man with shares in a copper mine in Nevada to sell, handed him the proceeds from the sale of the homestead, and never saw him again. Six months later, sick of the rain in Portland, he spotted a tree frog one morning and made Maxine start packing to go back to Nebraska. "Max," he said, "when it's so wet the frogs are takin' to the trees, it's time to go home."

Back in Nebraska, after seventeen years of an infertile marriage, I was born on his forty-eighth birthday. Eighteen months after that, he was driving the tractor pulling the harrow through the fields too fast because he wanted to make it to a barn dance that night, Maxine riding the harrow until he took a turn too quickly, flipped her off, and broke her leg—the second time she had suffered that particular accident, both times because he was in a hurry. She was in bed with the broken leg in a cast, and he was supposed to be watching me and wasn't. I got in the corral with a four-hundred-pound boar hog who tore my head open, probably with his tusks, split the skull in front, and almost ripped one eyelid off. Pop found me bleeding in the corral, carried me into the house, dropped me on the bed beside her, and said, "Max, I reckon the boy's dead." She screamed and grabbed, felt a heartbeat, called the doctor, who sewed me up good as new except for the split in my forehead which would never go away. She never forgave him for that, although I never understood whether she was angry because of the broken leg, because he let the hog get me, or because he told her I was dead, although it was probably a bit of all three.

There were other things she might have held against him. Until I was four we lived in a basement house, a one-story home set down in the ground so that only the windows peeked out. He drove her almost crazy, putting a ramp up to the edge of the roof where it hung down to the ground so he could race his motorcycle up and jump it over the house, a man past fifty years old still jumping motorcycles,

chasing women, riding wild horses, and dealing with any difference of opinion by knocking out the man who disagreed with him,
which tended to reduce her circle of friends. But after me there were
three sisters, and he did what he could to take care of us—meaning
that he worked, as he put it, from "cain't to cain't. So dark a man
cain't see when he starts, so dark he cain't see when he's done."

What land we had left started as a three-hundred-acre farm down
between the edge of town and the North Platte River. He sold it off
piece by piece because, hard as he worked, he was too preoccupied
with horses and boxers and women to make a go of it in the ruthless
business of farming. Instead he tucked hay for a living at four dollars
a ton and trained horses for the love of it, and I was seven the first
time I drove the truck in the hayfields, twelve when I started working full days—every weekend, every holiday, every birthday. Every
day all summer unless it rained, Sundays included. Thanksgiving,
Christmas Day, New Year's Day, our shared birthday. On my twelfth
birthday we were supposed to be shoveling manure out of the corrals all day and I rebelled, fought him in a running battle all that
day and into the evening, found myself working in the headlights
of the truck until near midnight, scooping horse manure like I was
told. Winters we forked loose hay that sent cascades of snow sliding
down our necks, in summer we heaved seventy-pound bales all day
long when it was one hundred degrees up in the sandhills and the
stubborn deerflies made little cuts on your face that stung when the
sweat ran into the cuts. We went home at night stumbling tired with
cows to milk and pigs to feed, to bed on summer evenings with the
light still fading outside, not yet light next morning when I'd hear
him growl: "Let's go, Jack boy. We got hay to move. Up and at 'em."
If I didn't move fast enough to suit him he'd grab one foot and yank
me out onto the hard wooden planks on the floor.

We used to kid about how tough he was but it was a thing to
behold. He would get impatient waiting for me to bring a hammer and drive a bolt into the tractor with his bare fist, and I would
come back to find him cussing and licking the blood off his knuck-

les. When I was ten, he roped a mule and dallied the rope around a post. He caught three fingers of his left hand in the rope, and when the mule took off the rope sawed two of the fingers clean off and left the other dangling. He hauled the mule in, got the rope off its neck, picked up the severed fingers, drove himself to the hospital, and dropped the fingers on the receptionist's desk.

"Do you reckon you got anybody here can sew these back on?" he asked.

She fainted. The fingers stayed off.

I'm standing in the doorway now, just home from Miami, bending to give my mother a hug, seeing how stooped and gray and frail she is. Pop starts on me.

"Say, you gotta get a GI haircut before you go into the army, son. You can't go in to be a fightin' man when you look like a girl."

"Why would I get a haircut when they're going to shave my damned head anyway?" Knowing that if I push it, big as I am, he will cut me to pieces with those fists. Seventy-two years old and he can still throw punches from all directions in ways you can't stop. He has never hit me. He doesn't have to, because I've seen what he can do, and I know how quickly an argument with him can end with big, strong men lying unconscious on the ground.

As usual, we do some yelling instead of punching and sit down to dinner, tempests in our family like dirt devils on the prairie. They blow up quick and disappear quick. We shift to safer ground, the one thing we share—a passion for boxing and admiration for Muhammad Ali. Long before Ali won his title as Cassius Clay, Pop was saying he would be the greatest fighter who ever lived. Unlike most white Americans he never wavered, not when Clay became Ali, not when Ali refused to be inducted in 1967, not now. We don't see eye to eye on the war, but we agree on Ali. It's a start.

Chili and cornbread and carrot salad and a corn casserole all out on the table, apple pie in the oven. I am full of myself, bragging about the *Herald* and Mariela. We are all talking at once, trying to forget that I have a November 13 date with the Selective Service. As usual, Pop has a dozen questions I can't answer: How many presses do they have at the *Herald*? (I don't know.) Is Miami a port for Atlantic shipping? (I think so but I'm not sure.) When they built all those bridges out to the Florida Keys, how did they sink the supports in the ocean? (I don't know.) Are the big skyscrapers in Miami built to stand up to a hurricane? (I don't know.) Is there anything about Miami I do know?

My mother hates the war almost as much as I do. We wait to talk about it until he has finished dinner and is back in his easy chair, ten feet away but too deaf to hear what we are saying.

"You know, I think I'd almost rather have you in Canada than over there fighting this stupid war," she says.

"I know. I thought about it. I don't think I could stand the thought of being cut off from my country forever and ever."

"Well, it's better than you getting killed, isn't it? Or shot up so bad you spend the rest of your life in a wheelchair?"

"Mom, that's not gonna happen."

"You don't know that."

"They have to end this war. They can't keep fighting it. The whole country is against it. Nixon might bring everyone home before I get through basic."

I don't believe that, but I have to say it. Sitting in that kitchen where the linoleum is still cracked, where the single bare bulb in the kitchen still hangs from a cord heavy with electrician's tape, where the swaybacked ceiling looks like it might collapse over the dinner table, where the wind blows through the cracks in winter. She is almost sixty now and worn out, having raised four children in this tiny house, usually with no more than twenty dollars a week for grocery money, often with much less. I will never know how she got us through the winter when I was twelve, when Pop spent six months in the veterans' hospital in Cheyenne after falling off a hay truck and at the end of the winter we had nothing left to eat except cornbread with milk and butter from the one cow I had to milk morning and night.

We have been hurled into the world on the force of her dreams. Having come this far, she will concede nothing to a nasty war in a far-off place. There is nothing I can say that matters. When I leave the kitchen she is still sitting at the table, lips pursed, chin resting in her palm, thinking.

Sonny comes busting through the door late the next afternoon, just in time for dinner. Like he always did, like it hasn't been more than three years since we've seen each other, like we just walked home from school two hours before. Says he was driving by and saw my car with the Florida plates and hit the brakes. Comes in grinning that let's-get-into-some-trouble-tonight grin, still nearly eight inches shorter than me but heavier than he used to be by ten pounds of muscle—that and a tight khaki T-shirt the only sign he has been anywhere near Uncle Sam's army. He's been out just long enough to make it home from Fort Dix in time to catch me on the way in. He sits down and helps himself to meatloaf and scalloped potatoes and carrot and pineapple salad, the two of us hugging and backslapping and talking with our mouths full. Apart from Mariela, there is no one on the planet I would rather see.

Mom keeps a weather eye on Sonny. I was four years old first time we hooked up, the way kids do, his parents just moved into the first of the new houses they built where our farm used to be, the two of us out in the field chasing grasshoppers when we decided to be best friends for life. I invited Sonny into the kitchen where Mom was unpacking groceries from the co-op. He scrambled up onto the table and ripped open a box of corn flakes and started shoving the dry cereal into his mouth, and I thought it was the funniest thing I'd ever seen until Mom told me to get that kid out of the house and tell him he was never allowed in our kitchen again. That rule lasted about a day, but she always kept her eye on him anyway, just in case he decided to hop up on the table and attack the groceries.

Me, I'd find Sonny hard to forget even if I wanted to. I have a scar on my right forearm where I ran into the back of a pickup truck trying to catch a pass from Sonny while we were playing touch football on the street. A scar at the hairline on my forehead where Sonny threw a dirt clod at me and found out too late there was a rock inside, a fact we established after I finished pounding on him and went to the hospital for stitches. No scar at all where we tried to leave one, when I decided in fourth grade that I was in love with a girl named Vicki Ruplinger. We went fishing down by the Platte River and Sonny helped me carve her initials on my left arm with a dull pocketknife, a job that took most of the afternoon. The "V" was easy, the "R" hurt like hell. Both scabs healed and disappeared before my mother noticed what I had done to myself. No scar either from the time we were fishing at the gravel pit and the gravel along the shore caved out from under me and I fell in, a panicky, fully dressed ten-year-old, and Sonny stayed cool enough to pull me out with his fishing rod.

We hunted crawfish together along the banks of the Platte. We wrecked red ant hills just to see how long it would take the ants to build them back up again. We played marbles in the dirt along the street they would call Avenue F after they paved it, "potsies" where you drew a circle and tried to drive the marbles out of the circle with your shooter, "chasies" where you tossed a marble out and tried to hit it from five or ten feet away. We threw rocks at everything, especially stray cats, birds, streetlights, and little sisters. We played basketball and football and baseball, Sonny better at everything until I got too big for him to handle.

When I was sixteen and six foot five and could finally throw harder than he could, I put Sonny in the hospital playing sandlot baseball. I was pitching and fielded a ground ball and whirled to throw to second base. Sonny was sliding in and the throw caught him in the kidneys. When he could finally move I had to help carry him home. When he started urinating blood the next day, his parents took him to the hospital. It didn't matter. We forgave each other for everything. We took my .22 rifle and his .410 shotgun and blasted at everything that moved in the woods which ran from the edge of our old farm another mile down to the river. Sonny, following along behind me one day when we were thirteen or fourteen, blew a magpie out of a tree five feet above my head with the shotgun. Blood, guts, and feathers rained down on me. I ripped the shotgun out of his hands and pummeled him until he was as bloody as I was, then we got up and laughed over the whole thing, the pair of us covered with blood and feathers and bird guts.

When I wasn't out on the hay truck with Pop, we made up Robin Hood games and fired real arrows at the sheriff's men, cleverly disguised as bales of hay. We let a big, shambling neighborhood kid named Ron Bales follow us everywhere and play Friar Tuck while Sonny was always Robin and I was Little John, and we would have quarterstaff fights with long wooden poles. We played World War II, building snow forts in winter, dirt forts in summer where the new housing was going up. Ron always had to play the Nazi, Sonny and I were the GIs who blasted him out of his bunker on D-day. Ron never complained when we got a little rough. He was so big and strong he could have crushed either of us, but he was easygoing and patient and never lashed out except when we attacked the red ant hills. Ron said it was mean to pour kerosene down an anthill and light it on fire, especially when we put firecrackers in there, too.

We graduated from playing marbles in the dirt and throwing rocks at the streetlights to dragging Main chasing girls, but we stayed friends. We were together the night they fried Starkweather in Lincoln in the summer of '59, a bunch of us hanging out with some older kids a few streets away, everybody crazy because we knew Starkweather was going to die. Some kid who had been indoors listening to the radio came out to say that when they fried Starkweather at the state pen, it took so much current the lights dimmed in that part of Lincoln. We raced through the streets, played kick the can and necked with girls where we hid in the darkness under the hedges, high and crazy because we were young and alive and the killer with the Coke-bottle eyes was dead.

When I went away to the university Sonny stayed home, did a year at the junior college in Scottsbluff, finally gave up on school in 1967. That cost him his college deferment, and he was drafted and sent to Vietnam. Sonny doesn't talk about the army much now except to say that he hated it. When he got back from Vietnam the chickenshit at Fort Dix nearly drove him crazy, bitter noncoms and officers who hadn't been in combat riding his ass for no reason at all. He nearly got into a fight with one noncom at Fort Dix, went AWOL for a week, ended up going back to finish his hitch. That much he'll talk about, but if I push him about Vietnam, he clams up altogether.

My last night in Scottsbluff I head down to Sonny's after dinner. We have a couple of beers upstairs with his parents, take a six-pack down to his bedroom in the basement. There are mementos of Vietnam everywhere. Pictures of Sonny with his unit or in Saigon. A North Vietnamese helmet and pistol belt without the pistol. A bayonet. Sonny's old combat boots. I flop on his bed and open another beer and we sit there yakking about the Cornhusker football team and a girl Sonny liked in high school, speculating about where the army is likely to send me. Everything is cool; we're about two beers into the six-pack. We're quiet for a minute, and then Sonny looks at me with the expression of a man who has just run into his own ghost in a dark alley.

"You can't go," he says. "You just can't go."

"What?"

"You can't go into the army. I mean it. You can't go. You gotta go to Canada."

"Sonny, man—I can't do that. I told you. I thought about it every way there is and I've got no choice. I've got to go do my hitch."

Sonny shakes his head, staring at the floor.

"Look, I can't let you get drafted. I'll drive you to Canada myself. We can take off right now. You can't go through that shit. I took enough of it for both of us. We have to get you out."

"Thanks for worrying about me, man, but I did Marine Corps officer training. I know about the bullshit. I can take it. The army can't be as bad as the Marines."

"I'm not talking about chickenshit sergeants. I'm talking about Vietnam. You got no idea how bad it is there. You don't know how fucked up you're going to be if you make it back."

"You went, and you don't seem all that messed up."

He looks at me slow and steady, and I know what a dumb thing I just said.

"You can't go."

"I gotta go, man. I promised Mariela. And I can't do that to my folks. God, look how old they are. It would kill them if I went to Canada.

"It's gonna be worse for them if you go to 'Nam and get shot up. I had a piece of shrapnel go right through me, almost took my nuts off. I'm lucky to be sitting here right now. And that wasn't even the worst part."

He sits there rocking back and forth, arms wrapped around his ribs like he's trying to hold himself in.

"Look," he says. "I'm gonna show you some pictures. Nobody has seen this stuff except the guys who were there, but you have to see it because you gotta understand what you're getting into."

I put a hand on his shoulder again and try to steady him, but he doesn't want to be steadied. He pulls his old army footlocker over to the foot of the bed, opens the lock, pulls out two or three big stacks of photos, and sits down on the bed next to me. When we were kids we sat in this same room and thumbed through his father's collection of men's magazines from the '50s, all of them full of pictures of women with pneumatic breasts (the nipples always artfully concealed) and stories like "I Was a Nazi Love-Slave," illustrated with a drawing of a beautiful woman tied to a post, her dress ripped half off, a cruel Nazi colonel about to ravish her. What we are looking at now is obscene in a way those corny old magazines could never be.

For the next three hours Sonny does everything he can to persuade me to go to Canada. He doesn't say much, just a word or two to explain where a picture was taken, who was in it. The first photos are very ordinary, young soldiers stripped down to the waist, standing outside tents, playing cards, drinking beer, lying on their bunks. There are at least a hundred photos taken all around the helicopter base near Cam Ranh Bay where Sonny served as a perimeter guard—shots of him and his buddies smoking cigarettes and playing poker, *Playboy* pinups on the wall in the background, all of them grinning like they were away at Boy Scout camp for the summer.

Sonny pulls out a shot of some of the helicopters, then one of the guard towers, another of him with a German shepherd.

"See these dogs, they're supposed to warn you if anything is coming. I was in-country a week, I did my first shift on night guard duty. Scared shitless, you know. Like it's just you and your rifle and the dog and it's dark as hell and you know you're not going to make it till morning. The sun comes up and we find the guy on the next tower, him and his dog, both of 'em with their throats slit. We didn't hear a fucking thing, but they're both dead. That poor damned dog never even got a chance to bark."

Sonny had to go back on guard duty after that. Night after night, week after week. Waiting for sapper attacks, holding a .12-gauge shotgun to hit an enemy at close range in case the Viet Cong broke through the perimeter and were on top of you before you saw them. Waiting for night when they would sneak in, moving into the wind so the dog wouldn't pick up their scent, killing you quiet. The Viet Cong never got any of the dogs or the guards again while Sonny was there. They didn't have to.

He keeps leafing through the photos. Guys in his unit strung out on patrol in one photo, and you can almost smell the boredom and sweat and fear. Another shot: three body bags, dead GIs killed in a sapper attack. More photos: soldiers smoking potent Vietnamese dope, using the barrel of an M-16 as a handy pipe. "Guys were wired all the time," Sonny says. "Speed and weed. The speed hops you up so you hear everything, the weed cools you out so you don't jump right out of your skin. Beer, scotch, tequila, some kind of killer hooch the Vietnamese make. Anything, just so you stay fucked up."

Sonny was out on patrol one afternoon and his platoon fell out for a break. He went off fifty yards into the jungle to take a shit in peace. He had his pants down around his ankles when a small man in black pajamas came around a bend in the path a dozen feet away, AK-47 dangling at his side. Sonny brought his M-16 up and panic-fired the entire clip on full automatic, all twenty rounds. M-16s on full automatic have a tendency to climb, so he fired the first shot over the head of the V.C. and the rest of the clip into the trees and was left holding an empty rifle with the muzzle pointed at the sky. The Viet Cong was a kid—sixteen, maybe seventeen years old. He pointed his AK-47 at Sonny's chest, aimed—and for no reason at all just melted away into the jungle without firing a shot. The rest of Sonny's squad came crashing through the bush a minute or two later, but the kid was long gone.

The mortar attacks were bad, the suicidal sapper attacks were worse. Viet Cong sappers carrying satchel charges to blow up the helicopters attacked the wire at night, night after night. It should have been impossible for them to get through but they got through anyway. There was coiled razor wire around the perimeter, and there were Claymore mines rigged with tripwires low to the ground, and GIs with radios, shotguns, rifles with infrared night scopes, spotlights and flares and M-60 machine guns and all the rest of the hardware supplied by the richest nation on earth, and still the Viet Cong slipped through, sometimes in twos and threes, sometimes swarming the wire in company-sized attacks. A few got as far as the helicopters and the big birds went off like fireworks on the Fourth of July, making targets of the GIs silhouetted against the burning choppers. When the Viet Cong came in strength there were massed attacks on the razor wire, Claymores exploding, pitched battles at close range with the Viet Cong screaming and the guards firing blindly into the darkness with their .12-gauge shotguns and M-16s, never knowing whether they hit anyone until they found the bodies on the wire next morning.

That's how we come to the worst of it, photos taken the morning after one of the assaults on the wire. Dead GIs zipped into body bags, Viet Cong in their black pajamas still draped over the wire, some with chunks of their bodies blown away by the shotguns. Soldiers with dead eyes stare into the camera, grinning, necklaces made of Viet Cong ears around their necks.

Sonny is not in any of the photos. I don't know if he took them or if they were taken by someone else in his unit or if Sonny was even present when they were taken. We're not talking a whole lot now, just staring at the pictures. There is no passing judgment on the GIs in the snapshots. They were in a nasty war ten thousand miles from home, their buddies dying around them for no reason they could understand. They had no one but one another. They killed in furious combat and then, half crazy with fear and blood and triumph, took their trophies. They were operating in a country where every smiling kid on a bicycle might be carrying a grenade or a satchel charge, where every mama-san might be a Viet Cong.

No wonder the guys who were there went a little crazy: One day you're hanging out with your buddies in the parking lot of the A&W trying to pick up girls. Four months later you're killing a man with a shotgun in the dark, cutting off his ears, grinning for a buddy with a Kodak. You do your tour, fly home to The World, find it nothing like the world you left behind, go back to the A&W, try to pretend everything is the same—and the first thing you learn is that no one wants to hear the stories you don't want to tell.

There's nothing I can say to Sonny that won't sound cheap and dumb. He packs the photos back into the footlocker, padlocks it without saying a word. We pop open the last two beers, sit there looking at our feet.

"Y'know, the only way I can go to sleep, I have to turn on every light in the room and leave the radio on. Even then, most nights I just lay there."

"Maybe you should see if they'll give you a little help. You know, help you get back into the world."

"Shit. I can't go talk to some shrink, some asshole's gonna tell me to feel good about myself. I know what's there and I know what's here and, man, you just can't go from there to here. One way or another, you have to stay out of the army."

"I can't, Sonny. I just can't do it."

"You can't go, man. You just can't."

"I have to."

We sit there quiet for a while, finish the beer, make plans for Sonny to drive me to the bus station the next afternoon for the trip to the induction center in Denver. I walk home, crawl into bed, lie there staring at the ceiling, thinking about the memories Sonny takes to bed every night. Grinning GIS and body bags, the smell of blood and cordite, the chatter of AK-47s, moans of the dying, the coolness of damp clay when your face is pressed into the dirt and the earth shakes from the concussion of mortar rounds, shrapnel screaming through the night.

At 4 a.m. I hear Pop get up right on time, stomp around getting dressed, make a racket before heading out to do his chores. I'm too wired to sleep, too tired to help him with the livestock. I pull the blankets up to my chin, shivering with cold, wait till sunup to crawl out of bed. Mom has coffee on, pancakes, fried eggs, bacon, orange juice. She asks me if everything is OK with Sonny.

"Yeah, Mom. He's just fine."

Excerpt from *When I Was a Young Man: A Memoir*

BOB KERREY

In the spring of 1961 before high school graduation I decided to go to the University of Nebraska in Lincoln. I did not consider any other college. The university was the hometown school where my brother had gone before me and many of my friends were going. And the pride a Nebraskan feels for the university—even before our football team became famous—is something that cannot be understood by residents of states where the college scene is dominated by a venerable but private institution.

Most of my high school class of more than three hundred did not go on to college. They went right to work in factories where wages were still high enough to support their families. There were good jobs at Goodyear Tire and Rubber, the Burlington Northern Railroad, Western Electric, Cushman Motors, Gooch's Mill, and other smaller manufacturing businesses. Every male knew that two years of military service was required by law, but only if there was a shortage of volunteers. The need for recruits was too small to present any real risk to us of being drafted. The Vietnam War was not much of an issue for the class of 1961.

I chose pharmacology because I loved chemistry and because a university counselor explained how I could complete my pharmacy training in four years by taking a heavy load and going to summer school. That convinced me. I was eager to finish school and get out into the world on my own.

In August before classes began I ventured outside the safety of my hometown for the first time. Three fellow Angles and I drove to New York City. We saw all the tourist attractions—the Statute of Liberty, the Empire State Building, and Ellis Island. We saw Mantle and Maris play at Yankee Stadium. And we went to Greenwich Village where we had our portraits sketched by a street artist and managed to get into the Bitter End for a performance by John Coltrane. We were four square young men from Lincoln, a universe away from the people we saw here. Driving out of New York we laughed at how different everyone in the city was—but knowing that we were the ones who did not belong.

I was beginning to sense that I could no longer remain outside the flow of world events. Newly elected President Kennedy had said in his inaugural address on January 20, 1961, that Americans were willing to "pay any price and bear any burden" to win the battle against communism. Two months before I graduated from high school in 1961, he authorized a CIA-supported invasion of Cuba at the Bay of Pigs. And the tensions were not confined to Cuba. In 1960 Soviet surface-to-air missiles had shot down an American U-2 spy plane and captured the pilot, Gary Powers. In August 1961 East Germany closed the border between East and West Berlin and constructed the Berlin Wall. Also in 1961 the Soviet Union detonated a thermonuclear device that was the largest ever exploded; its shock wave was felt around the world.

Around the world four hundred years of Western empires were coming to an end, in some cases peacefully and in some cases not. Colonies in Africa, Asia, and South America were becoming independent nations and some became Cold War battlegrounds. I would not have pretended to understand or care about the underlying nature or history of these conflicts. And as for emotional engagement, compared to the genuine sadness I felt when rock-and-roller Buddy Holly's plane flew into a snowstorm after a concert in Clear Lake, Iowa, on February 3, 1959, these other events barely registered with me.

When I entered college, I would have done poorly on any test that asked me questions about the origins of our country or about the great narratives of the men and women who built it. I would have done well on a test that asked about the periodic table and algebraic, geometric, and trigonometric problems. I did not understand the history of people, their lives, deaths, successes, failures, destructive ways, and creative abilities. I knew or cared little about the world outside of Lincoln.

I had one girlfriend who went to Alabama with the Freedom Riders in May 1961 just before we graduated. She told me how frightened she was by the police who stopped the bus she was riding in and by the hatred other white people showed toward her. I thought it was brave of her to go but had no interest in joining her.

For a story to reach me it would have to be in a movie theater. I went to most of the new movies that opened in Lincoln. In 1961 they included Jackie Gleason and Paul Newman in *The Hustler*, Stanley Kramer's *Judgment at Nuremberg*, and *A Raisin in the Sun* with Sidney Poitier. I saw Audrey Hepburn in *Breakfast at Tiffany's*, *The Guns of Navarone* with Gregory Peck and David Niven, Marilyn Monroe and Montgomery Clift in *The Misfits*, and Vincent Price in *The Pit and the Pendulum*.

I read what my mother recommended to me. Usually it was a Book of the Month Club selection, her source for books, or something she saw in *Reader's Digest*. In 1961 the only book I read that came out that year was Joseph Heller's *Catch-22*. Beyond that I had no contact with the world of culture. I knew a guy who became a painter, but in 1961 he was too strange for my company. I could not have told a Picasso from a Miró and did not know who Stella, Twombly, de Kooning, Johns, or Warhol were.

My pharmacy courses were mostly in the sciences—chemistry,

math, physics, and pharmacology. I especially loved chemistry and its magical color changes, energy releases, and precipitations of newly created substances. In the dark labs smelling of strong acids and bases I learned to test for nitrates, sulfates, and phosphates and to tell which metals were present in various liquid and solid substances. I learned to measure precisely and to record the results meticulously in spiral notebooks that quickly gathered the stains of the laboratory reagents and dyes.

My only liberal arts courses were in elementary philosophy and elementary literature. I barely understood the difference between deductive and inductive logic. I was confused by the arguments, and did not know if I was a fatalist who believed in predestination or a determinist who believed I was the master of my own fate. In English I could not make sense of metaphors or muster excitement for the stories we were assigned to read. The only nonscientific course I remember well is economics, only because the lectures were broadcast from two television sets mounted from the ceiling in the front of a large room; they reliably put me to sleep.

In order to belong I joined a fraternity, Phi Gamma Delta, and lived by its written and unwritten rules. Some of my friends did not because they would not bend to the conformity that dominated every fraternity house. Those who did not fit in for physical, psychological, religious, or racial reasons—and a man could be blackballed for any of these—did not get in. I accepted the exclusionary conditions without hesitation; I was in and that was what counted most. The fraternity did give me a chance to lead. I was elected president of the house. Buoyed by this success, I ran for president of the student council and lost. I ran for vice president and won. In the spring of my junior year I was one of twelve men chosen to be members of the senior honors society.

The experience on the student council was blemished by a decision I made to take over a project organized by a graduating friend. The project was a student discount card that entitled students to lower prices from merchants who were eager enough for the business to pay to have their names on the cards. The cost of the cards was a few hundred dollars less than the revenue from the merchants. I got approval of the project from the council without disclosing that I was earning money, which I presumed, was obvious. The presumption led to a call for an investigation, which concluded I had done nothing wrong. But my integrity had been called into question because I had not been careful about the appearance of a conflict.

I decided not to approach the council with a problem created by the only failing grade I earned in college in a semester course in the Air Force Reserve Officers' Training Corps. The instructor judged me to be incorrigible and undisciplined during close-order drill and inspections. Because the university required all men to complete four semesters of ROTC in order to graduate, I needed to either get the rule changed or alter my behavior. I chose the first option, and led a grassroots campaign to persuade the university chancellor to change the policy. In my fourth year the university made the courses optional.

Before I could qualify for a pharmacist's license, I had to work for a year as an intern under the supervision of a licensed pharmacist. One of my best friends in the fraternity lived in Rushville, a town of twelve hundred in the heart of Nebraska's Sandhills, three hundred miles north and west of Lincoln. His father was publisher of a weekly newspaper. They knew the local pharmacist, who was looking for a low-cost employee. I took the job and lived with my friend's family.

Rushville is a dusty town, and if you approach from the east or west on U.S. Highway 20 when the grass is high and green it looks like a raft at sea. Driving northwest on a steady wind, you can be tricked into seeing the hills move like rolling waves. Looking north of Rushville a ridge of pine trees marks the beginning of a large Lakota Sioux reservation across the Niobrara River and the border into South Dakota. In all other directions hills of grass roll as far as the eye can see. At night when the sky is clear and the stars are bright, you can drive a car along the back roads without headlights.

And if you lie on the ground and stare up at those stars, everything suddenly seems possible as if you are possessed by magic.

The writer Mari Sandoz grew up near Rushville. She wrote *Old Jules*, the story of her Swiss immigrant father, and *Cheyenne Autumn*, the story of Red Cloud, the last Sioux rebellion, and pursuit by the U.S. Army. I read both that summer and had my view of the west transformed.

Sandoz describes the two great conflicts of the west. The first was the conflict between the settlers and the natives, whose attitudes toward the land were incompatible. The settler needed title to his property. The Native Americans were still hunter-gatherers and could not survive in a world where land was subdivided and sold to private owners. The second conflict was between the rancher who wanted grazing land and the farmer who brought the plow to break and turn the sod. Disease and force resolved the first conflict with the Native Americans in favor of the settler. Though there was violence between the rancher and farmer, it was drought that gave victory to the rancher.

The settlers who survived this country were not timid souls. They risked their lives in the pursuit of their dreams, and they never knew what lay ahead of them. Some knowledge guided their choices, but it was mostly the instinct for living free and unencumbered that drove them. Of course a prairie blizzard can change a snug little sod house into a frozen cell and make a person—often a young wife left alone while her husband made a long trip to the closest town—so lonely and dejected that death was preferable to life.

So I learned early that romantic dreams of the west are best left in the movie house. *Old Jules* typified the extremes of the western personality in a single man who was brave and determined with an explorer's spirit. And that same man hated the idea of his daughter becoming a writer. He called writers "the maggots of society" in part because he regarded any activity that did not produce something practical to be a drain on the energies of those who did the real work.

On my first weekend in Rushville I went to a fundraiser at the American Legion Club sponsored by the Catholic Church. The party featured gambling, whiskey, and Rocky Mountain oysters, a delicacy made of thinly sliced beef or sheep testicles. That evening I met two sisters from Hay Springs, a town ten miles west on Highway 20. One was my age and the other two years younger. My second weekend they invited me to go swimming at Smith Lake. We stayed at the lake until the sun set and the stars came out. My imagination had not prepared me for this moment. Suddenly the world had become a much larger and more exciting place.

The world of voting in real elections was opened to me during college. In 1964 I reached twenty-one and cast my first vote in that year's election. My host family in Rushville heavily influenced the choices of political party and candidate. The father believed in limited government, which meant he usually lined up with Republican views rather than Democratic. I heard those views every Thursday night after he had finished printing and distributing his weekly paper.

On Thursdays he came home stained with ink and lead type. He engaged us in a lively discussion of history and politics. He was well read, strongly opinionated, and understood the lessons of history better than any person I had heard until then. He preferred freedom to government interference, advocated risk instead of guarantees of security, and preached the gospel of solving your own problems rather than complaining that life had treated you unfairly.

When I returned to classes in September 1963 I felt more aware of the importance of national politics thanks to these Thursday night discussions. But nothing that year affected me more than November 22, 1963, when Lee Harvey Oswald assassinated President John Kennedy. I was in the university library when I heard the news and quickly walked down R Street to my fraternity house to watch television. I stood in the card room of our house with other men who could not believe what they were seeing. I had not known such events were possible. They happened only in history books. Now the violence described in these books was visiting our lives.

Heavily influenced by my Rushville experience, I registered as a Republican. In November 1964 I cast my vote for Barry Goldwater, the man who was described as too extreme and bloodthirsty to be trusted with the nuclear button. My first vote was for a losing cause. Johnson's landslide victory included a Democratic win in Nebraska, a nearly unheard-of event. I was told that if I voted for Barry Goldwater America would get deeper into the Vietnam War. Well, that is exactly what happened.

In the summer of 1964 as the presidential campaign was heading into its convention stage, I was taking a course in physics at Creighton University in Omaha. I had rented an apartment and found part-time work. President Johnson did not appear to be in any real trouble, but he was still concerned that Goldwater was scoring political points by accusing him of being weak on communist aggression against South Vietnam. The president was looking for a chance to display his toughness. In the first week of August, two American destroyers were attacked in North Vietnam's Gulf of Tonkin, giving Johnson what he needed. He went to Congress and requested enactment of a resolution authorizing him to use whatever force was needed to respond to this aggression. On August 7, as my family was celebrating my mother's fiftieth birthday, both houses of Congress passed the authorization. With the passage of this resolution, life as I knew it was over. I did not know it at the time but within a year I would.

Black Elk, a famous Lakota Sioux medicine man, told the poet John Neihardt, "It is in the darkness of their eyes that men get lost." This darkness is a blind spot that prevents us from seeing that which we need to know most of all. The darkness makes it more difficult for us to tell right from wrong. We sleepwalk and respond to commands we do not challenge. We are guided by blind habit. When I left college in the spring of 1965 I was very much the sleepwalker. Looking back, the darkness in my eyes covered a very large territory.

Excerpt from *Being Home*

RUTH RAYMOND THONE

In those days, most of the magic and mystery of the
Capital City centered on the bell tower and shadowed
courtyards of Plymouth Congregational Church—First
Plymouth, one learned to call it later.

It might have been magic only to a high school girl
from Scottsbluff, ingenuous in that she thought herself
sophisticated, as cheerleaders are wont to do.

The mystery might have come from the moonlit
night and the heady adolescent thrill of having a date
with an older boy from the big city.

This later awareness notwithstanding, Lincoln during the state basketball tournament, at least some thirty
years ago, was as exciting a place as a small-town teenager's heart was likely to know.

There was only the boys' tournament in those days,
and all classes played their games in the old Coliseum,
followed then as now by hundreds of cheering, crying,
devoted, loving fathers and mothers and little brothers
and sisters and coaches and principals, and teachers and
girl friends and proud neighbors and friends.

The Scottsbluff Bearcats usually made it to the state

tournament, since they had a tradition of good basketball teams and were the biggest frog in the pond in western Nebraska, representing the partially disenfranchised counties of the Panhandle along with teams from smaller schools.

No doubt about it, we were the aliens, the ones that were different in Lincoln at tournament time. They all lived closer together in the heavier-populated hills of eastern Nebraska, in the first place. We drove the longest distance to come to the tournament, much farther than to go to Cheyenne, Wyoming, to a dance or to Laramie on senior sneak day, or to Denver to shop at the old Denver Dry Goods store.

We were awfully proud of our western heritage. In fact, we might have had just a tinge of self-righteousness about how plain and pure and clean our flat ranchlands made us.

The mothers drove us to Lincoln and chaperoned us every step of the way, especially after we got to town. One time, after an overnight stop at a motel on old U.S. 30, we were chagrined that the head mother figured out we'd been smoking cigarettes in our room. Nice girls did not smoke cigarettes in their rooms. Nice girls did not smoke cigarettes, nor drink alcohol. The boys did, but certainly not while in training for big athletic victories. High school sports was a real cause for them and they had their coaches. We cheered for them and tiptoed our own way through growing up.

We were never set loose in the city. We must have been herded back and forth between the old Cornhusker Hotel and the Coliseum—or timidly herded ourselves. (The "old" becomes a standard prefix in one's vocabulary at a certain point in life.) We might have been frightened at venturing too far into the city, even if the mothers' strict rules had permitted that.

The evening idyll at First Plymouth with a Lincoln High romeo must have been the farthest away this (old) cheerleader could stray, since its ambience has stayed clearly etched in my memory all these years.

Yet the Coliseum and the Cornhusker were riches aplenty for

us—with an added stop in between at Hovland's or Miller's, envying our friends whose parents had charge accounts there and let their children use them.

The old Cornhusker helped chaperone us, too. The lady at the desk certified that you were registered and then Al Lew, towering manager, escorted groups upstairs to their proper places. Heaven forbid that one of the mothers should catch you in the wrong room, or that anything beyond the wildly daring situations of boys and girls chatting in a bedroom with the door propped open would even occur to us.

Too bad for those fine young men who played their hearts out in local and district basketball tourneys. We loved them, but what we really wanted was a trip to Lincoln. We would live until school was out on the memories. But perhaps they could, too, those memories of the supercharged atmosphere inside the Coliseum, as many as four games played at once, each surrounded by its own intensely devoted yelling, screaming fans.

There's a new Cornhusker rising in Lincoln's skies these days, the old Coliseum has been replaced by the Bob Devany Sports Center and Pershing Auditorium, and television and Sputnik and interstates and computers have changed us enormously and forever.

Yet this middle-aged heart hopes there still glows in the hearts of outstate high schoolers the dream and promise and joy of getting to go to Lincoln for the state basketball tournament.

Excerpt from "Children of Hope, Children of Tears"

MARY PIPHER

Home is where you hang your childhood.

—WRIGHT MORRIS

In southwestern Minnesota, there is a quarry for pipestone, the rock used by all the Plains Indians to make
peace pipes and many other sacred objects. It is a soft,
carveable rock that glows red at sunset. Pipestone quarry was a sacred site where all the tribes came together
in peace. While they were there, a truce existed; all the
tribes mined side by side, then parted to fight on other
ground.

Pipestone is a good metaphor for schools. Schools are
the sacred ground for refugees, and education is their
shared religion. At school, the Croats and Serbs study
together, as do the Iranians and Iraqis and the southern
and northern Sudanese. Outside school, groups may
feud, but inside school, they will be respectful so that
they can all quarry the American educational system.

Before their first day of school, many children from
traditional cultures have never been away from their

mothers for even an hour. At school, they may feel far from home. Everything may be different—the language, customs, the colors of the people, the clothes, the foods, and even the play. Developmental levels of children are not uniform either. Five-year-olds from one culture have very different skills, relationships to family, and comfort levels with strangers than do five-year-olds from another culture.

Schools are often where kids experience their first racism and learn about the socioeconomic split in our country. There is the America of children with violin lessons, hockey tickets, skiing trips, and zoo passes, and there is the America of children in small apartments whose parents work double shifts.

English as Learned Language classes are taught by teachers who are responsible for everything from cultural orientation to teaching English and basic academic skills. The students are grouped according to their ability to speak English, and kids from as many as twenty different language groups may be in one class.

School may be overwhelming at first, but it is school that will enable children to make it in America. School offers students the freedom to develop and to dream big American dreams. In spite of their disadvantages, refugees have lower drop-out rates and better grades than native-born kids.

A determining factor in kids' success is the quality of their family lives. Well-loved, well-nurtured kids from all over the world have a tremendous advantage. Mothers and fathers who carefully select the best from both the new and old cultures have the best-adjusted children. Parental involvement in education varies. In general, refugee parents have high expectations, but limited contact with the schools. They feel that education is the job of the teachers. Parents may want to be involved, but may not understand how to be involved. Also, work schedules, transportation, and language problems make contact with schools difficult.

Schools are therapeutic environments. Half the world's refugees are children and adolescents, many of whom arrive in the United States malnourished and with health problems. Many students have lost siblings, parents, or other family members. Teachers may not deal with trauma directly, but they are part of the healing process. They give their students order and predictability. After the chaos and confusion of their lives, nothing is more comforting than routines. Kids like the same things to happen at the same time with the same people. Students need to receive the message that school is a safe place. Order, ritual, and predictability are part of this reassurance.

Relationships with kind, consistent adults are deeply healing. Good teachers, to quote Nellie Morton, "hear people to speech." They give children lap time, pats, and nonverbal reassurance that they are going to be okay. Physical affection and smiles can occur in the absence of a common language. A hug has a universal meaning.

Teachers connect the dots between the world of family and of school, the old culture and America, the past and the future. They help children understand how their worlds fit together and they teach empathy and good manners. Children become moral beings, not through lectures, but through countless daily encounters with moral people. They learn how to be good through stories about honesty, kindness, responsibility, and courage. Moral behavior is essentially a set of good habits. Good teachers help children form those good habits.

The class story that follows is about ELL students and their teacher, who is a cheerleader, an instiller of hope, a cultural broker, a therapist, and an occasional comedian. I worked in elementary schools and summer ELL camps. Over the course of my research, I met hundreds of children, all of whom had interesting stories. However, for the purposes of this book, I will limit my discussion to one classroom at one school, which I'll call Sycamore Elementary School.

The class actually had twenty-five kids, too many for one teacher. Grace was an excellent teacher, but there wasn't enough of her to go around. Many kids who were eager to work couldn't get the help they needed. For this story I chose to describe only ten of the kids. I picked both kids whose parents were doing a good job making choices in America and kids whose parents were choosing all the wrong things. And I picked kids who varied in resilience and overall adjustment to America.

SYCAMORE SCHOOL

The number one thing is to care for children.

Class Roster:

| Abdul | Ignazio | Ly | Trinh | Deena |
| Pavel | Khoa | Mai | Walat | Fatima |

September 6, 1999

Sycamore Elementary School is a three-story redbrick building just off a busy street that is lined with a McDonald's, Arab and Mexican markets, liquor stores, pawnshops, and a Vietnamese karaoke bar. The houses around the school are small, close together, and dilapidated. Police cars cruise the area. Unemployed men stand on the corners and in the alleys. The school was built for the children of Czechs and Germans, but it now welcomes students of all colors and ethnic groups.

Walking in the first day, I admired a sycamore tree with its sheltering white branches and big greeny-gold leaves. There is something about the shape of a sycamore that reminds me of embracing arms. On the playground, a Latino boy scored in a vigorous soccer game and his team shouted and high-fived each other. Soccer is the universal solvent in Lincoln—Vietnamese, Mexican, Haitian, Romanian, and Serbian kids all like soccer.

Inside the school a boy who looked like a biker's kid, wearing black jeans and a black T-shirt, watched a girl with dreadlocks twirl in circles, singing to herself. A teacher listened to an Arabic-speaking mother in a hijab. The mother was surrounded by her four wide-eyed kids, the youngest of whom clung to her skirt. The teacher imitated talking on a phone, then she wrote down a phone number and handed it to the mother.

I walked past a sign that said YOU HAVE ONLY ONE CHANCE TO HAVE A CHILDHOOD. I examined pictures of houses from all over the world—a Thai houseboat, Panamanian hutches, a Somali camp—and a display of macaroni-and-cereal necklaces, some of which had been nibbled on.

I signed in at the front office and a third grader named Judy Running Wolf escorted me to a portable classroom, a trailer outside the main building beside the clothing and food distribution center. My new class was a ragtag group, dressed in Salvation Army clothes, with an amazing array of bad haircuts. Most of them looked between eight and eleven, although some might have been small twelve-year-olds.

They were holding Village Inn menus and practicing how to order. The kids giggled and pointed at the glossy pictures of cheeseburgers and blueberry pie. In a dozen languages they discussed the pictures as if they were rare objets d'art. These kids came from many religious traditions and had food taboos and preferences. Some kids don't eat lettuce. Others didn't like milk. But today several ordered pretend hamburgers and boasted they had eaten before at McDonald's. Others ordered the most expensive dishes on the menu and bragged about how much it cost.

Their teacher watched them converse. Grace was a pretty woman in her late thirties. She didn't miss much and nothing rattled her. She spoke softly, laughed easily, and kept the room reasonably calm without making threats. As the kids ordered pretend meals, she told me a little about each of them.

Grace's biggest worry was Abdul, a beautiful kid with nut-colored skin and deep dimples. He was an Iraqi boy who had watched his younger brother freeze to death in the snow when his family walked barefoot across mountains into Turkey. Possibly he was brain damaged from gas attacks during the Gulf War. Abdul rarely did his work and he didn't seem to connect with anyone. Other teachers thought he should be in special education classes, but Grace wanted to give him a chance to adjust. She said many of the ELL kids look like special education kids at first, but then they adapted.

Pavel sat beside Abdul. He was a big awkward kid from the Former Soviet Union (FSU) with tangled blond hair and his shirt half tucked in. Grace said he was much indulged by his parents. Pavel was good-natured, but restless and lazy. He preferred playing with Nibbles the rat to doing his studies.

Ignazio was a good-hearted Mexican boy whose parents worked long hours at a sugar beet refinery. Nobody at home seemed able to help him with his studies. He was lovable and well behaved, but not very focused. Grace worried that Ignazio might be picked on because he was chubby and innocent.

Khoa was skinny and wore tight polyester pants that didn't reach his ankles. He wore a torn Star Wars T-shirt and his shiny hair badly needed a wash and a cut. He was clowning and hamming it up, making everyone laugh at his outrageous order of four hamburgers and three malts. Grace said his family had experienced great trauma getting to this country from Vietnam. In Lincoln, he lived in a rough neighborhood and his older brother had been in trouble with the law. Khoa was a fan of violent video games and twice Grace had confiscated nunchakus from him. Still, she felt he was essentially a good person.

Beside Khoa sat three Vietnamese girls. Grace said, "I put them beside Khoa because he can make them laugh."

Ly was a Vietnamese girl from a big hardworking family. Her parents were strict and Ly had extremely good manners. Her schoolwork was consistently A-plus.

Mai was a small angry-looking girl on the edge of the group. She had lost her mother when she was three, just before she and her father came to America. Her father had remarried and Mai lived with her father, stepmother, and new baby brother. Mai was troubled and had few ways to deal with her troubles. She scratched her arms or pulled her hair when she was upset.

Beside Mai, Trinh stared at her glossy menu. Grace said, "Trinh will not answer questions. I haven't heard her speak yet." Her parents had drowned crossing from Vietnam into Thailand. She lived with her grandparents, who had told Grace that Trinh spoke occasionally at home.

Walat was a handsome, self-contained, and competent boy from Iraq. His family was part of the close community of Kurds. His dad had been an engineer in Kurdistan and, even without credentials, he had found related work in America. Walat's mother was able to stay at home, study English, and help the kids with their homework.

As Grace told me about Deena's life, the small blond-haired girl ordered an imaginary ice cream sundae. She had seen her grandparents and uncles killed in Bosnia, then she and her parents had been herded into an internment camp. Her mother was depressed and her father was incapacitated by stress. Solid, energetic, and intelligent, Deena spoke the best English in her family and was often kept out of school to translate.

Next to Deena, Fatima held up her menu and, like Deena, she ordered a pretend ice cream sundae. Fatima was a Kurdish girl who'd been burned on her face and arms when Iraqis bombed her village. Grace told me that her scars had caused her some trouble at school. Some ELL kids came from cultures where deformed people are shunned. These kids did not want to hold her hand. "In America," Grace had explained, "We treat all people with respect." Fatima's father could not work, and her mother supported the family of five by working at a food-processing factory. Grace said, "Fatima can wear me out asking for validation."

Grace tapped on her desk and the kids stopped ordering food and looked up. She introduced me as "Miss Mary" and the kids stared at me with interest. Ly smiled. Khoa loudly declared that I looked old, very old. He kept saying this and finally I said to him, "Yes, I could be your grandmother." After that, he stopped.

Grace picked the name of a helper out of a hat. Today it was Fatima, whose job it would be to feed Nibbles and distribute supplies. Grace had the class look at a calendar and take turns saying, "It's Tuesday, September 6, 1999." She asked what kind of weather it was. "Clear," shouted Khoa, and Grace smacked a yellow plastic sun on the calendar board.

As Fatima, Deena, and Ly worked at their spelling, Khoa talked about poop and eating boogers. He looked like he needed every-thing—a bath, a good meal, a full night's sleep, and lap time with a patient adult. He watched me as closely as I watched him, and he winked whenever our eyes met.

Pavel twisted in his seat as if he were being tortured, broke his pencil, and wrinkled and smeared his papers. But like Khoa, he somehow managed to be disruptive and sociable at the same time. Together they gave the class a certain energy that wasn't all bad.

Grace went over the spelling words: "father," "mother," and "uncle." Then she began a discussion of what people needed to do at home. She wrote down phrases on the board such as "sew clothes," "mow yard," "cook food," "change baby's diapers." When she said this, Khoa shouted out, "Change the diapers or the baby will get stinky butt." He laughed uproariously at his own joke. Grace cleared her throat and asked what else should families do at home.

Ignazio shouted, "Buy food." Deena said, "The number one thing is to care for the children." Ignazio elaborated, "Without food you might die." Fatima said, "Buy clothes. Without clothes you can't go outside." Mai said, "Take care of the baby."

Grace asked what chores were not so important to do. Pavel shouted out, "It's not important to pay the bills." Grace said gently, "In America that is pretty important."

Grace asked the class to write a story about a family who forgets to do some jobs. I pulled my little chair up by Abdul. He bristled and turned away as if he were allergic to me. However, for the first time that day, he did some work. He hunched way from me, work-ing on his assignment so that I wouldn't stay with him. Grimly, I reflected that I was helping him, but it wasn't much fun. When he finished, I checked his work. Then I turned to Pavel who had been waiting impatiently for help. He was a big teddy bear of a kid. He wrote, "Good dads take their sons fishing."

I asked him if he liked to fish and his eyes brightened. Stupidly, I said maybe the class could go fishing sometime. Pavel was riveted by the suggestion. He asked, "Tomorrow? Where? How would we get there? Could I bring my own pole?"

I realized what I had done and tried to put the rabbit back in the hat, but, of course I failed. Other kids also got excited. We never finished the spelling words.

It was time to go. Fatima picked up papers and pencils. I helped Ignazio with the broken zipper on his coat. Ly flashed me a smile and said, "I'll see you next Monday, Miss Mary." Trinh and Deena slipped out, but Fatima waved shyly at me. I gave Abdul a hug, but he shrugged it off. Pavel had one last fishing question and I smiled sheepishly at Grace, remarking, "I've created a monster." As Khoa dashed out the door with his shoelaces untied, he asked me, "Will you come back tomorrow?"

As I watched Mai walk across the yard into the main school building, I thought about her complex situation. I wanted to help her with her feelings about her baby brother, her stepmother, and even about her mother's death. She was raised in a culture that teaches the suppression of negative emotions. It was unlikely she knew what to do with her troubled feelings.

Her scratches were a call for help. I recommended that Grace do all she could to feature Mai in class, to give her some power and visibility. I suggested a Big Sister from the YWCA so that she could have one person who cared just for her.

These children had many complicated needs, including the need to heal from great sadness. Some dealt with the sadness by withdrawing, others by clinging. Trinh, Deena, Mai, and Abdul needed therapists, but they all came from places where mental problems were unacceptable. Many students came from cultures where creative expression in children isn't valued. Yet they had great needs to understand and share their experiences. Group storytelling would be great, and art and music therapy might work because children don't need verbal skills for them. Play and laughter are therapeutic. I had never been around kids who loved to laugh as much as ELL kids.

The ELL kids needed help with self-definition. I wanted to put their birthdays on the calendar and take their pictures. I wanted to identify what each child did best. Question games might help. What was their favorite food? What games did they like? What was the scariest thing they ever did? The bravest thing? What was their earliest memory?

With ELL classes, I really understood the value of classrooms small enough that each child could be given individual attention. The kids were at very different developmental and acculturation levels. Some kids were precocious from war experiences but had missed kid experiences. Some children cared for younger siblings, cleaned and cooked, or even did factory piecework at home. A few had no play in their lives.

There were differences in intelligence, motivation to learn, energy, confidence, and likeability. There were differences in the amount of trauma the kids had experienced and in the amount of family and community support they received in America. They all had much in common—they were strangers in a strange land, eager to be accepted. They liked games, music, puppets, and cookies. And they had a thousand needs. Compared to American kids, they tended to be better behaved, more respectful of adults, and less spoiled. Grace said the longer they were in America the more likely they were to act up.

It helped me to remember that these kids had simple needs as well as complicated ones, needs to be hugged, helped with spelling words, smiled at, and read to. Even small acts of kindness made a difference.

I had been in class three hours and was ready for a nap. How do teachers do this five days a week, eight hours a day?

Immigration, Technology, and Sense of Place

EAMONN WALL

Those days when I wasn't working I enjoyed going 'round the corner to Chris and Louis Discount (they were immigrants from Greece), buying a newspaper, a cup of coffee ("Best coffee in New York," Louis said), and some sweets for the kids and then heading up Broadway, pushing the stroller in the direction of Inwood Park. I was Louis's sometime secretary: If he was having difficulty communicating with the *Times*, the *News*, or the *Post*, he'd ask me to phone on his behalf. He thought that I spoke the same kind of English the people in the billing sections of the city's newspapers did. I shouted at the people on the other end of the line to get their respect. Shouting became my standard telephone technique; it was the only method that worked for me in New York.

Louis's hands were black from handling the papers and I remember him bent over the sports pages of the Greek newspaper reading the reports of soccer games from Europe. We shared a common language—Gullit, Shearer, Platini, Barcelona, Maradona —which brought us close, separating me from the Americans —or Yankees, as he called them with a smile—who came into his shop. This is why some mornings Louis would place a stack of bills on the counter, hand me the phone, and say the coffee's free today. Of course, the Dominicans spoke this language too, but they had their own newspaper shops, their own loyalties. It was to their bodegas I went in the evenings for bottles of beer and quarts of milk. There men stood talking in groups and parted to let me through. The Dominicans knew, too, that Jack Charlton managed the Irish soccer team.

One morning, in typical New York fashion, the shop was closed, Louis was gone, and the rumor went around that he was working in a restaurant in Connecticut. So I transferred my business, for what it was worth, to a shop on Broadway owned by a man from Galicia in Spain—"We are both Celts," he said to me when he got to know me better. Later, when I told him I was leaving New York to live in Nebraska he shook his head and moaned, "You are leaving New York to live in America. God help you!!" I still can see Pedro leaning across the counter to make a point; he is always smiling.

I often think of Louis in Connecticut working in a diner, if they have diners in Connecticut. He must be the counterman pouring coffee, yelling orders taken over the phone at the chef, smiling as he hands you back your change. Maybe he's telling the customers that he's happy to be out of the crazy city, or maybe he remembers New York fondly. I know he misses Greece and is saving money to go home: the old story. I think too of the immigrant businesses which define New York for me—newspaper shops and kiosks underground, bakeries, diners, delis, and fruit vendors. I think too that each moment in the city men and women are reading, or looking forward to reading, newspapers which tell the news of their homelands, and I see myself leaning over their shoulders, sharing in their excitement and anticipation, like a child who, unable to read, studies the pictures carefully and invents the narrative.

Up Broadway we went—past the shops and the old Dyckman House. At 207th Street (to the right) stood the Tara Gift Shop where each Monday night a crowd of Irish people waited to buy

Irish newspapers hot off the plane. Piles of local papers, just like at Eason's bookshop in Dublin, and Irish hands and Irish eyes eager for the news of home. After a couple of years, I gave up buying these papers: It was unsettling to get this news so fast, to seem to be living in Ireland, but to be so distant from it. The *Echo* and the *Voice*, both published in New York, provide the sports results, my dad the local news, and that's all I need. Which coalition is in power or what Fianna Fáil is up to doesn't bother me; I don't care about that stuff.

Now, ironically, a few years on, living in Nebraska and far away from an Irish center of influence in America, it's become even easier for me to get the news from Ireland. And it's free. Each morning at work, I turn on my computer and read the *Irish Times*. Everything is there at my fingertips. I can even convince my superiors that this reading is related to my writing and research. It is quite a measure of success for me as an employee to be able to tell my employer that spending the first half-hour of company time reading a newspaper is vital to my work. Even more of a triumph is to know that my superiors will believe me, encourage me, and suggest that soon I'll need to be provided with a better machine so that the graphics will come up clearer and the text will appear with greater speed. I know I have made it in America! The first section I read is the sports; then I work my way backward through the other sections. This is the way I have always read newspapers, my tao of reading. It seemed so natural to me as a child that the first page of the *Irish Times* contained the national and international news and the second the daily racing runners and riders. How could it ever be possible to justify another set of priorities?

Yet despite the convenience and addictiveness of the Internet, a part of me regrets its power, presence, and intrusiveness. Certainly it is exciting to get Irish news so easily, to have at least a sense that I know what is happening in Ireland. In the old days you had to be an embassy employee to get news that fast. It fascinated me as a student in Dublin to look at the antennas on top of Iveagh House and to think of all the secret communiqués which the Department of Foreign Affairs were sending out to their ambassadors and consuls throughout the world. With hindsight I suspect that the diplomatic staff awaited the same news I hungered for—scores from championship matches and county finals.

But the immigrant needs also to be able to forget, to be able to walk away down some distant road, to look ahead and see bright neon signs and people on benches in the sun who are curious about him or her. Turning to look behind, the immigrant should find revealed a clear, open sky. Of course, we cannot forget. I will always walk from my parents' house to school: each morning noting the presence of the train, the presence of the river, the time on the clock above Kerr's shop, these minutes before nine o'clock when the life of the town seemed mute and suspended. The Internet provides us with information, but it doesn't allow us the illusion of forgetting and fails to nourish us. We are reminded that we are not over there, which makes adjustment to America more difficult. To survive, we need to be able to begin the process of forgetting. Paradoxically, being Irish, our deepest desire is to remember and recreate everything.

On those weekday mornings the streets were alive and sparkling, and I felt very strongly the romance of living in New York. When we sat on a bench outside the Dyckman House I'd watch what my kids were watching, knowing what they were learning was not what I had learned on the Square or on the prom in Enniscorthy in the 1960s. Because it was so different, it seemed richer. And just as the street sweeper (the cleaner, not the gun) transfixed my children so too I was transfixed by their intense watching. And we observed the man on the next bench who fed corn to the squirrels, who called them out from the trees by the names he'd christened them—Jenny, Terry, and Sara. The buses and gypsy cabs paraded up and down Broadway all day long, and I was a child again among children, feeling intensely privileged, beginning (I was thinking) to finally understand America. Occasionally, theater stopped the world:

a fire department truck and hook-and-ladder convoy was called out to a false alarm on 215th Street.

When we got to the playground, the children ran to the equipment and sandbox while I sat down to drink my coffee and read my paper. It was great not to have to work every weekday. At that time I was working part-time in the Bronx at Hostos Community College on 149th and Grand Concourse where it seemed every student was from another country. One day I asked the students what the Gettysburg Address was all about, but they had never heard of it, and this made me feel right at home since there have been so many ordinary things about America which I have had to learn too. One day not long after I arrived, a woman I was chatting up asked me if I liked Pop Tarts, and she couldn't understand why I hadn't heard of them and thought I was some sort of freak. I'm not a freak; I'm an alien. My wife has taken on the job of explaining America to me, of cutting through this confusion. It was she who put together my packet for immigration after I had failed at the task myself and was pushed away from the grill in Federal Plaza. At night, before falling asleep beside her, the blinds closed, the air conditioner humming dreamily, I feel so firmly rooted here.

The teaching work was okay because it brought me into new neighborhoods and introduced me to new people. Some mornings on the way to the Bronx, while waiting for the bus at 145th and Broadway in Harlem, I'd hear (when I closed my eyes) the jazz of older times, the voice of Billie Holiday, and smell the sweet aroma of perfume from an elegant lady stepping from a huge, late-model Eldorado. Then, to match my mood, I'd recite to myself some lines by Langston Hughes:

> Have you dug the spill
> Of Sugar Hill?
> Cast your gims
> On this sepia thrill:
> Brown sugar lassie,

Caramel treat,
Honey-gold baby
Sweet enough to eat.
Peach-skinned girlie,
Coffee and cream,
Chocolate darling
Out of a dream.

"HARLEM SWEETIES"

Between 7 and 7:30 a.m. the streets were quiet. I waited with a bunch of kids in uniforms headed for Cardinal Hayes High School across the river, and we all got into the bus via the rear door. One day I remember our bus passing Mitch "Blood" Green, who'd fought Mike Tyson in the ring and on the street, and the kids waved and hollered at him. Another day, an old hand in the department I worked in answered my comment that the boss seemed a decent sort of guy with the comment that "he should be institutionalized." A year later, I sat in the office of the English department awaiting news of my teaching load and responsibilities for the semester, with my contract in my bag. It seemed I sat for hours until I was told there was no work. This is how my career in the Bronx ended.

While the children made friends with one another, I made friends with the mothers and fathers. Every stereotype and cliché that I'd ever heard about the city and its people was exploded by these encounters in the playground. New Yorkers, I discovered, are a gentle, friendly, and communal people, despite all the negative hype. Because we lived so intensely and close to each other in such a crowded city, we were forced by circumstances to get on with each other, to be neighborly, to be friendly, to talk to each other on the stairways of our apartment buildings, to sit together on the benches in the park watching our children play. One day a bookish-looking mother sat beside me and produced a sheet of paper from her tote bag and placed it in my hands. "I've been reading

The Commitments," said she, "and don't know what these words mean, and since you're from Ireland. . . ." I looked at the sheet and laughed. It read "bollix" and "gobshite." Bollix I dispatched in my best Bakhtinian metaphor/metonomy fashion, but gobshite was more difficult. I told the lady that if you didn't recognize a gobshite when you saw one, you had a problem. I understood that just as there were things about America I would never understand, there were also things about Ireland I could never satisfactorily explain to someone who'd never lived that singular, Irish life.

When my son Matthew started school he went to P.S. 98: He was in a bilingual English/Spanish program. His teacher said he had a real flair for Spanish and one day asked me whether I spoke Spanish and helped him. I (proudly) declared to her: "Well, I've picked up a lot of Spanish since coming to Inwood. I listen to the super of my building speak Spanish, I listen to the men in the bodega and the diner. . . ." She stopped me dead in my tracks and said, pointing a finger at me, "Under no condition speak Spanish to your son," and she pulled him toward her to protect him from his Spanglish-speaking father. Or Spanglish with an Enniscorthy accent which would surely qualify as a new dialect. Once in the bodega on the corner I asked for razor blades and was given flypaper. And I was so proud of my Spanish!

One Sunday morning last summer I was standing on top of Vinegar Hill and looking down on my hometown: Enniscorthy, County Wexford. I noticed how compact the town was, how an American town with a similar population would need three or four times as much space, and it dawned on me why I had always felt so at ease in Inwood. Both Inwood and Enniscorthy are squeezed, compact, warm, and comfortable. To grow up in a small close-knit Irish country town is a good preparation for life in a New York neighborhood. In both you are part of your neighbors' lives: You smell their food, hear them making love. In Nebraska, where rugged individualism is favored over gentle communality, you are separated from your neighbors. Consequently, the day-by-day culture is often conducted in monosyllables or at a distance: We speak across fences or over the buzz of snow blowers.

When I arrived in Nebraska, one day I took my kids to Memorial Park at a time when I felt that other children would be playing there. But it was empty; there was no need to be out under a hot sun since houses have backyards and the streets are quiet enough for playing. Now there are no opportunities for me to sit down outdoors on neutral ground with neighbors and strangers, to enter into their lives, hear their stories, and learn some more about America. There are no fire hydrants turned on for kids to run through. And in the beginning, I sensed that people didn't want to talk to me, didn't need to know my story. However, because I didn't go away people have opened their arms, offered food in their houses, conversation, and friendship. Still, this is a more formal world which requires invitations for dinner, the checking of calendars, the cleaning up of houses, and the elaborate preparation of food. There's no middle ground of park or bar where parents and children can hang out and let their guards down, where the grownups can play like their kids. Although I can relax with friends, I still long for the casual informality of the chat on the street. Sitting on the benches in Inwood Park, listening to the voices of mothers and children, I was so aware of the swish of great trees of the park, of the screeching of brakes on the parkway and bridge, and of the insistent, welcoming songs of the Hudson and Harlem rivers. The nearest I have come to re-experiencing such communality has occurred after heavy snowfalls when we gather in the park, close to the war memorial, and lunge, screaming, downhill on sleds.

It's difficult to socialize with people my own age, as most are locked into fixed ideas of family and parenthood, both of which preclude having a few drinks in a bar on a regular basis or coffee in a diner. I believe my neighbors should get out more, to spend more time with young adults, to abandon their television sets and fixed ideas. I look out the front window of my house at the bright sidewalks on which no one walks and experience an intense loneliness. The prairie is lonely and vast, and far from the ocean. Yet, as Kathleen Norris has pointed out in *Dakota: A Spiritual Geography*, it too is wondrous and a gifted teacher. Slowly, I open to it, learn its language, and enter into its mysteries. My kids have settled in to roam the alleyways behind the houses and claim the comfort of their block, and nothing gives me more pleasure than to press my face against the window and watch them roll about each winter in the snow.

I live in the city, not a suburb, but I think that after living in New York most other American cities will seem suburban to me. Fifteen months after we left Inwood we returned for a day and neither of my kids recognized our old apartment building. If I hadn't been there to point it out, they'd have walked right past it. This devastated me because I felt I'd pulled them out of childhood violently, and I feared, or even knew, that they would never have that strong sense of place I so deeply profess, that they had begun this impossible process of forgetting much sooner than I had, and that moving from the source of early experience had damaged them.

The other day I was listening to a pizza advert on the radio and the speaker claimed that now you could get New York–style pizza here in the "Heartland" without having to put up with New York–style rudeness and attitudes, and I thought to myself that they could keep their pizza—just let me have one slice of that rudeness and attitude for old times' sake. When my kids get cheeky, I don't complain too much—I say to myself, "They can't help it, they're New Yorkers," and I sit back and enjoy the banter. But I like where I live now, like being able to get out into the country in a few minutes, though I feel very strongly that when I left Inwood, I left home. And it bothers me that shouting at people on the phone gets me no respect here; it has taken the fun out of being hassled. Sometimes I suspect that people have trouble distinguishing rudeness from style. But I know I have settled and am happy. When I am away from here, I look forward to returning, and I long for those Nebraskans from whom I have learned what it means to be generous.

Concerning Freaks, Book Clubs, and the Unbearable Distances of the Plains

RON BLOCK

Not so long ago I moved away from Nebraska. It wasn't the first time. I've left Nebraska for New York, Minnesota, Louisiana, Maine, Wisconsin, and even North Dakota, but something about the place keeps pulling me back, as though it isn't quite finished with me.

This time I'd been living in the western part of the state, where the Blocks have resided for over 120 years. If I could get you to follow me three miles north and seven miles east of the town of Gothenburg, where I was born, I would show you the prairie dog–riddled patch of sod where my great-great-grandfather Marten Block was buried in 1890. My ties, as they say, to the region are deep.

But even so, when I was offered a better job in the East, I loaded up my family into a rented truck and drove them fifteen hundred miles across country to New Jersey, a place where many educated people don't have a grasp of where Nebraska is. Some don't even know enough about the place to formulate a sensible question.

For example, not long after the move I was interviewing a job candidate at the college where I now teach. She was a smart woman, well traveled, multilingual—but when I began to talk about my recent cross-country trip over lunch, I was startled to hear her ask in all apparent earnestness, "So then tell me, what is the biggest difference between Nebraska and New Jersey?"

I looked at her. For a moment I hardly understood her question at all. It was as though someone had suddenly asked me to explain the difference between a Black Angus and a pit bull. I hardly knew where to begin. Many Nebraskans upon hearing a question like that would have burst out laughing. And yet her question seemed like a sincere one, so I wanted to give her a straight answer—but instead I said something that I hardly understood.

I said, "New Jersey is the most densely populated state in country. But no place is more crowded than a small town on the Plains."

As the candidate stared at me I suddenly realized that I had overstepped the bounds of interview decorum, pushing her rather aggressively into the heart of a paradox, and I didn't even have time then to explain my Zen-like answer, which faded into the distance the way many discussions of Nebraska do, the way Nebraska itself does.

But now as I think back on this, I actually think that I was saying something halfway true—because Nebraska actually is a very densely populated place, especially when you get away from Omaha and Lincoln. Ask anyone who lives in the western part of the state, where the population drops to under five people per square mile, and they might very well tell you that no place is more crowded than a little town where everyone knows everyone else.

This is the kind of town where I grew up: Gothenburg, Nebraska, where people get along because they really have no choice, and where memory is long and enemies can't be avoided.

People in a town like this don't have much aside from each other, and so old grudges are passed down like family heirlooms through the generations. Everyone knows everyone's business, so much so that the forced intimacy of a small town like this often feels like the tight air of an impending storm.

And yet this closeness is also a kind of paradox, because each time you drive down a road or go out into a field you see nothing but the vast, open distance of the landscape all around you. You might even start to feel the closeness of the small town and the distance of the land as being something inseparable: the distance presses in on the small town, packing the people there more closely together, and the people in a small town look out at the distance, filling it up with all the longings and misgivings that give the distance its *distance*.

Outsiders often look at the land and say nothing's there, as though the landscape is invisible to them. But to those who grew up in this distance or who pass through it with open eyes, this is a landscape as open to possibility as an empty page—except that like any empty page, it's not really empty at all. It's full of all those things that we experience by their absence, such as loss and regret, but most of all desire. Of course, many Nebraskans are not all that comfortable with a landscape of desire with its napes and mirages and shoulders and bluffs, and so we measure it and section it into manageable spaces contained by barbed wire. But even so, if you live in a landscape like this for a very long time, you might start to adapt to the distance. It fills up your mind. It alters your vision. And suddenly you don't look *across* the distance anymore; rather, you are looking *into* it, and there you are able to see, like Steven's snowman, the "nothing that is not there and the nothing that is."

No wonder that so many writers who come from Nebraska continue to write about the place long after they have left, which is strange because the rest of the country seems to have little interest in Nebraska at all. It's almost as if there is a riddle here that we can't let go until it's resolved—which may take a long time because it takes language fit for paradox to describe such a place, the way the distance separates us and joins us, pushing us together and pulling us apart. As we move across the distance, even if we try to move *away* from the distance, it seems to travel with us, receding before us, closing behind us.

Even for those writers who choose to stay put, the distance has a way of entering everything we do, the way dust does, working its way into the smallest crack. Its vacancy surrounds us. It presses in on a small town and makes the town feel even smaller. Out of isolation and estrangement, it forces a bloom of familiarity. It alters our vision, inviting us to be farseeing even if we blind ourselves to what is nearby. It alters our sense of scale. If we look into the distance, the miles seem like inches. In this sense the place seems to be a map of itself, and like any map it makes us feel two places at once. It concocts mirages that we can never quite reach, and so it distorts our sense of distance itself. But perhaps even more fearful for writers (or teachers or any other kind of *soothsayer*) is how the distance seems to affect our ability to be candid. The openness of the land might even tend to close us off and shut us up, making us cagier than we'd have to be in the tight streets of the anonymous city. But I don't think I really understood all this until I returned to the state to become a distance-learning teacher.

Let me explain. For the seven years prior to my most recent move from Nebraska I had been teaching a strange class, conducted on fiber-optic cable and two-way television, and sometimes by NebSat satellite. My students, who were in the Sandhills and other remote areas, could see me on a TV monitor, and I could see them, and we could speak to each other, but we never shared the same space. I was teaching them short stories, poetry, and how to write an essay. But since we call this kind of class "distance learning," I occasionally wondered if the true subject of the class was *distance* itself, and on bad days I wondered if that was the only thing I was teaching them.

This distance, of course, is a central quality of the place that I still call home. Cattle aside, there's little else there aside from the distance. For example, my students who were in Hyannis lived in a region where the population drops off to a single person per square mile, and when I asked them which square mile was theirs, they did not laugh. Sometimes they didn't know what to make of me. I was a stranger to their community, a televised face composed of pixels with no knowledge of what happens in their hallways, much less on their back roads, whose idea of their school was composed by the narrow view of a TV camera hanging from the ceiling in the front of a class. In their close world I was the outsider, and so I often wondered, How could I be their teacher when I wasn't a part of their community?

Compounding the estrangement was the fact that many of the stories and poems I assigned were "weird" to them, and they would tell me so, keeping their distance from their difficult lessons. And it's odd, but even though my students were some sixty to one hundred miles away, they often sat at the back of their respective classes. Even at this distance it seemed that there wasn't distance enough.

In some ways I might have even been a bit of a threat to the values of their community, a liberal emanation from a college classroom, an infiltrator bearing a foreign ideology, the very man that AM radio warned them about. That's a bit overstated I know, but many of my students were still in high school, taking my class for college credit, and more than once I saw the head of a principal popping into the frame of my monitor, as though in warning whenever I broached even the most mildly "controversial" topic. I was using a fairly standard literature anthology, where gay men actually spoke aloud in the warmest tones, and Eastern Europeans agonized and doubted God, and a few dead authors said *fuck* with impunity, while I seem to be governed by rules more stringent than the FCC's.

What's more, the arrangement of these monitors and cameras were such that people could watch me, and I would not know that they were there. Once a member of our Board of Governors complimented me on my teaching, and I thanked her, cautiously, knowing thereafter that she was watching me. Yet another time a teacher popped up in the monitor of a distant site and offered an impromptu lecture on Spanish surnames. I realized then that she had been watching me, too. The fact is that at any particular moment, in the strange environment of the distance-learning classroom, I didn't know who was monitoring me, and every word I said, every gesture I made was being recorded onto videotape. Knowing this, I will confess that I sometimes practiced self-censorship—not always out of cowardice, sometimes only to be polite, because I often didn't understand if I was a guest in their house or if they were a guest in mine. Whose house rules were we following? Just where *is* the picture on a two-way television monitor, especially one that's viewed several places at once?

Perhaps the oddest aspect of this environment is how it eventually began to feel completely normal to me. At first, I thought that I was merely growing accustomed to the technology of dislocation. But now I realize that as a writer, especially as a writer who comes from a small town, I have lived in an environment like this for many years—because what else is writing if it's not another distance learning technology?

There are, after all, great similarities between my experiences in the distance learning classroom and the experiences of writers, especially those who live in a Plains community. As writers, we might become confused about the degree to which we belong to these small towns. A sense of distance, maybe even from the lonely act of writing itself, creates distortions in our sense of community. We stand apart a little from the lives we are trying to describe, and so in time we might ask ourselves, What is our relationship to this distance? Should we bridge this distance, which might mean that in the cause of making ourselves acceptable and possibly connecting with our neighbors we practice self-censorship? Or should we tell secrets or speak candidly about the problems of our homeland, which might mean that we merely alienate our neighbors?

The rest of America tends to dismiss our homes in the Plains as not being worthy of consideration. They don't even know enough about us to ask the right questions. Given this, is our role as writers to celebrate these out of the way and remote places? On the other hand, the communities themselves tend to invent a mythology and a sentimental history. Is it our role, either when we write or teach, to set our neighbors straight by telling the truth—or what we think is the truth?

These questions became even more real to me when I discovered—just about the time I was beginning to navigate the freakish geography of distance learning—that New Rivers Press was going to publish a book of my short stories, a collection that in part involved themes that many people in my hometown would find deeply disturbing. Something happened to me then that I had not anticipated. I began to feel paranoid about how my home community would react to the book. In some ways I was prepared for these feelings because a number of years earlier I had read a wonderful book by Kathleen Norris called *Dakota: A Spiritual Geography*, and so I remembered how during a previous move from Nebraska, from the safe vantage of Milwaukee, I had admired Norris's clear explanation of how the closeness of a small town affects the candor of the writers who happen to live there. But now my admiration for that book was shaded by a deeper sense of apprehension. To admire a book is one thing, but to reenact it quite another.

As Norris notes, "Many writers depicting rural and small-town America . . . have found it necessary to write about that world from a distance." In fact, I had that kind of geographic distance when I wrote these stories. Norris continues: "But the writer who is thoroughly immersed in Dakota's rural milieu," or Nebraska's for that matter, "where nearly everyone is related, faces a particularly difficult form of self-censorship." While I had not exactly immersed myself in the "day to day realities" as much as Norris, I was close enough, and my family is large enough, to feel my hometown's silencing influence. But in my case the paranoia of self-censorship came after the fact.

Perhaps this paranoia happens to many writers no matter where they live. When we compose short stories or poems or imaginative essays, the possibility of even having an audience is not a sure thing, and we know this, so we may not give the idea of audience much thought. In fact, in this very lack of an audience, we might experience a sense of freedom from self-censorship that we might come to value. A blank page always listens, and you can always tell it the truth.

And even when you share your writing with a select group of friends before it is published, your strangeness, or what you might call your freakishness, can be put in perspective and tempered by good will. After publication, however, your writing falls into the prying hands of strangers. As the old writer says in Wim Wenders's movie *Wings of Desire*, "My readers used to sit in a circle, but now they have dispersed, and not one of them knows any other."

Sometimes I wonder why anyone would want this. Publication is a strange kind of disembodiment. Your thoughts disconnect themselves from your body, your life, and go off on their own. What's more, you no longer choose your audience. Your audience chooses you. You might start to feel, as I have felt, that you have revealed too much of yourself. Frankness between friends is one thing, but confessing your neuroses and malfeasance to strangers is quite another.

So then why publish? There are answers to this question, of course, even apart from vanity and careerism. First off, the eyes of a stranger can clarify your own writing. But the eyes of a stranger have their cost. You have to accept a certain degree of estrangement from that work you have known intimately. And if the subject of your writing is estrangement itself—as it is in part for me—then to have that strangeness reflected from a stranger's eye can make that writing seem even stranger still.

One Sunday morning a friend called and told me that *The Dirty Shame Hotel*, my book of short stories, had been reviewed in the Minneapolis *Star-Tribune*. Standing in a kitchen in North Platte, Nebraska, not far from the little town where I was born, I begged him to read the review to me, and so with a voice full of portent and drama he read the headline: "TALES OF TWISTED LIVES." I tensed for what was to come, but for the most part, the review reserved judgment and merely summarized:

> In "A Bed-Time Story" the narrator sets out to tell his grandchildren of their mother's childhood visit to a pumpkin farm and ends up telling them of the systematic slaughter of the

denizens of a back-yard zoo. In "Demon in the Closet," a demon moves in with and becomes a closeted member of a family that never "hides things."

It is a convention of short story reviews to give a one-sentence summary for several stories in the collection. Here's another synopsis, from *Minnesota Monthly*: "A lonely librarian catches a worm from a book. An old girlfriend turns into a scary clown. A marching band marches into oblivion." Although the reviews were generally positive, I was still a little dismayed by these characterizations since the stories seemed bleaker than I had thought. In fact, a reviewer in *Kirkus* described the title story as having "the bleakness of an Edward Hopper painting." I kept coming back to this phrase. Was this the book I'd written? Somehow, when summarized, everything about my book seemed more extreme and demented than I ever realized.

Now, at readings you can pick out the sweeter stories, the ones more palatable for a general audience of friends, family, and strangers who might like some Chicken Soup for the Soul. But then, upon publication, you have to think about the audience you did not really intend to reach: the administrative deans and fundamentalist friends and people who know that some of this is not fiction. All these people can choose *you* now, choose to read what you've written, and you cannot stop them. And then you recall something that one of the strangers said:

"Some of the stories are unpleasant" (*Minnesota Monthly*).

Mind you, the idea that some of these stories are unpleasant has occurred to you before. Let's say that you were in a bookstore, checking the shelves to see if your book was there. And *yes*, you do find a few copies. Racked with guilt, you look around, your heart pounding, and you shove the other books down the shelf, arranging your own book so that it is face out, with that beautiful cover showing. You half suspect that the cover is better than the book, and you are not afraid to take advantage of this fact.

And then you do not linger. You're on your way out of the store, when suddenly you find yourself in the self-help section. All around you, dwarfing the poetry section or anything else that interests you, you see the healthy, socially conscious, and morally uplifting texts that promise personal and professional achievement and growth. They fill the aisles of the bookstore like virile plants that offer herbal remedies and promises to straighten up your life, and then you flash back to that Sunday morning review, the banner headline "TALES OF TWISTED LIVES!"

Suddenly you think of your old Sunday school teacher, one of the few people in your hometown who seemed to respect you for reading books, a man who laid a heavy hand upon your shoulder when you graduated and said, "Ron, be a good boy, and try to make a buck along the way. . . ."

You suddenly wonder how *he* will react to this book.

I used to think that such concerns were beyond the writer's care. In my romance with freedom of expression and independence, I thought that writers were supposed to chase the horizon, heedless of social inhibitions. But I now knew that writers worry, or at least some of the ones who live far away from the anonymous cities do.

Let me quote Flannery O'Connor:

I once received a letter from an old lady in California who informed me that when the tired reader comes home at night, he wishes to read something that will lift up his heart. And it seems her heart had not been lifted up by anything of mine she had read. You may say that the serious writer doesn't have to bother about the tired reader, but he does, because they are all tired. One old lady who wants her heart lifted up would not be so bad, but you multiply her two hundred and fifty thousand times and what you get is a book club.

Now, honestly, I did not really think about this kind of audience as I was composing my stories. I always have some imaginary reader in my mind, prompting me, reacting. I did not, however, imagine a fundamentalist minister reading over my shoulder. And yet, in a small town, ministers read. They are one of the few groups you can *count* on to read something you wouldn't want them to read.

What's more my family is huge. In Gothenburg, a town of three thousand, there are thirty-three listings in the phone book for "Block." The Blocks of Gothenburg are, as one friend described them, a "quiet dynasty," filled with silent farmers, school teachers, ministers, active members of the church council, but not many writers. But they like the idea of local authors, at least in theory, and so the local TV station ran two stories about my book. *The Gothenburg Times* wanted to do an interview and feature, and suddenly the distance I had imagined that would protect me from my own excesses wasn't there. People were excited for me. They wanted to read my book. They wanted me to autograph it.

And then a couple of book clubs contacted me. Now, we're not talking Oprah here. We're talking about small groups of sincere individuals, mainly women, mainly older, who gather in the living rooms of places like Paxton, home of Ole's Big Game Bar, and Arnold, the Queen City of Custer County. Perhaps I'm dealing in stereotypes here. Paranoia feeds on stereotypes. Even so, I couldn't quite imagine sitting down in someone's living room with coffee and maybe a Bundt cake to discuss animal apocalypse or ritualistic humiliation involving sex and clowns or the other strange tropes within my book. In Gothenburg people always thought I was a little different. Now with this book in their hands they might discover they didn't know the half of it.

So let me tell you what happened. When I received these invitations I felt compelled to issue a warning. My stories, I said, might be considered by some to be disturbing, even offensive. Not all of them. Just some. And I succeeded in scaring the book clubs away. I actually felt good about this, that I was altruistically saving these good people from an afternoon of unpleasantness, but when I told a friend from New York City about these exchanges, he challenged my motives and my commitment to my stories. He was honestly shocked that I would not take every opportunity to discuss my stories, if indeed, I felt committed to them.

Why was I so nervous? Growing up in a small town, I sometimes went out of my way to shock my elders, say by walking around with a copy of *The Communist Manifesto* sticking out of my back pocket, just to tick people off. People who really knew me as a child would not be that surprised. I was the little kid sent home from a sleepover because I had told a story that made all the other children cry. I was a small-town rebel. I enjoyed this role, but now I was a grown man. My mother was embarrassed by the title of my book, and my father put it to me straight, "Why don't you write about . . . nice things?" And I have to admit that shock for the sake of shock wears a little thin shortly after adolescence. As embarrassing as it is to admit, I felt that I had to make an accounting of my motives at least to myself so that I could have the guts to visit the book clubs and stand behind my work.

What I write here may only seem to be a matter of personal archeology, reconstructing the intensions of my book of stories after the fact. It may even be a cardinal sin to write this, since we are instructed to let the writing speak for itself. It may be mere narcissism, but on the other hand not to speak of my motives might just be another form of self-censorship, and so allow me, at least provisionally, to claim a higher purpose, because I hope that what I have to say might be useful for other writers working in the Plains who might be called up by their friends, family, and neighbors to rationalize their love for what is sad and strange—and one might say *grotesque*.

Let's consider that word for a moment. Originally *grotesque* referred specifically to the ornamental arts discovered in the excavations of the caves and grottos of Rome. To say something was grotesque was to say that it was like the art uncovered from the caves. It was *grotto-esque*. Unlike Classical ornamentation with its concern with idealized beauty, this art form often dispensed with balance and proportion and involved the amalgamations of seemingly incompatible elements: human torsos tapering into the stems of plants, becoming the limbs of animals, metamorphosing into monsters.

Now, in common usage, *grotesque* refers to something that is merely disgusting, but in literature, it refers to a combination of elements that are not always easy to classify, such as laughter and whimsy occurring simultaneous to feelings of repulsion or dread. It is an art of ambivalence. But the definition of the grotesque that is most useful to me comes from Wolfgang Kayser, in *The Grotesque in Art and Literature*, where he writes in capital letters: "THE GROTESQUE IS THE ESTRANGED WORLD." If it disregards exacting description for exaggeration and distortion, the grotesque provides an image that it is recognizably our world, and while it is difficult to define, it is for the most part easy to recognize.

In Flannery O'Connor's "Good Country People," the grotesque is not so much Hulga's artificial leg: it is the Bible salesman who steals it. In *As I Lay Dying*, the grotesque characterizes the journey of the Bundrens to bury Addie, fulfilling her wishes far beyond the limits of good sense. In "A Rose for Emily," the grotesque characterizes that certain something that Miss Emily Grierson is keeping in her attic. Faulkner's metaphor is fleshed out like this: to hang on to the past, he suggests, is a form of necrophilia. This, of course, is an unpleasant idea, but oddly enough, there is something sweet about each of these characters, too, and this is something I will explore towards my conclusion. Humor, to my mind, is also a central facet of the grotesque, which often makes us smile, perhaps in a guilty fashion. As Angela Carter said, "A child's laughter is pure, until that child first laughs at a clown."

Part of the reason why I feel that I have to make an accounting is that I don't know if the grotesque has been considered to have much of a place in Plains writing. On the other hand, the grotesque is pervasive in the literature of the South, so much so that "Southern" can be a kind of shorthand designation for the grotesque, as acknowledged by Flannery O'Connor when she said, "Whenever I'm asked why Southern writers particularly have a penchant for writing about freaks I say it is because we are still able to recognize one."

It's a good answer, but a flip one, and of course she doesn't leave it there. It does seem, however, that *recognition* is part of the issue: the grotesque is a mode of creating estrangement so that we can rediscover what we have lost the ability to see. This is why I feel that the grotesque, or any other mode that seeks to emphasize strangeness, is an important approach to getting at the truth of small towns in the Plains.

I used to think it took a kind of subtlety and precision to discover and express the beauty of the Plains, and I still think this. But sometimes it seems to me that instead of precision, strangeness and distortion are necessary to get past what André Breton called "the beast of custom," the habitual forms of seeing that are a form of blindness. In a small town you feel that you see the same things every day. You stop paying attention. You don't even notice what it is that you do not notice. And so that's why I feel the stranger is necessary. The stranger points out things that are dense, complex, ambivalent, and even freakish—things you do not even see anymore, they are so close to you.

In saying this I find myself perhaps at odds with a more traditional perception of Plains writing. In the essay "Horizontal Grandeur," which might be called a classic expression of the core motives of writing coming from the flatlands, Bill Holm puts it like this:

> There are two eyes in the human head—the eye of mystery, and the eye of harsh truth—the hidden and the open—the woods eye and the prairie eye. The prairie eye looks for distance, clarity, and light; the woods eye for closeness, complexity, and darkness. The prairie eye looks for usefulness and plainness in art and architecture; the woods eye for the baroque and ornamental. . . . Sherwood Anderson wrote his stories with a prairie eye, plain and awkward, told in the voice of a man almost embarrassed to be telling them. . . . Faulkner,

whose endless complexity of motive and language take the reader miles behind the simple facts of an event, sees the world with a woods eye.

I have two things to say about this. First, for "prairie" read "Plains." Outsiders don't know the difference anyway, which has mostly to do with grass height and rainfall. Second, I *love* Holm's analogy, and I think that it is wonderfully informative. But I can't really say that anyone would find it a healthy situation when only one eye tends to dominate one's vision. My son has a condition where he has problems focusing one eye. If left uncorrected the brain would stop using that eye, and he could go blind in that eye, and so when he was a year old we put him in glasses.

A baby in glasses strikes people as both incongruent and unbear-ably cute, and this is, again, another little parable—because, to my mind, being open to the incongruent qualities of life in the Plains is almost like corrective vision. It is a means to make sure you keep looking with that second eye. It creates estrangement. It allows us as writers and readers to stand back a bit to be able to see what is too close to see. And, like a two year old in glasses, it may allow us to see the sweetness in the oddest contrast.

Now, according to Holm I don't have a prairie eye, and perhaps neither does anyone else who writes about the complexities of liv-ing in the Plains. But then again I don't really think that Sherwood Anderson had a prairie eye either. After all, he wasn't just looking at the prairie. He was looking at the ordinary residents of a small town, which he very self-consciously labeled as "grotesques." I think that Anderson wanted us to look at these ordinary prairie people through the strange eye of the woods, in terms of their "closeness, complexity, and darkness." In doing so Anderson helped me to see my own little town differently, seeing it at a distance, but also see-ing it more clearly. And even if these depictions involved a degree of distortion, then they were still eerily familiar.

So then rather than, like Holm, saying Anderson has the eye of the prairie, I would rather think of him and other flatland writers in the way that Flannery O'Connor thought about herself: as a "realist of distance"—which is "a matter of seeing near things with their extensions of meaning and thus seeing far things close up." It is a kind of realism that negotiates the distance even if it distorts what it sees. She continues by stating, "The prophet"—that is the one who sees far—"is a realist of distance, and it is this kind of realism that you find in the best modern instances of the grotesque. It is a realism which does not hesitate to distort appearances to show a hidden truth." In part, this clarifying distortion is acquired by taking a distant view, a more estranged view.

You might feel that Plains people do not need to achieve this kind of distance because we live in the distance. Here in the Plains, we live in the distance the way some people live in the mountains. We live *on* the distance. Although the word is abstract, we can see it. It has a sensual force. Sometimes distance is all that we can see. And so it's often seemed to me that a sense of distance so dominates our view that Nebraska writers find themselves translating other kinds of distance—emotional distances, aesthetic distances, distances of time and affection—into geographic distance.

Sometimes, if you look at land with a poet's traveling eye, you might see how a distant cloud contains a father's disaffection; and where the rows of corn converge and vanish, you might find a memory, misplaced in your childhood. Older now, you can see how the alienation of the worker becomes the distance he must travel, keeping to a schedule where the miles equal money. Or you might see how each rise in the land hides an unknown future where each rolling horizon is a traveling illusion, holding everything you hoped for and didn't get, or everything you had and lost, or anything else that scares you with its absence.

Through the eyes of that old distance-learning teacher Willa Cather, you might see how the breadth and scale of the Plains can cause a pioneer girl, seeing that distance for the first time, to feel as though she is as negligible as a single word on a nearly empty page:

"Between that earth and that sky I felt erased, blotted out. I did not say my prayers that night: here, I felt, what would be would be."

Or if you look through the eyes of the poet Ted Kooser, you might see how the distance is the ambiguous common ground between living writers, farming their paper, and our Dead Forebears—and as our common ground it signals our mortality: "a lone oak cackling with blackness off in the distance."

Our common ground is this distance we share, and this distance has even become a medium for our art. But this distance is not characterized by a deadening sameness and monotony, as outsiders might think. Our sense of distance is diverse, as is our presbyopia, and it has many paradoxes and ambiguities to it.

Here is yet another one.

Traditionally, Nebraskans have always viewed themselves as farsighted. We live in a place of deferred expectations. If there is drought this year, we hope for the next. Historically, as settlers, we have viewed everything in terms of its potential. But farsighted people need corrective vision as much as nearsighted ones do. In seeing far, we might distort what is near especially in our small towns, where nothing new seems to happen.

On the Plains your line of sight is so open, so clear, some people might start to feel they can see the future. It is, after all, the same thing that happened yesterday. And in this clairvoyant declaration we may become false prophets. At the very least we become inflexible and habitual in our perspectives.

In "The Book of the Grotesque" Anderson tells of an old writer who "had quite an elaborate theory" about people who grow rigid in their outlooks. Recognizing that there were many truths, "It was his notion that the moment one of the people took one of the truths to himself, called it his truth, and tried to live his life by it, he became a grotesque and the truth he embraced became a falsehood."

For Nebraskans one of these so-called truths that we embrace is that we are *ordinary* people, salt of the earth, regular folk—which might just be a desperate way of insisting that we are not freaks, or at least not in a way that we recognize.

You see, this was in part the real issue with my fear of small-town book clubs. Was I to hold up the mirror of the lonely, obsessive people in my stories, and say, "This is me, and this is you." Would they recognize this? If Southern writers write about freaks because they are still able to recognize one, must we then say that Plains writers do not write about freaks because we *cannot* recognize them—which means we deny that they are among us, that we cannot recognize that we are the freaks?

In a Nebraska small town we might have a tendency to believe that freaks are outsiders. They are in California. At worst they are no closer than Boulder. And we might even be able to hold the freaks at that distance until we have a native-born son or daughter, who for some odd reason decides to write poetry or stories or a strange little memoir—because writers are born to be outsiders. And I would say that a place needs its writers. They are our freaks in residence, and they offer corrective vision.

Of course, a small town quite naturally wants straight-thinking kids. Let me take myself as an example. In my first real awareness of the distance of the Plains, I am riding a tractor, sentenced by my father to ride it all day. It is difficult to plant straight rows of corn if each row is a quarter mile long. If you focus on the ground, the rows are crooked. So my father taught me to focus on some far point, a fence post, a telephone pole, a lone tree, and he told me that if I would drive toward that point, then the rows would keep relatively straight. This is of course another parable, and it's a good lesson.

But on that tractor, staring into the distance, my mind began to roam. I had to daydream because otherwise I could not deal with insane boredom of the distance, and so I stared into the distances inside my head—and I made crooked rows. My father was unhappy, but I enjoyed the daydreams and profited by them, and in time I began to think that the ability to daydream was my redemption or even my ticket out of town.

And so the daydreams started to separate me from those around me who started to notice the distance in my eyes. I became, at least in my own mind, a stranger among them, and the people I loved became ghostly figures on the rim of the sky. They turned into odd creatures, partly real, partly imaginary. They become grotesques, and yet in this distortion I started to see something about them that I could not see before. I felt it was something they would not understand. It was a paradox, a contraction, something that seemed almost impossible to explain, but I recognized it almost immediately when I was still a kid and I came across this passage in Anderson's "The Book of the Grotesques":

> You see the interest in all this lies in the figures that went before the eyes of the writer. They were all grotesques. All of the men and women the writer had ever known had become grotesques. The grotesques were not all horrible. Some were amusing, some almost beautiful. . . .

"The grotesques were . . . almost beautiful."

He is talking about us, you know, about Plains people or anyone else who lives out in the open, or anyone open enough to write about the experience. This is what I should have explained to my distance-learning students. Yes, distance education *is* an education about distance, as is every good book, because in the distant, self-estranged view that writers have, the sad and strange—the freaks among us, the freaks we are—are not repellent. You do not have to distance yourself from them. If we understand this, then we can cross the distance. The distance collapses.

I think this idea is best stated in Anderson's story "Paper Pills":

> The story of Doctor Reefy and his courtship of the tall dark girl . . . is a very curious story. It is delicious, like the twisted little apples that grow in the orchards of Winesburg. In the fall one walks in the orchards and the ground is hard with frost underfoot. On the trees are only a few gnarled apples that the pickers have rejected. . . . One nibbles at them and they

are delicious. Into a little round place at the side of the apple has been gathered all of its sweetness. One runs from tree to tree over the frosted ground picking the gnarled, twisted apples and filling his pockets with them. Only the few know the sweetness of the twisted apples.

Perhaps it is this very neglect, the lack of attention from an audience at large or the country as a whole, which provides the sweetness of Plains experience, which year by year grows stranger to the eyes of mainstream America.

Only the few know the sweetness of the twisted apples.

This is the point I wanted to get across to the small-town book clubs, or whatever readers I might yet have. This is the reason why our stories are so sad and strange. Even if we were born on the Plains and prairies or in the tall cities, we're all from the neck of the woods where the Grimm brothers live. It is a place full of weird paradox, a state of mind full of distance and density and desire, and so we cannot stop looking at it, trying to resolve it, if only now in memory. That's why, even after moving away from the state, I must keep writing about it. Nebraska is never really through with us, because it keeps pulling us back to the heart of a mystery.

But I suppose any place can do that, too, once it gets inside your head, and so let me push toward yet another parable and say we are all distance-learning students. Increasingly, our world is like theirs, mediated by pixilated images that are supposed to cross the distances but create new ones instead. We may enjoy the daytime TV spectacle of what's sad and strange, but we don't want to be moved by it for fear of contamination. We want our consumer products to reassure us, even with lies. In the landscape of commodities, one does not want surprises. We don't want to bite down on a Big Mac and be surprised. We don't want politicians who express ambivalence. We are perhaps more afraid of strangeness now because it's a stranger time. Why would we want to add to the strangeness?

I think there's actually a moral answer. When I was a young man, my friends and I would sometimes greet each other by saying, "Hey, freak!" My wife still says this to me, and it's a good thing, an acknowledgment of openness. Acknowledging we are strange is the very opposite of estrangement and maybe an invitation to candor, and maybe by this we can close a little of the distance between us. For all my gray uncertainties, I am certain that *this* has to be one of the major roles of writers in small towns on the Plains.

And if you wonder what a small town has to do with you, then think of an office, a neighborhood, a college—or a family, the smallest and most densely populated town of them all. That is why each of these places needs their writers. Because if our writers can show us the sweetness of the twisted apples, then maybe we could proceed to the more difficult idea, an ancient idea really, deeply imbedded in the art of the grotesque and liberating to our appreciation of the Plains, an idea can allow us to bridge the unbearable distance between us:

"There is no beauty without some strangeness to its proportions."

Because if you can hold on to that idea, the beauty of strangeness in all of its ambivalence, then you can live *in the open*. You might even be able to say, like Kathleen Norris, that you live inside a spiritual geography—even if you now live in New Jersey.

Source Acknowledgments

"The Land That Time Forgot" by Ron Hansen is reprinted from the book *These United States: Original Essays by Leading American Writers on Their State Within the Union* edited by John Leonard. Copyright © 2003 by The Nation Institute and Avalon Publishing Group. Appears by permission of the publisher, Nation Books, a division of Avalon Publishing Group.

"Myths of the American West: Two Views of the Oregon Trail" by Michael Anania is reprinted with the permission of Moyer Bell and is from the book *In Plain Sight: Obsessions, Morals & Domestic Laughter* published by Asphodel Press.

"Preface" from Ted Kooser's *Local Wonders: Seasons in the Bohemian Alps* is reprinted by permission of the University of Nebraska Press. © 2002 by the University of Nebraska Press.

"Nuts" by John Price was first published in *Orion* v. 21 (Winter 2002). Reprinted by permission of the author.

"Far Brought" by Lisa Knopp is reprinted from *The Nature of Home* by permission of the University of Nebraska Press. © 2002 by the Board of Regents of the University of Nebraska.

"An Indian Candidate for Public Office" by Mark Monroe is from *An Indian In White America* by Mark Monroe, edited by Carolyn Reyer. Reprinted by permission of Temple University Press. © 1994 by Temple University. All rights reserved.

"Weighed Down by Buckskin" by Delphine Red Shirt is reprinted from *Bead on an Ant Hill: A Lakota Childhood* by permission of the University of Nebraska Press. © 1998 by the University of Nebraska Press.

Excerpt from "From Pine Ridge to Paris" by Joe Starita is reprinted from *The Dull Knifes of Pine Ridge: A Lakota Odyssey* by permission of the University of Nebraska Press. © 1995 by Joe Starita.

"In the Time of Buffalo" by Alan Boye is reprinted from *Holding Stone Hands: On the Trail of the Cheyenne Exodus* by Alan Boye by permission of the University of Nebraska Press. © 1999 by the University of Nebraska Press.

Excerpt from Merrill Gilfillan's *Magpie Rising: Sketches from the Great Plains* is reprinted by permission of the University of Nebraska Press. © 1988 by Merrill Gilfillan.

Excerpt from "Tending to Ruin" by Jack Todd is from *Desertion: In the Time of Vietnam*. Copyright © 2001 by Jack Todd. Reprinted by permission of Houghton Mifflin Company. All rights reserved.

Excerpt from chapter 9 of Bob Kerrey's *When I Was a Young Man: A Memoir*, copyright © 2002 by J. Robert Kerrey, is reprinted by permission of Harcourt, Inc.

Excerpt from *Being Home* by Ruth Raymond Thone is reprinted by permission of the author. Copyright © 1993 Ruth Raymond Thone.

Excerpt from "Children of Hope, Children of Tears" from Mary Pipher's *The Middle of Everywhere*, copyright © 2002 by Mary Pipher, is reprinted by permission of Harcourt, Inc.

"Immigration, Technology, and Sense of Place" by Eamonn Wall is from *From the Sin-é Café to the Black Hills: Notes on the New Irish*, © 2000. Reprinted by permission of The University of Wisconsin Press.

Contributors

MICHAEL ANANIA is a native of Omaha and attended the University of Nebraska–Lincoln and the University of Nebraska at Omaha. The author of many books, including several collections of poetry, the novel *The Red Menace*, and a collection of essays, *In Plain Sight: Obsessions, Morals & Domestic Laughter*, he is a professor of English at the University of Illinois–Chicago.

RON BLOCK grew up in Gothenburg, Nebraska, and attended the University of Nebraska–Lincoln. A professor of English at Rowan University in New Jersey, he is the author of two collections of poetry and a short-story collection, *The Dirty Shame Hotel*.

ALAN BOYE grew up in Lincoln, Nebraska, and is a graduate of the University of Nebraska–Lincoln. His books include *Guide to the Ghosts of Lincoln*, *Complete Roadside Guide to Nebraska*, *Holding Stone Hands: On the Trail of the Cheyenne Exodus* (University of Nebraska Press, 1999), and *Tales from the Journey of the Dead* (University of Nebraska Press, 2005). He currently teaches writing at Lyndon State College in Vermont.

BOB GIBSON is the author of *Stranger to the Game*. Born and raised in Omaha, Nebraska, he attended Creighton University and went on to a winning career as a pitcher for the St. Louis Cardinals. He was inducted into the Baseball Hall of Fame in 1981.

MERRILL GILFILLAN lived and wrote in western Nebraska for a period of several years. He is the author of many books, including *Magpie Rising: Sketches from the Great Plains* (reprinted by University of Nebraska Press, 2003), winner of the PEN/Martha Albrand Award, and *Chokecherry Places*, winner of the Western States Book Award in 1989. He currently lives in Boulder, Colorado.

RON HANSEN grew up in Omaha, Nebraska. He is the Gerard Manley Hopkins Professor of English at the University of Santa Clara, and the author of numerous books, including the novels *Mariette in Ecstasy*, *Atticus*, and most recently *Isn't It Romantic?* a short-story collection entitled *Nebraska*, a children's book, and two screenplays. In addition he is the author of a collection of essays, *A Stay Against Confusion: Essays on Faith and Fiction*.

JOHN JANOVY JR. is the Varner Professor of Biological Sciences at the University of Nebraska–Lincoln and the author of many books, including *Keith County Journal* (reprinted by University of Nebraska Press, 1996), *Yellowlegs*, and *Back in Keith County* (University of Nebraska Press 1984).

PAUL JOHNSGARD is the winner of the 2004 National Conservation Achievement Award and recipient of the Lifetime Achievement Award (2001), both sponsored by the National Wildlife Federation. An emeritus professor of biological sciences at the University of Nebraska–Lincoln, he is considered one of the world's foremost authorities on ornithology and bird behavior. He is the author of numerous books, including eight published by the University of Nebraska Press, most recently *Prairie Dog Empire: A Saga of the Shortgrass Prairie* (2005).

BRYAN JONES is a farmer and reading teacher in McCook, Nebraska. He grew up in small towns in Nebraska and returned to the state after graduating from Roosevelt University in Chicago and attending graduate school in New Orleans. He is the author of *The Farming Game* (University of Nebraska Press, 1995) and *Mark Twain Made Me Do It and Other Plains Adventures* (University of Nebraska Press, 1997).

BOB KERREY grew up in Lincoln, Nebraska and is an alumnus of the University of Nebraska–Lincoln. A former governor and U.S. Senator from Nebraska, he is now the president of the New School in New York City. He is the author of the memoir *When I Was a Young Man*.

WILLIAM KLOEFKORN was named the Nebraska State Poet in 1982 and is an emeritus professor of English at Nebraska Wesleyan University. He is the author of many collections of poetry and two collections of short fiction as well as three memoirs, *This Death by Drowning* (University of Nebraska Press, 1997), *Restoring the Burnt Child* (University of Nebraska Press, 2003), and *At Home on This Moveable Earth* (University of Nebraska Press, 2006).

LISA KNOPP lives in Lincoln, Nebraska, and is the author of three collections of essays: *Flight Dreams: Life in the Midwestern Landscape*, *Field of Vision*, and *The Nature of Home* (University of Nebraska Press, 2002). She teaches creative nonfiction at the University of Nebraska at Omaha.

TED KOOSER, one of Nebraska's most highly regarded poets, is a recent Poet Laureate of the United States. He is the author of three books of nonfiction, *Local Wonders: Seasons in the Bohemian Alps* (University of Nebraska Press, 2002), *The Poetry Home Repair Manual* (University of Nebraska Press, 2005), and *Writing Brave and Free* (University of Nebraska Press, 2006), as well as ten collections of poetry. His most recent poetry book, *Delights and Shadows*, is the winner of the 2005 Pulitzer Prize for Poetry.

KENNETH LINCOLN grew up in northwest Nebraska, where his great-grandparents homesteaded along the North Platte River and in the Sandhills. He is currently a professor of Contemporary and Native American Literatures at UCLA. His books include *Native American Renaissance*, *The Good Red Road: Passages into Native America* (University of Nebraska Press, 1997), *Indi'n Humor: Bicultural Play in Native America, Sing with the Heart of a Bear: Fusions of Native and American Poetry, 1890–1999,* and *Men Down West.*

KEM LUTHER is a poet, writer, teacher, and genealogist who was born in Broken Bow, Nebraska. He is the author of *Cottonwood Roots* (University of Nebraska Press, 1993) and lives in Victoria, British Columbia.

MARK MONROE is the author of *An Indian in White America.* Born on the Rosebud Reservation in South Dakota, his family moved to Alliance, Nebraska, when he was a child. Monroe served as the Director of the American Indian Council in Alliance, Nebraska, the Vice President of the Nebraska Indian Commission, and the President of United Indians of Nebraska. Sadly, Mark Monroe died during the time this anthology was being gathered.

MARY PIPHER is a clinical psychologist and an adjunct clinical professor at the University of Nebraska–Lincoln. She received her Ph.D. in Psychology from the University of Nebraska–Lincoln and is the author of several *New York Times* bestselling books including *Reviving Ophelia: Saving the Selves of Adolescent Girls* and *The Middle of Everywhere: The World's Refugees Come to Our Town.*

JOHN PRICE is an associate professor of English at the University of Nebraska at Omaha. He is the author of *Not Just Any Land: A Personal and Literary Journey Into the American Grasslands* (University of Nebraska Press, 2004) and was awarded a 2004–2005 fellowship by the National Endowment for the Arts. He is the proud father of two boys.

DELPHINE RED SHIRT is an Oglala Lakota who grew up both on and off the Pine Ridge Reservation in western Nebraska. The author of two books, *Bead on an Anthill: A Lakota Childhood* (University of Nebraska Press, 1997) and *Turtle Lung Woman's Granddaughter* (University of Nebraska Press, 2002), she is a professor at the University of Arizona.

MICHAEL RIPS was born and raised in Omaha, Nebraska. A graduate of Oxford University, he has served as a law clerk to a Supreme Court

Justice and is now an advisor to several museums and foundations. He is the author of *Pasquale's Nose: Idle Days in an Italian Town* and *The Face of a Naked Lady: An Omaha Family Mystery*.

BOB ROSS was born in Brown County in north-central Nebraska and currently lives near Ainsworth, Nebraska, occasionally teaching part-time at Sinte Gleska University. He is the author of *In the Kingdom of Grass* (University of Nebraska Press, 1992), a book of essays with photographs by Margaret MacKichan, and *Solitary Confinement*, a book of poems.

JOE STARITA was born in Lincoln, Nebraska, and graduated from the University of Nebraska–Lincoln. After a distinguished career at the *Miami Herald*, he returned to Lincoln with his family. He is the author of *The Dull Knifes of Pine Ridge: A Lakota Odyssey* (University of Nebraska Press, 2002), which was nominated for a Pulitzer Prize. He is now the Pike Professor of Journalism at the University of Nebraska–Lincoln.

RUTH RAYMOND THONE is a former First Lady of the state of Nebraska, and the author of two nonfiction books, *Women and Aging: Celebrating Ourselves* and *Fat—A Fate Worse that Death? Women, Weight, and Appearance*, as well as a collection of essays, *Being Home*.

JACK TODD was born and raised in Nebraska and is a graduate of the University of Nebraska–Lincoln. He left the United States during the Vietnam War and settled in Canada, where he is now a sports columnist for the *Montreal Gazette*. His books include *Desertion: In the Time of Vietnam* and *The Taste of Metal: A Deserter's Story*.

ROBERT VIVIAN grew up in Omaha, Nebraska. He has had over twenty plays produced off-Broadway and several have been published, with monologues appearing in the international anthologies *Best Men's and Women's Stage Monologues* from 1995, 1996, 1997, and 1998. He is the author of the novel *The Mover of Bones* (University of Nebraska Press, 2006) and *Cold Snap as Yearning* (University of Nebraska Press, 2001).

EAMONN WALL was born in Enniscorthy, County Wexford, Ireland. Until recently, he was an associate professor of English at Creighton

University in Omaha and is currently the Jefferson Smurfit Professor of Irish Studies at the University of Missouri–St. Louis. He is the author of *From the Sin-é Café to the Black Hills: Notes on the New Irish* as well as several collections of poetry.

ROGER WELSCH is a humorist, folklorist, and essayist born in Lincoln, Nebraska, and currently living and writing in Dannebrog, Nebraska. He is the author of many books, including *It's Not the End of the Earth, but You Can See It from Here* (reprinted by University of Nebraska Press, 1999) and *You Know You're a Nebraskan*. His "Postcard from Nebraska" was a biweekly feature on CBS's *Sunday Morning* and he is also the host of *Roger & I* on Nebraska Public Television. He has taught at Dana College, the University of Nebraska–Lincoln, and Nebraska Wesleyan University.